IF YOU REALLY WANT TO HEAR ABOUT IT

# IF YOU REALLY WANT TO HEAR ABOUT IT

WRITERS ON J.D. SALINGER AND HIS WORK

*Edited by Catherine Crawford*

THUNDER'S MOUTH PRESS
NEW YORK

IF YOU REALLY WANT TO HEAR ABOUT IT
*Writers on J. D. Salinger and His Work*

Published by
Thunder's Mouth Press
An Imprint of Avalon Publishing Group, Inc.
245 West 17th Street, 11th floor
New York, NY 10011
First printing, June 2006

AVALON
publishing group incorporated

Library of Congress Cataloging-in-Publication Data is available.

ISBN-10: 1-56025-880-2
ISBN-13: 978-1-56025-880-3

9 8 7 6 5 4 3 2 1

Book design by Maria E. Torres

Printed in the United States of America
Distributed by Publishers Group West

*For Mac, Oona, and Smiley*
*(the one I can't wait to meet)*

# CONTENTS

# PART II: CRITICS AND CRANKS

## PART III: DECONSTRUCTING JERRY

## PART IV: FAMILY, FRIENDS, AND FANATICS

# INTRODUCTION

I've always thought that if I ever wrote a screenplay, the story would (not so originally) rely heavily on my college experience. Those four years were spent, or really misspent, at the University of Santa Cruz in California in the mid 1990s. In truth, I haven't worked out many details besides the setting, but there are one or two images burned on my brain that would definitely find their way in.

Although the passage from high school to college did alleviate many of the pains of adolescence, there were still a few lingering twinges of discomfort for me. I used to feel them most acutely at parties. As an English major cavorting with mostly English majors, there was always pressure to appear erudite and cool. One particular night, I found myself trapped in the kitchen near the keg, listening to a seemingly self-assured hipster interpret Sonic Youth lyrics for a small, seemingly interested group. I wanted to be free. I remember looking up to find a waif-like, perfect female hipster leaning against the refrigerator reading a paperback. Although she was in the shadows of the kitchen, she couldn't be missed with her long blonde hair and red studded sweatshirt. It didn't seem to register to her that she was at a party. Initially I was outraged—what a phony! This wasn't fair play. It would never wash. She did not have my vote as an interesting person. But then I looked closer and recognized the familiar book jacket. She was reading *Nine Stories*. Whether she found the book lying around at the party and, once she'd picked it up, couldn't put it down, or she knew that it was the perfect accessory for the desired affect—I no longer cared. Imagining what was going on in her tormented little head while she read some of my favorite writing was diversion enough.

By now, Salinger is more than an author; he is an affect. His small but powerful body of work has been contemplated by nearly everyone I know, and by many of the world's foremost critics and writers. I'm still slightly baffled when I meet someone who doesn't like Salinger. To me, it's like not liking ice cream. Or gin and tonic. The world he created, though not exactly familiar or even sometimes realistic, is so engaging and impassioned that I have no resistance. Salinger stopped publishing almost a decade before I was born. By the time I was reading his work in high school, Salinger's eccentric habits and the many endeavors to infiltrate his New Hampshire haven had attracted as much attention as the literary merit of his writing. He's defended his privacy with a fierce intensity, but his stories and characters have so deeply affected readers that his efforts are never enough. It was interesting to see how many writers were still conflicted about their published pieces on Salinger. On the one hand, many of them would like to respect his pleas for privacy; on the other, there's the feeling that his talent is too great, his influence too keen to warrant keeping readers away from the man.

It was this conflict that, in part, made the process of acquiring pieces for this book a serious challenge. As it turns out, very few writers, readers, or fans have managed to penetrate Salinger's Fortress of Solitude, as Superman or Jonathan Lethem might call it. Those that have succeeded, therefore, were immediate candidates to be contributors. Salinger's reticence, however, seems to be contagious, and I was surprised by the many walls I had to scale to acquire reprint rights. Although all of the pieces in this collection are previously published, more than a few writers simply said they were "uncomfortable" with their articles. I found myself wondering if they feared Salinger's opinion of their complicity, or if their opinions had changed about their subject. Perhaps in the case of early critics, no one expected Salinger's appeal to survive for so long. A critic's job is to criticize, but after fifty years of Salinger's unwavering popularity no one wants to be a pill at a great literary party.

One of the most interesting cases of writerly angst came from Betty Eppes, who is credited as the author of the famous *Paris Review* piece, "What I Did Last Summer." Betty is incredibly sharp, gracious and kind. Her breed of charm is distinctly Southern, so it's not surprising that she wrote for the *Baton Rouge Advocate*. For subscribers of the *Paris Review*, she is remembered as the sexy bimbo who used her female wiles to finagle an interview with Salinger. According to Ms. Eppes, however, this image is the result of heavy editing and artistic license at the hands of George Plimpton and his staff. She still experiences pain when reminded of the unauthorized changes to her original story. It was not easy for Ms. Eppes to grant this reprint, and I am forever grateful to her ability to recognize that any collection of writing on Salinger would be incomplete without her *Paris Review* piece.

With a surprising dearth of Salingerian commentary available, I clearly had my work cut out or me. One friend suggested I contact various government agencies to obtain Salinger's records through the Freedom of Information Act. So I did. A few weeks later I received a response from the CIA: They were willing to send anything they had on J. D. Salinger, provided I could furnish proof of death or permission from the author. Many similar notices from other agencies soon followed, and each time I experienced a small fit of laughter when I read "permission from the author." If I could get that, after all, I'd have an entirely different book on my hands. As for the proof of death, I imagine (and hope) that this is a long way off. By all accounts, Salinger takes his nutrition as seriously as he does his writing. Although it's been a while since we've had a firsthand account, there is every reason to believe that each day he follows strict dietary regulations—involving mostly raw food—and writes away the morning hours. There have also been reports of dedicated meditation, homeopathic medicine, and a lot of yoga—sure, it's not the most glamorous routine, but if it means that one day J. D. Salinger is going to spring on us a final, fantastic and utterly unphony book, well, I guess I can forgive him for the lack of fireworks.

## PART I:

## IN SEARCH OF SALINGER

# Interview with J. D. Salinger

SHIRLIE BLANEY

During the preparation of the recent student edition of the *Daily Eagle*, Miss Shirlie Blaney of the class of 1954 at Windsor high school, spied Jerome David Salinger, author of the bestseller *Catcher in the Rye* in a Windsor restaurant. Mr. Salinger, who recently bought a home in Cornish, obliged the reporter with the following interview.

An author of many articles and a few stories, including *Catcher in the Rye*, was interviewed and provided us with an interesting life story.

A very good friend of all the high school students, Mr. Salinger has many older friends as well, although he has been coming here only a few years. He keeps very much to himself, wanting only to be left alone to write. He is a tall and foreign looking man of 34, with a pleasing personality.

Jerome David Salinger was born January 1, 1919, in New York. He went to pubic grammar schools while his high school years were spent at Valley Forge Military academy in Pennsylvania. During this time he was writing. His college education included New York university, where he studied for two years.

With his father, he went to Poland to learn the ham shipping business.

He didn't care for this, but he accomplished something by learning the German language.

Later he was in Vienna for ten months, but came back and went to Ursinus college. Due to lack of interest, he left at mid-years and went to Columbia university. All this time he was still writing.

Mr. Salinger's first story was published at the age of 21. He wrote for two years for the *Saturday Evening Post, Esquire, Mademoiselle,* and many more. He later worked on the liner "Kungsholn" in the West Indies, as an entertainer. He was still writing for magazines and college publications. At the age of 23, he was drafted. He spent two years in the Army which he disliked because he wanted all of his time to write.

He started working on *Catcher in the Rye*, a novel, in 1941 and finished it in the summer of 1951. It was a Book-of-the-Month club selection for the month, and later came out as a pocket book.

The book is a study of a troubled adolescent boy. When asked if it was in any way autobiographical, Mr. Salinger said: "Sort of, I was much relieved when I finished it. My boyhood was very much the same as that of the boy in the book, and it was a great relief telling people about it."

About two years ago he decided to come to New England. He came through this section. He liked it so much that he bought his present home in Cornish.

His plans for the future include going to Europe and Indonesia. He will go first to London perhaps to make a movie.

One of his books, *Uncle Wiggley in Connecticut*, has been made into a movie, *My Foolish Heart*.

About 75 per cent of his stories are about people under 21 and 40 per cent of those about youngsters under 12.

His second book was a collection of nine stories. They first appeared in *The New Yorker*.

# The Search for
# the Mysterious J. D. Salinger

ERNEST HAVEMANN

## The Recluse in the Rye

On one of the unnamed, unnumbered dirt roads that struggle up, down and around the 36 hilly square miles of the town of Cornish, New Hampshire.

I went exploring the roads a few weeks ago and can testify that I know them well. There stands a rural-route mailbox laconically lettered with the single word SALINGER. It is a totally undistinguished, everyday sort of mailbox and it could belong to a Tom, a Dick or for that matter a Harry Salinger in which case it would hardly have been worth my search or your attention. As it happens, however, this isolated and austere mailbox is an American landmark, for it constitutes the sole existing link between the outer world and J. D. Salinger, who at 42 is the most influential man of letters in the U.S. today and also the most inaccessible, mysterious and fascinating recluse in all U.S. literary history.

Through the galvanized membrane of the mailbox ooze Salinger's rare contributions to the world, materializing as if drop by drop. *Franny and Zooey*, published this autumn (Little, Brown) is his first book since 1953. And against the box, despite his meager output and his intense desire for privacy, presses the world's curiosity: hundreds of letters, thousands of questions a year from fans, critics and scholars all over the globe. (Salinger's stories, although written mostly in colloquial New Yorkese, are very big in England and in their German, Swedish, Finnish, and Japanese translations.) None of the questions that assail the mailbox is ever answered. Salinger does not reply to letters, sign autographs or give lectures. He has never consented to have his biography in *Who's Who* and he has an unlisted telephone number. He emerges from his house only to pick up the mail, buy groceries and books, and make an occasional business trip. Few people have seen him; fewer still have spoken to him, and almost none have had the privilege of hearing him answer back.

## Best-sellers with Lasting Impact

The reticent owner of the mailbox is unquestionably more widely read than Nobel Prize winner William Faulkner has ever been, and is probably a stronger literary force than even Ernest Hemingway at the height of his fabulous popularity in the '30s and '40s. The final haunting words of Hemingway's *A Farewell to Arms* (". . . and walked back to the hotel in the rain") would seem to be unforgettable to anyone who had ever encountered them. Yet I remember that a professor who made a survey in the early '30s, when I was going to college, was shocked to find how few of us students around the U.S. could recognize them. Salinger's *The Catcher in the Rye* begins with the most commonplace, low-key sort of words, ("If you really want to hear about it . . ."). Yet the moment the quizmaster on a recent television contest for college students started reading the open lines, I noted that ever hand in the place was quickly raised.

To today's youth, Salinger seems to be Hemingway, Faulkner, Mark Twain, and Walt Whitman rolled into one. *Catcher*, his only novel, published in 1951, has sold more than 1.5 million copes in the U.S. and continues to sell at the rate of more than 250,000 copies a year in four different editions, mostly to youngsters who have just begun to read serious books. College literature teachers no longer bother to put it on their list of required reading; they know that all their students with any interest at all in modern literature have already read it.

"Franny" was published by *The New Yorker* in 1955 and "Zooey" in 1957, yet last month's book combining the two old stories was eagerly sought by three of the book clubs. (Characteristically, Salinger has turned them down; he wants no artificial aids to the circulation of his works.) *Franny and Zooey* shot to second place on the best-seller lists almost immediately. It has been the chief topic of discussion in countless campus bull sessions and the subject of serious front-page reviews by leading critics. In every respect, it is *the* U.S. literary event of 1961.

What is the secret of Salinger's hold on his readers, and why does he shun the public that adores him? While *Franny and Zooey* was on the presses, I went to his lair to try to find out.

Even the mailbox was hard to din. It rises above a fork in a deserted road, a lonely mile east of the nearest paved road and nearly a rugged mile straight up. The roads at that point are steep and narrow tunnels cut through a heavy growth of birch and pine trees, banked by tall ferns. There is no sound, no house to be seen in any direction, just that silent and cryptic sentinel.

I nearly missed the mailbox—and although I happened by luck to take the right fork, although I drove as slowly as I could and gawked like any tourist hanging out of a sight-seeing bus, I completely missed the Salinger house.

The house sits back from the road at the crest of the highest rise of all, and is totally hidden behind a solid, impenetrable, man-tall woven wood fence. I shot past it for all my caution, like a man on a roller coaster. One moment the blank wall of fence struck my eye; the next moment I was over the top of the hill and plummeting down the other side. I was gone before I knew I had been there, and there was nothing to do but wait for a chance to make a painfully cramped turn and go back.

### A Gate Closed to Every Stranger

At one side of the road, on a brief clearing which serves as an outdoor garage, stood Salinger's two cars: his old beat-up Jeep, a new gray

Borgward. On the other side was that forbidding fence. I parked next to the Jeep and walked to the gate. It was solid like the rest of the fence, and was locked. I called hello. It was a rather tremulous hello; I confess it. I was intimidated by that fence.

On the other side a baby began to cry. A screen door quickly slammed. A woman's voice quietly comforted the child. And then the gate opened—not wide, a mere tentative slit. A young woman with blondish hair, barefoot, and without make-up, stood there, holding her startled baby in her arms. Behind her was a little girl who had a friendly and expectant look as if she hoped I had brought her a playmate. I was meeting the author's 27-year-old wife, British-born, Radcliffe-educated Claire Douglas Salinger, his 5-year-old daughter Peggy and his 18-month-old son Matthew. Beyond them I had a glimpse of a square, two-story red house. An icebox house, as New Englanders call it.

By and large, journalists receive a fairly warm welcome wherever they go. Not that we necessarily have such delightful personalities—but most people seem to view us as the representatives of their own curiosity about current events and current personages; and also most people like the idea of seeing their names in the paper. At the Salinger home, I can report that I was definitely not invited in to tea. When I announced myself as a journalist, Mrs. Salinger's eyes said unmistakably, "Oh, Lord, not another one!" She sighed and told me that she has a set piece for visitors who want to meet her husband, the gist of it being absolutely no. There was no point in making her recite it. I knew that Salinger resolutely refuses to meet the press in any shape or form, and I had merely called at the gate partly for the record and partly in the hope that I might catch him in an unguarded moment of unprecedented gregariousness. The hope had proved futile, as I had expected. I mumbled my goodbyes to Mrs. Salinger, who was looking more distressed by the moment, and the gate closed. Driving away, I looked back and caught another glimpse of the house through a gap in the birch trees. Behind it someone has put up an old Army-surplus green pyramid tent for the children to play in.

## Schoolgirl's Scoop at a Soda Fountain

Only one journalist has ever interviewed Salinger. She is a young woman named Shirlie Lamothe who has since become a wife and mother and now lives a half hour's drive from Salinger's house. When she interviewed Salinger her name was Shirlie Blaney; she was 16, a "pretty little golden-haired girl," as her teachers recall her, and her niche in the journalistic world was as one of the seven or eight students who prepared a monthly high school page for the Claremont, New Hampshire *Daily Eagle*. Anyone who seeks the facts about Salinger must visit Shirlie. I found her moving into a new house, which she and her husband, who runs a diner, had just rented. What she told me of her meeting with Salinger deserves reporting in full detail, with background supplied by some additional inquiry among Salinger's friends, neighbors and acquaintance, past and present.

Salinger bought his house in Cornish around New Year's Day of 1953, which was his 34th birthday. He was between marriages at the time. The details of his first marriage, like most of the incidents in his life, have to be reported with reservations. His mother, father, and sister, who presumably know more about him than anyone else, will not talk about him. Nor will such close friends and fellow authors S. J. Perelman and Peter De Vries, to whom he has also apparently talked frankly. His more causal acquaintances can never be quite sure of the facts.

## End of Marriage, Start of a Retreat

In the first place he seldom talks about himself, and in the second place many of the things he says seem to be exaggeration or inventions. (As we shall see later, Salinger is a great kidder, almost a practical joker.) But it is definitely established that Salinger married a woman whom he met while serving overseas with the 4th Infantry Division in World War II and divorced her in Florida in 1947 after the briefest of marriages. She seems to have been French and a doctor, almost surely a psychiatrist. I imagine that she was the inspiration for Salinger's onetime interest in psychiatry, which was apparent in *Catcher*, on which he was working all through the '40s, and in the short stories *A Perfect Day for Bananafish* (published in 1948) and "For Esme—with Love and Squalor" (1950). At one period all Salinger's heroes either had just gone to a psychiatrist, were going or were about to go. In the stories since his divorce there are only a few brief mentions of psychiatry, mostly unfavorable.

At any rate Salinger was living the life of a bachelor in 1953 and had been doing so for six years, first in New York City and then in Tarrytown, New York, and Westport, Connecticut, as he migrated farther and farther out in his search for privacy. When he moved into the red house up on that woodsy road in Cornish, he cooked his own meals or ate them in the restaurants in Windsor, Vermont, which is the nearest little city. He did not have a phone; his literary agent and publishers had to call the home of an artist who lived at the bottom of the hill, and the artist or his wife then had to drive to the top of the hill to summon Salinger. He bought a gasoline-powered chain saw and began clearing off some of the hundred acres that went with the house. He listened openmouthed, like anybody born and reared in New York City, while his neighbors explained that corn had to be planted in double rows, to cross-fertilize—but lost his crop anyway, to the weeds. He put in some rosebushes. He lived, in short, much like his character Buddy Glass, the narrator of "Seymour: An Introduction," the most recent of his short stories, which was published in *The New Yorker* of June 6, 1959.

Perhaps Salinger was a little more lonely in Cornish than he had intended. He was working very hard and on occasion with exhausting intensity; his acquaintances of the period have told me that he sometimes kept writing right through the night, or awoke in the early morning, say at 3:30, with an uncontrollable itch to get something down on paper. Sometimes, they say, he disappeared for days or weeks and showed up afterward unshaven, noticeably thinner but full of the air of accomplishment. Between his longer bouts of work he began what for him was an absolute orgy of sociability. He dropped by the artist's home on his way up and down his hill, often stayed for dinner and sometimes played giant steps and little steps with the artist's children on the broad lawn in the twilight. He went to cocktail parties with some of the local teachers, writers, and retired military officers, and entertained them occasionally in return. On one memorable evening at his house he began talking about Zen and yoga and his guests decided to try to get into the lotus position, sitting on the floor with legs crossed, feet resting sole upward on thighs. One young woman who made it promptly got a leg cramp, and it took the combined efforts of all the guests to get her untangled again.

His chief friends, however, were the students at Windsor High School, classes of '53 and '54. He went to all their basketball and football games, sitting with them in the students' section, and afterward shot the breeze with them at their hangout, a lunchroom called Harrington's Spa. When there was an out-of-town game as many of the youngsters as could were welcome to pile into his keep. His full name is Jerome David Salinger, and the youngsters all called him Jerry. When they spotted him on the streets of Windsor they could call to him and wave, from as much as a block or more away, and he would invariably look up, grin, and yell back. He was practically one of the gang. In the evenings, when a group of the students had got together in a car and had no place else to go, they took to riding up the hill and visiting Jerry. There was no fence in front of the house in those days; they could walk right up and knock at his door. Some of them had read *Catcher* and liked it; some had tried to read it and had bogged down, and some had hardly even heard of it. This seemed to make no difference. If anything, Salinger seemed to prefer the poor students, the boys who were skirting the edge of trouble, like young Holden Caufield in *Catcher.*

One of the prominent members of the Class of '54 was Shirlie Blaney, blond, pretty, and popular—and also quite smart and sensitive. She remembers, she told me, seeing Salinger at the football and basketball games, very tall, and casual, wearing tweed jackets with leather patches at the elbows. She also remembers that she was somewhat aghast the first time one of her friends said, "Let's ride up and visit Jerry"—for she was more aware than most of her friends of his literary reputation, although she herself did not especially like his stories. "I knew all about him before I ever met him," she said, as we talked about these events eight years later in the living room of her new house.

## Teen-age Nights at Jerry Salinger's

Despite her doubts she went along with her crowd and presented herself at Salinger's door. "He seemed to be delighted," she recalls in some wonder. "He cried, 'Come on in' and started bringing out the Cokes and potato chips. After a while he began playing some records on his hi-fi; he had hundreds of records, classics and show tunes. We were there a long time and I finally told my date, 'Come on, let's get out of here; Jerry doesn't want to be bothered with us.' But every time we started to leave Jerry would say, 'Stick around. I'll play another record.' I couldn't understand why he put up with us, but he didn't seem to want us to go."

After that Shirlie went to Salinger' house many times. "I never saw anyone fit in the way he did," she told me. "He was just like one of the gang, except that he never did anything silly the way the rest of us did. He always knew who was going with whom, and if anybody was having trouble at school, and we all looked up to him, especially the renegades. He'd play whatever record we asked for on his hi-fi—my favorite was *Swan Lake*—and when we started to leave he'd always want to play just one more."

It was a small house, Shirlie Lamothe remembers, and the living room took up the entire downstairs, except for a tiny kitchen at the back. Salinger was a good housekeeper; his place was always neat. He had a dog—she thinks it was a big English sheep dog—which always lay in the middle of the floor, oblivious to the music and the conversation. Salinger himself was nearly as quiet as the dog; he was a friendly and eager host but he sat smoking his pipe or one cigarette after another, not saying much, mostly listening. "He seemed to love having us around," she says, "but I'd sit there and wonder, why is he doing this? Finally I decided that he was writing another book about teenagers and we were his guinea pigs. I don't mean that he was looking down his nose at us, or had us on a pin or anything like that. He was very sincere. There's nothing phony about him. He's a very nice person. Once I told him I thought I'd like to be a writer, that I was lying awake at night trying to think of ideas. He nodded very sympathetically and said, 'That's the best way. Be sure to get up and write them down, so you don't forget them.' "

One day in the fall of 1953, Shirlie and her fellow high school journalists were in the Windsor office of the *Daily Eagle*, racking their brains. "Our page came out once a month," she says. "That is, if we were lucky. There wasn't much news in Windsor. We were having our usual trouble filling the page this day and then I happened to look out the window—we were up on the second floor—and there across the street was Jerry. I told another girl to come along and ran downstairs after him, I had a wonderful idea."

She and her friend cornered Salinger in front of Harrington's Spa. "Jerry, I need a story for the paper," she said. "Tell me something I can write about."

He looked doubtful. "What paper?"

"Our high school page in the *Eagle*."

He relaxed. "Sure," he said. "Let's go inside."

While Salinger ate his lunch and the two girls drank Cokes in one of the Spa's wooden booths, journalistic history was made. Shirlie Blaney and the *Daily Eagle*, without quite knowing what they were doing, pulled off one of the great scoops of literary history.

The Windsor High School page came out the following Monday. To Shirlie's dismay, her interview was not there. That evening Salinger called her at home—a surprising action, it seems to me, for a man who hates publicity—and said, "That story wasn't in the paper. What's going on?" She reported that she was baffled too, and they chatted a few moments and said goodbye.

The story turned up four days later, in splendid prominence on the *Daily Eagle* editorial page. The strange thing is that Shirlie Blaney Lamothe does not know to this day whether Salinger ever read it, or is even aware that it appeared. That telephone call was the last conversation that she or any of the Windsor High School students ever had with Salinger. The next time a carload of them drove up to Salinger's house he did not seem to be at home, although his Jeep was parked across the road. The next time they found the fence blocking their way, and nobody answered their calls.

They heard that their friend Jerry had gotten married; they could only speculate as to whether he was no longer lonely, was through writing stories about teen-agers, or was just too busy and preoccupied to want to see anybody at all.

## Painstaking Effort that Pays Off

Salinger has worked, since his children were born, in a little studio built of concrete blocks set far down the hill, invisible from the road and even from his house. He goes there very early in the morning and almost always works at least until noon and often much longer, well into the afternoon and evening, sometimes 15 hours or more at a stretch. The studio has a fireplace, two windows and a plastic roof which serves as a sort of skylight; its walls are covered with cup hooks on which he keeps clip boards to which his noted are attached. He writes, rewrites, polishes, and at the end throws most of his words away. According to his friends, *Catcher* was at one stage four times as long—some say 10 times as long—as the version which was published. Most writers who are slow bleeders, as the profession calls them, have trouble earning a living. Salinger is the lucky exception. He still gets royalties from *Catcher* and from *Nine Stories*, a collection of his short stories in 1953, and *The New Yorker* pays him a sizable annual retainer, regardless of whether he comes up with a story or not. But money does not seem to interest him particularly. Most writers pray every night for an offer from one of the book clubs, but Salinger apparently regrets that he let the Book-of-the-Month Club have *Catcher* and is determined not to let it happen again. He has also—ever since Hollywood did what he considered grave violence to the short story that was made into that 1949 movie called *My Foolish Heart*—consistently and sometimes angrily rejected all movie and television.

The author's father is Sol Salinger, son of a rabbi, now about 80 and still active as an importer, chiefly of European cheeses and hams. His mother is Scotch-Irish and at the time of her marriage changed her given name from Marie to Miriam to fit in better with the Salinger family. He has one sister, six years older than he, a buyer at Bloomingdale's department store in New York.

### Literary Start for a Dull Scholar

Unlike the children in the mythical Glass family about which Salinger has been writing in *Franny and Zooey* and all his other recent stories, J. D. was anything but a prodigy. He struggled along painfully in the New York City elementary schools—he was known as Sonny Salinger in those days—and when sent to a private high school promptly flunked out; his record as a freshman shows an I.Q. of 111, a shade above average, and grades of 80 in English, 77 in biology, 66 in algebra and 66 in Latin. His family finally sent him to Valley Forge Military Academy as a sort of last resort—a blessing in disguise, since it gave the world *The Catcher in the Rye.* Later, in a short story class at Columbia, Salinger made a poor first impression on his teacher, the noted editor Whit Burnett, who says, "He was a silent fellow. Almost never a question. Never a comment. I thought he was nothing." Then at the very end of the semester Salinger turned in his first manuscript—so good and so carefully polished that Burnett could publish it at once in his *Story* magazine, without changes.

He was in the Army for three years and I have no doubt that he hated every moment of it. He never did acquire a military bearing or learn to look at home in a uniform. He was a loner who was constantly offended by his hard-drinking, profane companions. But he became a staff sergeant, went in right behind the Normandy invasion forces with an intelligence unit of the Fourth Division and earned five battle stars. He undoubtedly felt about war and soldiers as did the sensitive sergeant in his "For Esme—with Love and Squalor," although he did not, like his sergeant, wind up in a psychiatric ward. At one of the cocktail parties he attended during his gregarious period in Cornish, somebody asked him if "Esme" was autobiographical. One of the guests that evening has told me, "He blew up. He denied hotly that anything he ever wrote was autobiographical. It was as if the question had touched a nerve."

There is one story about Salinger as a soldier which seems almost too pat to be true, but one of his old army buddies swears to it. Ernest Hemingway once visited the unit, and Salinger arranged to meet him—the sort of young writer's call on the master which Salinger now discourages. Hemingway looked at some of Salinger's work, and later, when asked by an officer if it was any good, said, "Yes. He's got a hell of a talent." But while Hemingway was with the unit he got to arguing about the merits of a German Luger he carried as opposed to the U. S. .45, and blasted off the head of a chicken to prove his point. If the story is true, it was probably the basis for the incident in *Esme* where the sergeant is nauseated by the Jeepmate's senseless killing of cat.

Salinger may or may not have been an entertainer on the liner *Kungsholm* at one time, as he told Shirlie Lamothe and as she reported in the *Daily Eagle*. I know for sure that he was interested in dramatics as a boy: the 1930 annual of Camp Wigwam in Maine, where his parents sent him to spend that summer, listed him as everybody's "Favorite Actor." His Zooey is a professional actor, and Franny aspires to become an actress. But the *Kungsholm* story is exactly the sort of tall tale that I have kept running into, that Salinger always seems to have enjoyed making about himself. When he was living in New York after his own divorce, and spending considerable amount of time with other young writers and editors in Greenwich Village, the girls he occasionally escorted to parties always seemed in the words of one of his friends at the time, to be "the youngest, most innocent kids he could find"—and he delighted in telling them wildly untrue stories. He persuaded one young lady that he was the son of an umbrella salesman, and went to elaborate lengths to convince another girl that he was the goal-tender for the Montreal hockey team.

## The Jokes that Hide the Suffering

The characters in Salinger's stories, I have noticed, are great jokers too. Holden Caufield in *Catcher* uses several assumed names and makes up a cock-and-bull story for the woman he meets on the train. Another Salinger hero tells people that his brother, who was actually a poet and a professor of English, is a chiropodist. The masquerades make very funny reading in the stories, and Salinger's friends say that his real-life masquerades were also good, clean fun; but I don't know. There seems to be a suggestion of malice in all of them. But perhaps that is unfair. The real explanation may lie in the comment of a somewhat older woman who went out with Salinger occasionally during his Greenwich Village days. "When there were other people around," she says, "he and I had complete rapport, but when we were alone our discussions always ended up lamely. I truly think that he was afraid. You see, I knew the routines and disguises he used with the college-age girls. He couldn't act for me. He had to be himself."

Salinger has suffered; anybody can tell that just from reading his stories. He suffered in his adolescence at the military academy; it is the suffering that makes *Catcher* so agonizingly identifiable to young people of all ages. He suffered in the war, and his war stories are great because every sensitive person suffered in the war, or expects to suffer in the next one.

Aside from the unmistakable core of suffering, every critic—indeed ever reader—seems to have his own impression of what Salinger is saying and what it is that makes his words so moving. This is perhaps one secret of his popularity. Like the Sphinx and the Mona Lisa, he is inscrutable; the argument over his message is endlessly fascinating. Some people think that *Catcher* is the saddest of contemporary novels, some that it is the funniest, some that it is almost unbearably sad and funny at the same time. In a way Salinger seems at times to be teasing his readers the way he once did his girlfriends. Holden Caufield, for example, appears in places to be an almost deliberately inconsistent character. He hates anything pretentious or hypocritical; his worst swear word is "phony." Yet

Holden himself does some very phony things, as in his masquerades; he is in some ways the biggest liar in the book. He is repelled by human weaknesses yet exhibits most of them himself. He is an idealist, saddened and defeated by a crass world; the reader is led to weep for him; older women have yearned to mother him and younger women to initiate him into sex—but at the end Salinger ships him off for psychiatric treatment, as if that was what he had needed all along.

When Salinger's short story "Teddy" was first published in 1953, arguments raged on campuses for months as to whether Teddy had or had not been murdered by his sister; some critics are still debating the point. When *Franny* first appeared, most readers leaped to the conclusion that her nausea and her abstractedness were the result of an unfortunate premarital pregnancy; it was not until the publication of *Zooey*, which more or less completes Franny's story, that it became unmistakably clear that her symptoms represented a crisis in religious experience. (The great debate over Franny, I have learned, infuriated Salinger, who seems to know a little more about his readers' reactions than he ever lets on. A woman who talked to him in that period told me that he said bitterly, "Here I am, supposed to be writing for the more intelligent reading public—and all that most of my readers got out of *Franny* was that silly question as to whether or not she was pregnant." But a writer of Salinger's skill can certainly avoid such ambiguities if he really wants to.)

### The Strange Ways of Seymour Glass
All the Salinger stories since 1955 and several published before that time, have concerned the Glass family in which Franny and Zooey are the two youngest children. Salinger's favorite in the family seems to be the oldest brother, Seymour; he has thus far written three stories which are mostly about Seymour and has referred to him at length and with great affection in several others. Yet Seymour is surely the strangest hero in all literature. Among the basic biographical facts about him are that at the age of 12 he threw a stone at a neighbor girl, doing nine

stitches worth of damage to her face; that at the time of his marriage at the age of 25 he had scars on his wrists, presumably from a suicide attempt, and was seriously contemplating psychiatric treatment; that he decided at that time to marry a girl of absolutely no intelligence or sensitivity whatever, despite the fact that he himself was a genius (he was the poet-professor); that he left her at the church; that he afterward eloped with her, and that after six years of marriage and some psychiatry he shot himself to death on one of the twin beds of a Florida hotel room while his wife lay taking a nap on the other bed. One might almost say that Salinger is taking the same position with Seymour that Mark Twain took in his perverse little novelette *The Mysterious Stranger*, namely arguing that insanity is the noblest state to which mankind can aspire. But he is doing whatever he is doing in such an immensely subtle, complex, tangential and beautifully artistic way that Seymour seems like a real person, a close friend and dear buddy of countless otherwise conventional and nonpsychotic college freshmen, English professors and middle-aged advertising men. A writer for the British magazine *Twentieth Century* reported recently: "One night in Rome . . . an American friend noted for his sobriety and serious mindedness phoned me in a state of great excitement to say that he had met Seymour Glass's brother-in-law in a bar and would I go and meet him. Feeling that the Salinger myth was getting out of hand I said no . . ." Many other Salinger admirers would have gone without question.

Salinger is no longer writing about adolescence or the war. He is now writing about religion; he seems to have resolved his personal suffering through religious ecstasy. Everything he has published since Teddy, which was a serious argument for the theory of reincarnation that is central to Mahayana Buddhism, has been not so much a story or even a poem as a religious tract. Some friends who seem to know have told me that he has become a Zen Buddhist, that Zen Buddhism is his entire life now, that everything he does, thinks and writes is influenced by Zen Buddhism. Certainly much of his recent writing would bear them out.

## To the Fat Lady, with Love

One of the basic elements of Zen is the experience called *satori*, a sort of mystical revelation in which the converts to Zen suddenly come to realize that everything in the universe is inseparable and diving; that there is no difference between good and evil, life and death, sleep and awakening, mind and matter, man and beast, that everything is part of the divine pattern and the divine cycle. In a number of places, Salinger has written about experiences which can only be described as *satori*. Teddy, for example, says, "It was on a Sunday, I remember. My sister was only a very tiny child then and she was drinking her milk, and all of a sudden I saw that *she* was God and the *milk* was God. I mean all she was doing was pouring God into God . . ."

*Franny and Zooey* is also climaxed by a sort of *satori* experience. All the children of the Glass family, it should be explained, took part, while growing up, in a radio program that Salinger had modeled after the old *Quiz Kids* show. Near the end of the new book Zooey tells his sister about the time that Seymour urged him to shine his shoes before appearing on the show. Zooey objected that nobody could see his shoes, but Seymour insisted: "He said to shine them for the Fat Lady. . . . He never did tell me who the Fat Lady was, but I shined my shoes for the Fat Lady every time I ever went on the air again. . . . This terribly clear, clear picture of the Fat Lay formed in my mind. I had her sitting on this porch all day swatting flies . . . I figured the heat was terrible, and she probably had cancer. . . ." Then Zooey goes on to say, "There isn't anyone *anywhere* that isn't Seymour's Fat Lady. . . . And don't you know—*listen* to me, now—*don't you know who that Fat Lady really is?* . . . It's Christ Himself, Christ Himself . . ." And upon hearing these words, Franny, who has been having the symptoms of a nervous breakdown in connection with her religious strivings, relaxes and falls into a deep and soul-satisfying sleep, and the story is over.

To pragmatic readers, Salinger's message may seem to be that we should all love the unattractive Fat Ladies of the world, for they too are God's creatures. Everything else in Salinger's nose-quivering prose and his withdrawn ways would indicate, however, that he himself cannot abide Fat Ladies; perhaps this is his personal battleground between good and evil. As for the religious implications, scholars will note in *Franny and Zooey* a peculiar mingling of the Zen notion of *satori* with Christianity, (especially since Zooey and Franny had previously been talking at length about Jesus and St. Francis of Assisi) and the Hindu nirvana, the mystical concept of sleep or nothingness as the ultimate bliss. I suspect that Salinger is using the members of the Glass family as spokesmen for various shades of religious experience—and hopes, when the saga of the Glass family is complete, to have written the definitive work on the religions of the world, slightly disguised as fiction. (There is one brother, thus far mentioned only in passing, who is a priest—and will surely turn up in the future as a representative of Catholicism.)

Can Salinger bring it off? Can fiction and religious debate be mixed? Can a man who flunked his classes as a high school sophomore blossom into history's greatest religious scholar? Can a former Montreal goalie unlock the secrets of the universe? These are the most fascinating literary questions of our time, perhaps of any time.

Certainly Salinger has the seriousness of purpose to accomplish what he sets out to do. His isolation, although it may have some neurotic overtones, is a form of almost slavish devotion to his work: he cannot stand to have it interrupted. The hours he spends at his labors are almost incredible to other authors, most of whom have trouble concentrating for more than four or five hours a day. His patience is amazing. Most authors can hardly wait to see their words in print, but Salinger holds the words back until they are exactly right, and does not seem disturbed at all by the fact that his total output, aside from some conventional stories written while he was learning his trade, now amounts to only one slim novel and 13 short stories.

## Writing as Tight as Violin Strings

Salinger also has the artistry. His stories, when he finishes writing, rewriting, throwing away, starting over, and rewriting again, are as tight as violin strings. Every phrase, every word is right. He is perhaps the greatest word-weaver in American literary history. His stories can be read, aside from any meaning they may or may not contain, as sheer poetry—which is perhaps what they are. In explaining why he refuses to meet his public, Salinger once said, "The stuff's all in the stories; there's no use talking about it." Perhaps it is as futile to inquire into the meanings of Salinger's stories or his authenticity as a religious scholar— despite the fascination of the argument—as to ask: What does *Hamlet* mean? What was William Blake trying to say in *Songs of Innocence*? What did Beethoven say in his *Fifth Symphony*, and what business did a deaf man have writing music anyway?

Aside from all these literary considerations, which could be elaborated endlessly, you are perhaps wondering if I ever managed to see Salinger in the flesh. I'll only say one thing: I certainly tried.

Shirlie Blaney Lamothe told me that she had seen him on innumerable occasions in Windsor just after school let out, around 3 or 4 o'clock in the afternoon. Other Salinger acquaintances told me that he could sometimes be seen in Windsor around 10 or 11 o'clock in he morning, buying a newspaper or shopping at the supermarket. A Windsor High School teacher told me that he had frequently run into Salinger and his family at the Howard Johnson restaurant in nearby White River Junction, Vermont, eating early Sunday dinner.

I drove through Windsor time after time, morning and afternoon, watching for an ancient Jeep or a new gray Borgward. I waited in the parking lot of the supermarket and then walked down Main Street and sat on a shaded bench in front of the Windsor cemetery. There was a monument behind me with the inscription:

*EDMUND SHATTUCK*
*Died Feb. 3, 1875*
*Aged 71 Years*

Shattuck is a highly esteemed name around that part of New England. I found myself wondering, over the space of several hours if Edmund Shattuck too had been a recluse. Probably not.

A gray foreign car approached but turned out to be a Volkswagen. A Jeep with a New Hampshire license loomed down the street. My heart beat faster, but the driver was a youth with a scraggly blond beard—a beat-type Zen, not the authentic version.

### Roadside Vigil by a Circus Poster

Perhaps Salinger used the back roads; perhaps the true recluse would scorn the main drag. I did some more exploring and found that there was no possible way that he could drive from his house to Windsor except across a covered bridge that spans the Connecticut River. I spent all one Sunday morning parked at the bridge, watching the warblers and song sparrows in the underbrush and studiously reading and rereading a red, blue and white poster, wrapped around a telephone pole down the highway, which announced that the King Bros. Circus was coming to town. A car with a New York state license stopped behind me and an elderly man and his wife got out to take a picture of the bridge. Two Jeeps drove by, neither of them carrying Salinger. It had been raining and when the sun came out steam began to rise from the pavement. The humidity inside my car became intolerable.

The hour hand on my wrist watch crawled toward noon, then toward one. I decided that Salinger had eluded me by driving toward the north, toward White River Junction, and made haste to follow him. But there was no Jeep or Borgward in the Howard Johnson parking lot, and nobody who even faintly looked like Salinger at any of the tables. I dawdled over dinner until my waitress lost patience, then paid my check, asking the cashier if a Mr. Salinger had been in that day. She had never heard of a Mr. Salinger.

I gave up. I had all sorts of pressing work at my office; I had better things to do than sweat out a glimpse of a man who did not want to be glimpsed. I started to drive back home, through a drizzle which had replaced the morning rain, and on impulse I took a little detour and drove once again up the hillside and past the mailbox and the impenetrable fence.

The Borgward was in the clearing; the Jeep was gone. Salinger had eluded me; perhaps everything about him was eluding me. He had probably pulled into one driveway of the Howard Johnson just as I, in my bad luck, was pulling out the other one. I drove on, disconsolate.

And then I saw him. His Jeep was well past the house, well down the hillside, parked at a reckless angle next to a little snow fence and garden patch. He was inside the Jeep, half hidden by the curtains, wearing a rain jacket, puffing reflectively on a pipe.

I had heard about that snow fence from one of the neighbors. He had been having trouble with woodchucks in his garden, and he had built the fence to try to discourage them. Woodchucks, however, can burrow; they are no respecters of fences; they can try a man's soul.

I don't know what Salinger was thinking. Perhaps Zen thoughts. But he looked to me at that moment like any other city-bred gardener, frustrated by varmints; he looked a little miserable himself, like the Fat Lady, and I only wished that I could have expressed my sympathy.

# What I Did Last Summer

BETTY EPPES

I decided one day in 1976 that I was so bored that if I hit another tennis ball I was going to go crazy. So I thought, Now wait a minute, there's a small weekly paper in town—the Baton Rouge *Enterprise*—and if they needed a tennis *columnist*? I was a pretty good tennis player—fluctuating between No. 1 and No. 3 at my tennis club in Baton Rouge, which is the Southwood Tennis Club. I work with weights, dead-lifting, squats, bench presses, and all that stuff.

But I had never written a word professionally. In 1974 I tried a novel—more or less a kind of purge—about a woman whose life was parallel to mine. But I had no training to do such a thing; I had not even graduated from high school. I grew up in Trenton, Mississippi, which is a crossroads in Smith County; my father was a dirtfarmer. We were very poor. I married very young and had three babies. I learned my tennis from a friend in Florida. I don't guess there *is* a tennis racket in Trenton, Mississippi. But everything I try I study at incessantly. That's what I did with my writing.

So I wrote six tennis columns for the Baton Rouge *Enterprise*. But they wouldn't publish them. So finally I took the articles to the *Morning*

*Advocate*, which is the major daily in Baton Rouge. They not only published the columns, but after a while they let me do just about anything that was almost a reasonable story. Not only did I do columns on Bjorn Borg, Billie Jean King, and Rod Laver, and why tennis skirts cost so much money, but I went to the New Orleans Saints footfall camp and did interviews with Hank Stram, and a lot of neat things like that.

It's very important for me to be super-excited about things. I have to feel challenged. Otherwise I get terribly bored and begin wondering if I shouldn't move on to something else. Last summer I started wondering what assignment I could take on for myself that would be challenging and super-exciting. I thought and thought. I told Larry Fisher, who is the owner of the bookstore where I was browsing, that I was thinking—hoping to come up with something really interesting. He said he'd think about it too.

A day or so later I happened to be leafing through an encyclopedia of writers. I turned to William Faulkner who is just my idol, my personal *idol*, and there were pages and pages on him. Then by chance, because I had just reread *The Catcher in the Rye* I thought, Well, I'll check out J. D. Salinger, which is what I did. There was one skimpy paragraph.

So I went to Larry Fisher and I said, Damn, Larry, there's nothing at *all* about Salinger. He said that was because nobody knows anything about him. He said, Hey! There's your interview! I said, That's a good idea. I think I'll so it. Larry laughed and said, I think you ought to go and walk on the moon, too!

But the more I thought of it, the more enamored of the idea I became. I thought, damn, I'm going to go for it.

Actually I had a small file on J. D. Salinger. I am a very practical woman and I file things I think might come in handy later on. J. D. Salinger and Howard Hughes happened to be the most interesting people I didn't know. Peculiar birds. I had little files on both. In Salinger's file I had a short item clipped out of *Newsweek*, I think, which reported that he shopped in a complex called Cummins Corner in the town of Windsor, Vermont, not far from where he lives in Cornish, New Hampshire. I thought, That's where I'll go to try to find him.

So I filed two stories in advance with my editor, Jeff Cowart, at the Baton Rouge *Advocate*. I didn't tell him what I was going to do. I knew he would have said, Eppes, people have been trying to get an interview with Salinger for twenty-seven years; forget it, and go on out there and meet your next deadline. Well, I didn't want to hear that. So I just bought an airline ticket to Manchester, New Hampshire.

Now, as I say, I'm a very practical woman. I'd checked everything out and discovered the whole trip was going to cost $1,000. I thought, Jesus God, Eppes, that's a lot of money to throw away. So I cast around in my mind for another person in that area I could get an interview with in order to pay off some of the expenses. The only person I could think of was William Loeb, the publisher of the *Manchester Leader*. He's not one of my most favorite people. He is just about the most out-spoken conservative man there ever was, making all sorts of crazy noises, a wild man, but on the other hand I didn't want to eat $1,000. So I called up his secretary to arrange for an interview. She said it would be fine. So I hopped on the plane and flew on up to Manchester. I spent the first night in Manchester asking the populace what it felt about Bill Loeb. I wanted to get some background. I interviewed fifty-seven people. Ten out of the fifty-seven didn't like Bill Loeb.

He is ill-at-ease answering questions, it seemed to me. But there was no doubt about his attitudes. Once, when I referred to his conser-vatism, he interrupted me and gave me to understand that he thought of himself not as a conservative but a red-blood American. He said that if I cared anything about my country I should go back to Louisiana and campaign hard for a Ronald Reagan presidency. His office was full of American flags. A big one stood in the corner. You would have thought he was a member of the House of Representatives. He has a lot of little flags on his desk. He had one in his lapel. Certainly he was very gen-erous with his time. He invited me to a banquet at which he gave an award to the bravest man in New Hampshire who was somebody who had jumped into a river to save a child. Mr. Loeb gave him a plaque. Afterwards, he let me sit in on the opening meeting at which anybody could come in and grill him on his policies. Of course, he has the option of skipping the questions but I didn't see him do it. He allows them to grill the hell out of him: *What kind of newspaper you running?*—very sarcastic and needling.

After I had done with William Loeb, I rented a sky-blue Pinto and headed into the Green Mountains to look for J. D. Salinger. I've never driven into the mountains—and there I was, hauling my ass around those strange hills in a sky-blue Pinto that could barely make it over the peaks!

On my way to Windsor I stopped in Claremont, New Hampshire, to visit the offices of the *Claremont Eagle*. In my Salinger file at home I had a clipping about a Windsor schoolgirl named Shirlie Blaney who had managed to get an interview with Salinger for the student issue of the *Claremont Eagle* back in 1953. She had seen him eating in a local restaurant and had walked up and simply asked him. He had said OK and he had given her—at least as far as I knew—the only interview he had ever granted. There had been such a rumpus about this interview—I mean the little girl suddenly found herself in correspondence with people all over the country—that it reinforced Salinger's determination never to give interviews again.

I thought I should read the Blaney interview at least to prepare myself. A fellow who works for the *Eagle* named Jefferson Thomas of all names (he said he had a terrible time in the Army where he had to give his last name first) helped me look for it back in the files. He was very helpful. It turned out he and I share the same birthday. It took us 2 1/2 hours to find the story which I read into my tape recorder.

I also dropped into the bookstore in Claremont. It's a small bookstore but being the only one in that area Salinger comes over from Cornish and visits it on occasion. I talked with the owner of the store about him. She said, He's such a peculiar man, not like any customer you ever saw. He'll come in and doesn't want to speak even. If you ask if he needs help, he just shakes his head and walks away. . . . One day my little girl was here with me when he came in. She was so delighted. She got a copy of a book of his and went and asked for his autograph. Then he turned on his heel and walked out. He is a very peculiar man.

I stayed in Windsor, Vermont, at the Windsor Motel. Salinger lives in Cornish, of course, across the Connecticut River in New Hampshire, which is just the smallest kind of hamlet. Windsor is the nearest place that has lodgings. The motel there looked like an old-time motor court from twenty years ago—very primitive, no phones in the room, but it's set in a beautiful rural area amongst all those hills. Windsor itself is about seven miles away.

In my room that night I spent some time listening to the Blaney interview and preparing my questions, writing one on top of each page of my little spiral notebook. In that interview Salinger had mentioned that Holden Caulfield was autobiographical and that it had been a great relief telling people about his own early life. I thought I'd ask him about that, and if he planned a sequel to *The Catcher in the Rye*. He had talked to Blaney about wanting to go to Indonesia. I wondered if he had ever gotten there, and what he remembered about entertaining troops aboard ship, which he had done in the West Indies. I thought I'd ask him about the American Dream. I had about twenty-odd questions in my notebook when I'd finish.

The next morning it was cold. An arctic front had come through that night and there was ice in the swimming pool next to the motel. Here it was in the middle of June and I was wearing the normal clothes you'd wear in Baton Rouge in the summer. Luckily, I'd thrown a long-sleeved sweater in my bag. If it hadn't been for the sweater I would have froze my ass off.

I drove to Windsor. It is a small country town—everything concentrated on Maine Street with Bridge Street crossing it and leading down to the covered bridge over the Connecticut River. The first thing I did was to go into the drugstore. I told the man behind the counter that I was interested in interviewing J. D. Salinger. He looked at me and said,

You're a journalist. Go away. He wouldn't say another word. And I thought, Oh God, here it was, the first time I'd mentioned his name, and it was like a door had been slammed on me. I couldn't afford too many more of *those*. So I went back out in the street.

The Cummins Corner I had read about in the news story in my Salinger file turned out to be a bunch of shops in a big old wooden, sprawling building—a grocery store, a liquor store, a barber shop, and an ice cream parlor, though needless to say no one was hurrying in to buy ice cream *that* morning.

I went into the grocery in Cummins Corner and told the man behind the counter that I had read in a story that J. D. Salinger often came in there. He looked puzzled and said, No. He didn't think so. But he was polite. He wasn't like the guy in the drugstore. In fact, this guy didn't really know who J. D. Salinger *was*. I said, Think. Really think hard.

So he did, and after a while he said, Well, that name does sort of ring a bell. I have this really strange customer who comes in once a week to do some shopping. As a matter of fact, this guy has an unlisted phone number—and that's a little freaky in these parts. He said he had the number on file because this guy was a customer.

So he pulled out the number, and sure enough in the card it had J. D. Salinger. I thought, Ah *hah*! I didn't ask for the number, because I was sure he wouldn't give it to me, but I asked if he would call the number *for* me. He said he would. He called the number and then handed me the phone. It was J. D. Salinger's housekeeper! I told her who I was and that I would like to see Mr. Salinger. She got very nervous and said that she shouldn't be talking to me. She said Mr. Salinger doesn't want to *talk* to anybody, he doesn't want to *see* anybody, he doesn't want to be *bothered*. If she helped me she'd get in big trouble. I tried to reassure her. I said, Honey, you don't have to help me; just tell me how I can get to see Mr. Salinger. She was so nervous by this time she could barely talk. She said that I should write him a note and post it. I moaned. I said it could be a week before he ever saw it. She went to suggest that if I handed the note to the girl in the

Windsor post office, Mr. Salinger would get it. She must have been very relieved when I thanked her and hung up.

Well, then I bought myself a Mead's spiral notebook with a blue cover in which to compose this letter to J. D. Salinger. I thought it would be tacky to send him a note from my own reporter's notebook which is so small that I would have to use up five or ten pages just to tell him I wanted to see him. I bought a Bic ballpoint pen for nineteen cents. I took the notebook out on the street and since there are no benches in Windsor I sat down on the curbstone to do the letter. I thought, Oh God! What do you say to J. D. Salinger? Good *night*! I mean he gets tons and tons of requests—what would make him answer mine?

I started off by telling him who I was, and that I earned my living writing. I did not mention *The Catcher in the Rye* or any of his work at all. It's true I reread *The Catcher in the Rye* twice a year, but Salinger isn't one of my favorite writers—I can't really identify with the characters. What had fascinated me was that as a girl in Smith County, Mississippi, where males and females are very secluded from one another, I had two older brothers, and reading *The Catcher in the Rye* was like opening a secret door into their private male world. I really learned from it and I can certainly recognize the man's literary skills. Of course, I didn't say any of this in the letter. I told him I wasn't a girl who had come to usurp any of his privacy; I was a woman who supported herself through writing and would very much like to see him. I wanted to know if he was still writing. I told him I was a novelist. I told him writing was so hard.

Then I explained that I was staying at the Windsor Motel where there were no phones in the rooms. Since he could not reach me, I wrote him that I would come back to Cummins Corner at 9:30 the next morning and wait for thirty minutes. If he didn't come, I would be there at 9:30 the *next* morning to wait for thirty minutes . . . and I told him if he didn't come then I was going back to Baton Rouge because I couldn't afford to stay in Windsor any longer.

I told him that I would be sitting in a sky-blue Pinto right by the corner and just up the road from the covered bridge and that I was tall with green eyes and red-gold hair. I finished the letter, "I will make no further effort to seek you out, not because of guard dogs or fences, but because I do not want to anger you or cause you grief." Then I put PS down at the bottom: "I see perfectly why you live in this area. Its beauty is awesome. Often I find myself whispering."

I took the letter into the post office and said I had a letter for J. D. Salinger. I got a pretty peculiar look as I handed it over. The people in Windsor seemed so determined to protect him. God *bless*!

After I'd done that, I went and brought some extra batteries for my tape recorder. I was being very cautious. After all, it was so cold the batteries I brought with me could have been affected and malfunctioned. It was best not to leave anything to chance.

Then I bought an eight-pack of Tab. It's my favorite drink. I drink Tab like most people drink booze: I really swill it down. I took the Tab back to the Windsor Motel and there I fell apart. It was interesting. Up to that point I had been very confident. I remembered how nice Salinger was to the women he wrote about in his stories and books. Sometimes he was very rough on the men, but he was gentle with females. Holden is so very tender to his sister in *The Catcher in the Rye*. It was going to be a piece of cake. But then in my motel room I began thinking of all the reasons for J. D. Salinger *not* to come. I really got panicky. I hate to fail. I tried to think of things to encourage myself—that Edmund Hillary had climbed Mt. Everest the same year that *The Catcher in the Rye* came out. It didn't work. I got so upset that I began swearing and pacing and worrying and trying to calm myself by drinking Tab and finally I said to myself, Oh well! And I went and pigged out on some fresh fruit. I eat fruit like I drink Tab.

In the middle of the night I woke up and I *knew* J. D. Salinger was going to come. I was so excited that I had to say to myself, Now Betty Eppes, calm down. I have these *things*. I always know when something really important is going to happen. I always have them when people are dying. They just come to me like revelations.

I got up at four in the morning and turned on the TV. All hell had broken loose in the environment. Mt. St. Helens had erupted. On the TV preachers were wailing about Hell and damnation and destruction. But I remember thinking that only some natural catastrophe like that was going to keep me from my interview with J. D. Salinger. I was really confident. At breakfast I left a five dollar tip. I *knew* he was going to turn up.

I drove up to Cummins Corner in my Pinto. I bought a Tab there. Then I positioned myself in the Pinto about fifty yards from the covered bridge that crosses the Connecticut. I knew Salinger would have to cross that bridge to come into Windsor. One great piece of luck was that the bridge was being repaired. People parked their cars in a parking area on the New Hampshire side and then walked across. I knew Salinger would have to appear on foot. So I checked the camera and got it ready for an approach shot. I aimed it towards the covered bridge. I got the tape recorder out and set it up. I knew that Salinger would be spooked by the sight of a tape recorder, but also that it would be crazy to try to talk to him scribbling away in his face. So I thought *Hell*, I'll stuff the tape recorder down my blouse under my long-sleeved sweater. It was difficult to do without looking like I had some kind of deformity. I thought, Jeez—I wouldn't want J. D. Salinger to think I've got a square boob. So I finally shoveled the tape recorder down the sleeve of my blouse right under my armpit where I could hold it in against my body with my arm. I thought, if I just keep my elbow in, everything will be cool.

It seemed like I had waited there in the Pinto for about three years. I was just beginning to read an article in that morning's Boston *Globe* entitled "What Is Luck?" when right on time—nine-thirty—he stepped out from the black of that covered bridge . . . J. D. Salinger!

He didn't look like I thought he would. He had white hair. That freaked me out. He came out of the dark and the sun lit his hair like a beacon. In all the pictures I had seen of him he had dark hair. I was not looking for a Holden Caulfield but I was probably *thinking* of a Holden

Caulfield. Not only that, but I was surprised by the intensity of the man. He walked almost like he was driven or pursued, his shoulders hunched up around his ears . . . it was almost a *run*. He looked neither right nor left but in my direction. As soon as I saw him coming I fumbled under my blouse to turn on the tape recorder and I opened the door and got out of the Pinto. He kept coming towards me. He had an attaché case stuck under arm. He walked right up to me and said "Betty Eppes?" which meant, of course, he had seen or had news of my letter. He mispronounced my name. "Eppès," he said. We shook hands standing beside the Pinto. He had on a pair of jeans, sneakers, and one of those shirt-jackets. He looked in remarkable shape—very slim, very healthy. After he shook my hand, he backed off a few steps. He's a very tall man so he looked down on me with eyes, very black, that seemed to glitter. I thought, Shit, I have just shaken J. D. Salinger's hand; then I realized that the Sony tape recorder was going to fall out. I could feel it beginning to slip down my side. It was terrible! I clamped my arm in to keep it from going any further. And then I realized I only had 29 minutes of tape to go and when the machine reached the end it would give off a little beep. I thought if that signal went off while I was standing in front of J. D. Salinger and he heard it coming out from under my sweater, I'd just fall down in a *faint*. It was terrible! You don't *know* how terrible it was!

He seemed just as nervous as I was. His hands shook. Here was J. D. Salinger and I thought, Shit, the man isn't going to stand still. I mean it was obvious that he didn't want to be there . . . he was going to bolt any second. Great God! I thought, Now, Eppes, if you don't get but one question in before he bolts, it had better be about Holden Caulfield, because he's the one everybody want to know about.

First, I thanked Mr. Salinger for coming. He said, I don't know why I did, actually. There's nothing I can tell you. Writing's a very personal thing. So why'd you come here? He said that my letter had been very brief.

I was very nervous. I said, I came not just for myself, Mr. Salinger, but as a *spokesman* for all who wants to know if you're still writing.

It was then he must have known—I was a journalist. After all, I was reading the questions off my notebook page, and scribbling notes.

I asked about Caulfield. Please tell me—is he going to grow up? Is there going to be a sequel to *The Catcher in the Rye*? All your readers want to know the answer to that question.

The whole town was gaping. I mean everybody. The old man in the Cummins Corner office had his nose pressed to the windowpane. The people in the laundromat came out and stood on the sidewalk. There were faces looking out of the windows of the apartments across the street.

I kept pegging away about Holden Caulfield. He said, It's all in the book. Read the book again, it's all in there. Holden Caulfield is only a frozen moment in time.

So I asked, Well, does that mean he *isn't* going to grow up—there won't be a sequel?

He said, Read the book.

Every question I asked about Holden Caulfield he replied, Read the book. It's all in the book. There's no more to Holden Caulfield. Over and over. Except when I asked him if the book was autobiographical. When I quoted to him what he had once said in that interview with the Windsor schoolgirl about his boyhood being like Holden's, he seemed to be make very uncomfortable by that. He said, Where did you get that stuff from? He looked at me very hard. I thought he was going to say, Read the book, again, and if he has I would have stomped on his foot! But this time he said, I don't know . . . I don't know. I've just let it all go. I don't know about Holden any more.

So I left off Holden Caulfield and began asking about other things. Christ! I just wanted to ask him a question he would answer. I began turning the pages of my notebook.

**EPPES:** Have you visited Indonesia?

**SALINGER:** I really don't want to talk about this.

**EPPES:** You told Miss Blaney you were going to London to make a movie. Did you?

**SALINGER:** Where'd you get all this old stuff?

**EPPES:** Did you make or work on a movie? Will you in the future?

**SALINGER:** Can we go on to something else?

**EPPES:** Of course. But just for fun, do you remember the name of the ship you worked on as an entertainer?

**SALINGER:** I do, yes. The Kungsholm.

**EPPES:** You were in the Counter-Intelligence Corps. How many languages do, or did you, speak?

**SALINGER:** French and German, but not very well. And a few phrases of Polish.

**EPPES:** Given your family background, why writing?

**SALINGER:** I can't say exactly. I don't know if any writer can. It's different for each person. Writing's a highly personal act. It's different for each writer.

**EPPES:** Did you consciously opt for a writing career, or did you just drift into it?

**SALINGER:** I don't know. (A long pause) I truly don't. I just don't know.

I wanted a Tab. It was so painful for him to answer. But he kept standing there. I hurried on with my questions. I said that I had heard he had done his writing in a special concrete workshop situated behind his house. I asked if he did his writing there.

He said, I have my work area set up the way I like, so it's comfortable. But I don't want to discuss it. I don't want people streaming up here trying to climb walls and peek in windows. I'm comfortable, he said, and that's enough.

I asked him if publishing wasn't important.

He said that was an easy question that wouldn't take any time to answer at all. He said he had *no* plans to publish. *Writing* was what was important to him—and to be left alone so that he *could* write. To be left in peace. He couldn't tell me *why* he felt he wanted to be left in peace . . . but that he had felt that way in grade school, at the academy, and before and after military service. And he felt it now, too. Boy! He kept harping on that!

So I asked him why he had ever published anything *at all* if he felt so strongly that it disturbed his private life.

He said that he had not foreseen what was going to happen. He said he didn't expect it, and when it did happen, he didn't want it. It meant he couldn't live a normal life. He had to put the roads near his home under patrol. His children suffered. Why couldn't his life be his own?

I asked his if that was so why he had bothered to see me. Why hadn't he stayed up on his mountain? Why hadn't he ignored my letter?

He said, You write. I write. He had come as one writer to another. Then he began asking me about my writing. Had I done a book yet? Goodness me! J. D. Salinger asking Betty Eppes about *her* work!

So I told him I had written a novel and given it to a regional publisher—Southern Publishing—but while the contract was being prepared, the couple who ran the company split up and the manuscript was lost. I only had a copy of the first two-thirds of the book. I told Salinger that I was so upset with myself for not keeping a copy, and with the two of them for losing the work, that I just hadn't had the heart to rewrite that last section.

Salinger nodded and said that publishing was a vicious, vicious thing. He said that so many unforeseen things happen when you publish. He said that I'd probably be happier if I never published. He said there was a certain peace in not publishing.

Then we began talking about autographs. I asked him why he hated to give them. He said he didn't believe in giving autographs. It was a meaningless gesture. He told me never to sign my name for anyone else. It was all right for actors and actresses to sign their names, because all they had to give were their faces and names. But it was different with writers. They had their work to give. Therefore, it was cheap to give autographs. He said, Don't you ever do it! No self-respecting writer should ever do it.

Well, I myself had never really thought much about it. I mean nobody had ever asked me for my autograph before—well, *once*, a little girl did, but she thought I was Jane Fonda. I signed "Jane Fonda"—I don't want to hurt the girl's feelings.

I tried other subjects. I asked about discipline in writing.

He said that discipline was no problem—that you either want to write or you don't.

His style? Well, he said he didn't know much about his writing style. Obviously a writer had to make choices. Decisions. But he really couldn't help me with that question.

So I tried politics.

He said, I don't care about politicians. I don't have anything in common with them. They try to limit our horizons; I try to expand our horizons. He said that not one politician stood out in his mind.

I tried economics—inflation, unemployment, energy . . . did he have any comments to make about *these* issues.

No. He said that none of this touched him personally. Not his area. He didn't know much about these things.

That was becoming such a stock answer—that he didn't know. It made me super-nervous. He was super-nervous, too. He kept moving that attaché case around, sticking it out in front of him and then tucking it under his arm.

Then we had this exchange:

**EPPES:** I've heard you're into organic foods. Do you feel eating food stuffs organically grown is that important?

**SALINGER:** Yes, or I wouldn't bother.

**EPPES:** Is it true that you'll eat fried foods only if they're prepared in cold-pressed peanut oil?

**SALINGER:** Yes.

**EPPES:** Why is that?

**SALINGER:** Are you informed on the differences between cold-pressed oil as opposed to oil extracted by other methods?

**EPPES:** Yes, I am. I don't use peanut oil but only cold-pressed oils. I make all my salad dressing from cold-pressed apricot kernel, sesame seed, sunflower seed oil. With a few herbs thrown in you come up with a super salad.

I didn't know how many people would be interested in Salinger on cooking oils, so I went back to something more general. I threw him my question about the American Dream. Did he believe in it?

He said, My own version of it, yes.

When I asked if he would elaborate, he said, I wouldn't care to, no.

So I said that the Constitution seemed to have been written by men for men and that it may not have been intended for women. That produced quite a response!

Salinger: Don't you accept that! Don't ever listen to that. Who says you don't have a right to the American Dream, who says? That's frightful. Awful! Don't you accept that. The American Dream is for all Americans. Women are Americans too. It is for you too. Proceed. Claim it if you want it. . . .

After a while, I got to wondering if Salinger was going to bring a halt to this, which was OK by me, because the tape recorder was getting pretty close to the end where the beep was going to go off. I couldn't look at my watch to find out how much time there was left because if I had lifted my arm to look, that damn tape recorder would have slid right down, and I would have died! If Salinger knew what I was going through he might have smiled.

As it was, he smiled twice. The first time was when in the middle of our conversation—I don't know if it was frustration, or intimidation, or awe, or what—tears began to roll down my face. . . . God, it was embarrassing! And I couldn't wipe them away—I had this friggy pencil in one hand and I couldn't move the other arm because it had the tape recorder wedged in under it. Salinger smiled sympathetically at this point; he reached across and wiped those tears off with a knuckle, and then wiped his knuckles on his jeans.

The second time he smiled was when I asked him if he really was writing every day what then was he working on? He smiled and said, I can't tell you that. I kind of understood what he meant.

Finally Salinger went off to get his mail. I went into Cummins Corner to get an 8-pack of tab. I must have stayed in there for about ten minutes. As I came out of Cummins Corner I saw Salinger coming back along the street from the post office. I jumped in the Pinto, changed tapes and shoved the tape recorder back down my blouse, turned it on, and then I grabbed my camera and took three pictures of Salinger, who had been stopped by the young owner of Cummins Corner market; the guy had come out put his hand on Salinger's arm. Apparently he wanted to shake Salinger's hand. That made Salinger furious. He came stalking across the street to the Pinto and leaning in the window right in my face he really got on my case! He chewed my ass *out*! He was wearing his glasses this time. His eyes seemed much larger behind them.

Here's what he said: Because of you, this man I don't know, have never even met, has spoken to me. Just walked up to me on the street over there and *spoke to me*. Just like that. Walked up and put his hand on my arm and *spoke to me*. I don't like that. There have been calls to my neighbors because of you and I don't like my neighbors inconvenienced. I want to be left alone, left to my privacy. That's why I moved here. I moved here seeking privacy, a place where I could lead a normal life and write. But people like you pursue me. I don't wish to seem harsh. It's just that I'm a private person. I resent intrusions. I resent questions. I don't want to talk to strangers. I don't particularly like talking to *anybody*. I'm a writer. Write me letters if you wish. But please, don't drop in.

I knew I had nothing to lose at this point. As he began to turn away, I said, I'm sorry you're upset, Mr. Salinger, but please wait. Just a moment more. *May I take a close-up photograph of you?*

He looked horrified. Absolutely not! No!

All right, Mr. Salinger, all right. I've put the camera down. It's down, Mr. Salinger, see?

As he paused, I put one more question to him. Tell me honestly, are you really writing?

I thought he'd run, But he answered, I am really writing. I told you. I love to write and I assure you I write regularly. I'm just not publishing. I write for myself. For my own pleasure. I want to be left alone to do it. So leave me alone. Don't drop in here like this again.

Off he went. As he headed for the dark entrance of the covered bridge I snapped a picture. Before I could think of anything else to call after him, he walked back into that bridge and disappeared.

I sent Salinger a copy of the story I wrote for the *Advocate*. Eleven days later I received two Photostats—copies of order blanks he had sent away to New York. They were signed by him, mailed in Windsor, and addressed to me care of the *Advocate*. I haven't any idea if he sent them to me. The order was addressed to the Chocolate Soup Company in

New York City and in it Mr. Salinger asked for two oversized schoolbags, gift-wrapped, from Denmark (at $16.50 each) that had been advertised in the then current *New Yorker*. Now why was that sent to me? It drove me just about crazy trying to figure it out.

After the article appeared, there was a lot more spooky little shit like that—just enough to drive you crazy. I have an accordion-file stuffed with job offers, letters, requests . . . people seemed to come out of the woodworks wanting things from me. There were two motion-picture companies who tried to get me to go back up there to convince Salinger to make a movie! In a way I guess it was a kind of education about what Mr. Salinger had gone through *himself* and what had turned him into the kind of person I found.

I want to tell you that interview with J. D. Salinger was the most difficult one I ever tried. The next most difficult was one I did with Edwin W. Edwards, the former governor of Louisiana, on gambling—stalking him around Las Vegas for three days. But he doesn't compare with J. D. Salinger. Those eyes of Salinger's . . . the strangest black eyes that glittered and just seemed to gaze right through you. So weird, weird, weird!

*This* summer I decided to go to England. I interviewed James Mason, the English actor. He was a piece of cake compared to J. D. Salinger. He turned up in a pink sweater. He looked gorgeous. I just wanted to munch on him.

# J. D. Salinger Speaks about His Silence

LACEY FOSBURGH

Goaded by publication of unauthorized editions of his early, previously uncollected works, the reclusive author J. D. Salinger broke a public silence of more than 20 years last week, issuing a denunciation and revealing he is hard at work on writings that may never be published in his lifetime.

Speaking by telephone from Cornish, New Hampshire, where he makes him home, the 55-year-old author whose most recent published work, "Raise High the Roof Beam, Carpenters" and "Seymour, an Introduction," appeared in 1962, said: "There is a marvelous peace in not publishing. It's peaceful. Still. Publishing is a terrible invasion of my privacy. I like to write. I love to write. But I write just for myself and my own pleasure."

For nearly half an hour after saying he intended to talk "only for a minute," the author, who achieved literary fame and cultish devotion enhanced by his inaccessibility following publication of *The Catcher in the Rye* in 1951, spoke of his work, his obsession with privacy and his uncertain thoughts about publication.

The interview with Mr. Salinger, who was at times warm and

charming, at times wary and skittish, is believed to be his first since 1953, when he granted one to a 16-year-old representative of the high school newspaper in Cornish.

What prompted Mr. Salinger to speak now on what he said was a cold, rainy, windswept night in Cornish was what he regards as the latest and most severe of all invasions of his private world: the publication of *The Complete Uncollected Short Stories of J. D. Salinger, Vols. 1 and 2.*

During the last two months, about 25,000 copies of these books, priced at $3 to $5 for each volume, have been sold—first here in San Francisco, then in New York, Chicago, and elsewhere, according to Mr. Salinger, his lawyers, and book dealers around the country.

"Some stories, my property, have been stolen," Mr. Salinger said. "Someone's appropriated them. It's an illicit act. It's unfair. Suppose you had a coat you liked and somebody went into your closet and stole it. That's how I feel."

Mr. Salinger wrote the stories, including two about Holden Caulfield, the pained, sensitive hero of *The Catcher in the Rye*, between 1940 and 1948 for magazines like *The Saturday Evening Post, Colliers,* and *Esquire.*

Prefiguring his later writing, they concern themselves with lonely young soldiers and boys who eat egg yolks, girls with "lovely, awkward" smiles and children who never get letters.

**"Selling Like Hotcakes"**

"They're selling like hotcakes," said one San Francisco book dealer. "Everybody wants one."

While *The Catcher in the Rye* still sells at the rate of 250,000 copies a year, the contents of the unauthorized paperback books have been available heretofore only in the magazine files of large libraries.

"I wrote them a long time ago," Mr. Salinger said of the stories, "and I never had any intention of publishing them. I wanted them to die a perfectly natural death.

"I'm not trying to hide the gaucheries of my youth. I just don't think they're worthy of publishing."

Since last April, copies of *The Complete Uncollected Short Stories of J. D. Salinger, Vols. 1 and 2* have reportedly been peddled in person to bookstores at $1.50 each by men who always call themselves John Greenberg and say they come from Berkeley, California. Their descriptions have varied from city to city.

One such peddler told Andreas Brown, manager of the Gotham Book Mart in New York City, that he and his associates did not expect to get in trouble for their unauthorized enterprise because, as Mr. Brown related, "they could always negotiate with Salinger's lawyers and promise not to do it any more."

Mr. Brown, who described the young man as "a hippie, intellectual type, a typical Berkeley student," said, "I asked him why they were doing it, and he said he was a fan of Salinger's and thought these stories should be available to the public.

"I asked him what he thought Salinger would feel, and he said, 'We thought if we made the books attractive enough he wouldn't mind.' "

Gotham refused to sell the books and alerted Mr. Salinger to the unauthorized publications.

"It's irritating," said Mr. Salinger, who said he still owns the copyright on the stories. "It's really very irritating. I'm very upset about it."

According to Neil L. Shapiro, one of the author's lawyers here, the publication or sale of the stories without Mr. Salinger's authorization violates Federal copyright laws.

A civil suit in Mr. Salinger's name was filed last month in the Federal District Court here against "John Greenberg" and 17 major local bookstores, including Brentano's, alleging violation of the copyright laws.

The author is seeking a minimum of $250,000 in punitive damages and injunctive relief.

The stores have since been enjoined from all further sales of the unauthorized books, and, according to Mr. Shapiro, they still face possible damage payments ranging from $4,500 to $90,000 for each book sold. Additional legal action, he said, was being planned against book-stores elsewhere.

The mysterious publisher and his associates remain at large.

"It's amazing some sort of law and order agency can't do some-thing about this," Mr. Salinger said. "Why, if a dirty old mattress is stolen from your attic, they'll find it. But they're not even looking for this man."

## Discusses Opposition

Discussing his opposition to republication of his early works, Mr. Salinger said they were the fruit of a time when he was first beginning to commit himself to being a writer. He spoke of writing feverishly, of being "intent on placing [his works] in magazines."

Suddenly he interrupted himself.

"This doesn't have anything to do with this man Greenberg," he said. "I'm still trying to protect what privacy I have left."

Over the years many newspapers and national magazines have sent their representatives to his farmhouse in Cornish, but the author would turn and walk away if approached on the street and was reported to abandon friends if they discussed him with reporters. There have been articles reporting on his mailbox, his shopping, and his reclusive life, but not interviews.

But last week, he responded to a request for an interview trans-mitted to him earlier in the day, by Dorothy Olding, his New York lit-erary agent.

Did he expect to publish another work soon?

There was a pause.

"I really don't know how soon," he said. There was another pause, and then Mr. Salinger began to talk rapidly about how much he was writing, long hours, every day, and he said he was under contract to no one for another book.

"I don't necessarily intend to publish posthumously," he said, "but I do like to write for myself.

"I pay for this kind of attitude. I'm known as a strange, aloof kind of man. But all I'm doing is trying to protect myself and my work."

"I just want all this to stop. It's intrusive. I've survived a lot of things," he said in what was to be the end of the conversation, "and I'll probably survive this."

# Catching the "Catcher in the Rye" J. D. Salinger

MICHAEL CLARKSON

I sat in my car in Cornish, New Hampshire, and waited. I was parked on a quiet, unpaved country lane, its name known only to the local volunteer rescue squad. Ferns pressed against the car in the narrow green tunnel, and white birches creaked overhead.

There was no sign, no mailbox at the foot of the long, spiral driveway leading uphill from my waiting place; in fact, feeling a bit as if I were trapped in "The Three Bears," I wasn't even sure whether there was a house at the secret summit or the man I was tracking was barricaded, bearded in the concrete bunker the stories described.

I wondered if I was any further ahead than the teen-ager who had hitchhiked from Sacramento, or the woman who had come from Europe proposing marriage, or the world's crack reporters and investigators or the thousands of other whose letters wound up unopened, in a post office wastebasket. Not one of them had gotten the time of day from J. D. Salinger since he went into seclusion in 1953.

Salinger stopped publishing fiction at the peak of his career in 1965 at the age of 46, creating the biggest riddle in the history of American letters. He has never answered his fans or his critics, and he has been known to flee if approached by a stranger.

After reading Salinger's novel, *The Catcher in the Rye*, I had a warm, personal feeling for the author; but here, sweating apprehensively in a trench coat after a 450-mile drive, I felt like an intruder. Inspired by a remark in *Catcher* from Salinger's alter ego, Holden Caulfield ("I'd pretend I was a deaf mute so I wouldn't have to have any stupid, useless conversations and people would have to write things on a paper and shove it over to me"), I had given a note for the recluse to a clerk in the variety store where he was rumored to surface occasionally to buy newspapers.

My note, the product of two months' labor, read: "A man is in Cornish. Amateur, perhaps, but sentimentally connected. The saddest—a tragic figure without a background. Needing a future as much as your past. Let me."

Without warning two European compacts varoomed from an opening in the bush. Sharply they braked near my car. A longhaired teen-ager sprang from the lead vehicle and, referring to the other driver as "Dad," faced me with a karate stance and three howling dogs at his flanks. A tall, thin, graying man emerged confidently from a gray BMW with a soccer sticker on its bumper. With a wave, he signaled the boy and the dogs away. A regimented, military walk brought the man, dressed neatly in a brown tweed jacket with leather patches on the elbows, black turtleneck and sneakers, to my window.

"Are you J. D. Salinger?" I managed to ask.

"Yes. What can I do for you?" he said earnestly through enamel-white dentures. It couldn't be Salinger. For one thing, a photograph taken 27 years before resembled somebody else; for another, he looked older than 59.

"I don't know. I was hoping you could tell me."

"Oh, c'mon, don't start that."

"Really. All I know is I left my family and job and came a long way to see you."

"You didn't quit, did you?" I shook my head. "Are you under psy-chiatric care?"

"No, I don't think that's the problem. I suppose I have a need to be published," I said, as best I could, considering my suspected mental derangement. "It's hard finding people I feel comfortable with, who I can share with." (Holden in *Catcher*: "What really knocks me out is a book that, when you're all done reading it, you wish the author was a terrific friend and you could call him up whenever you felt like it.")

"You'll eventually find somebody," he said, trying to make my life seem as important as his. A dignity exuded from him, from his deep, nasal, studious voice—accent bordering on British—to his drooping ears and fleshy nose. He seemed weather-beaten, homely, but in an attractive way; a distinguished clown whose soul didn't have to be painted on his face, but was projected through the serious expression and faraway eyes.

"Anyway, how do you know you'd be comfortable with me?" His forehead and eyebrows, outstanding beneath a thick mixture of gray and white hair, slicked straight back, were tight with what seemed like worry, or at least a headache.

"Your writing."

He grew six inches taller. "I'm a fiction writer!" As if a nerve had been bared, he pushed away from the window to display outstretched hands. "There's absolutely no autobiography in my stories. I've had those notes passed around before," he said with a pained wince. "They're self-destructive; you must get out of that frame of mind." Confused, I didn't answer.

"Do you have another source of income besides writing?" he asked in an outgoing style. I kept waiting for him to introduce me to the man I'd come to see.

"I'm a reporter, police beat," I said. He was back in his car before I could blow smoke down my nose. "But I'm here for myself, not my job." My voice broke.

"I certainly hope so, because I don't have it coming!" he announced, eyes contemptuous. For the first time in my life I felt really hated . . . and feared. "I've made my stand clear. I'm a private person. Why can't my life be my own? I never asked for this and I have done absolutely nothing to deserve it. I've had 25 years of this—I'm sick of it!"

His delivery, timing and flair superbly fit the message. It was almost like acting.

Dramatically, he left in a hail of pebbles and surprised me again—by elevating his gangling arm up through the open roof in a friendly wave.

In a few minutes, as I sat dumbfounded, the man I couldn't be certain wasn't A. J. Foyt returned and issued warnings about having me removed. I told him I'd written another note.

"Bring it here," he snapped.

I left my car and walked to his window for a change. The long arm reached for the note and another produced a pair of glasses from a case.

The note, digested with his heavy lower lip naturally ajar, seemed to embarrass him: "Jerry: I'm sorry. It was probably a mistake coming to Cornish. You're not as deep, as sentimental, as I had hoped. If someone had driven 12 hours after leaving his family and job, I'd sure have given him more than five minutes. If I was after a story, do you think I would have told you I was a reporter? You say that you're a fiction writer, but you touch other people's souls, there's more to it than that. The person who wrote those books I love. (Signature.) P. S. I'll be staying at the Windsor Motel until morning."

He shut his motor off, including the one in his car, and spoke softly, extra slowly. He seemed ready to burst into tears as he sat in his car and looked away from me.

"Yes, well, you have the right to be cynical . . . but I've gone through this so many times, there's no gracious way to tell you to leave. I'm becoming embittered."

When he pulled an ugly face somehow it didn't look right. The things I was asking him, telling him, he'd heard over and over again, he said, more to the trees and posterity than to me, head shaking wearily, his dialogue conservative and tightly edited, with no room for small talk.

"The words are a little different each time. People with problems, people needing to communicate, people wanting help for their careers. They've come from all over this country, Canada and Europe. They've collared me in elevators, on the street, here. Why, I've even had to turn and run from them. I get stacks of mail and questions every day."

I thought of another passage in *Catcher*: "Anyway, I kept picturing all these little kids playing some game in the big field of rye and all. And I'm standing on the edge of some crazy cliff. What I have to do, I have to catch everybody if they start to go over the cliff—I mean if they're running and don't look where they're going. That's all I do all day. I know it's crazy, but that's the only thing I'd really like to be."

His game face dissolved. He slapped his hands on the steering wheel and squeezed it repeatedly. "There are no generalizations. You grew up under different circumstances than I did; you had different parents. I'm not a teacher or seer, anyway. I pose questions a little differently, perhaps. But I don't pretend to know the answers." He constantly referred to his career in the present tense.

"Nothing one man can say can help another. Each must make his own way. For all you know I'm just another father who has a son." His eyes were a day's work to look into. It would have helped him, I thought, if he could have cried publicly. I considered offering him a cigarette, but there was no sign of the chain-smoking reported in his early years.

"When I started in this business I had no idea this was going to happen. In ways, I regret ever having been published; it's the insanest profession. If you're lonely, as most writers are, write your way out of it."

He said he couldn't give me "a magic quarter to put under my pillow to make me a successful writer by morning," but he kept talking about writing.

"You can't teach somebody how to write," he said. "It's the blind leading the blind."

For a time after enrolling in a short-story course in 1939, his prose was said to have suffered from a workmanlike falsity. "The only good thing about lectures is they offer you a chance to mingle with others who've had rejection slips and share something in common." He wasn't being funny.

Odd, how I considered us both to have a sense of humor, yet in all the time we talked, neither of us laughed.

He claimed writing was still an open field to those "with enough drive and ego," and that publishers still took time to read salable material. I wondered if he knew what it was like to have manuscripts returned, to be unloved creatively. To have no feedback.

"Writing for yourself can be rewarding," he said. "But if you want to be published, I'll tell you this—you'll never be an author from the words I saw on that note at the store. Nobody over 30 can make head nor tail of that cryptic language. You have to separate fact from fiction."

"Would a writing career be worth it in the long run?" I asked.

"Sure, if that's what you want."

"Sometimes I lose incentive."

"Write your way out of it. Put everything down. Otherwise, I have no answers for you."

I left when I decided I was standing below J. D. Salinger's driveway and not at the bottom of some crazy cliff.

### "Ideals in Cement Shoes"

Jerome David Salinger, the most influential literary force of the 1950's and early '60's, was followed by irony from his birth in New York City in 1919 on the most public day of the year, January 1. His Irish-Jewish parents were the owners of a prosperous ham-importing business, and his only sibling, Doris, became a dress buyer.

As an introverted, polite child of average intelligence, he liked to act and write and go for long walks by himself, but he didn't apply himself at school and he flunked out of several.

After a brief fling at writing Army publicity releases, Staff Sgt. Salinger won five battle stars with U.S. Fourth Division intelligence in World War II. All aspects of the fighting demoralized him (including a visit from war correspondent Ernest Hemingway, who tried to impress by decapitating a chicken with a German Luger). But it was in Europe that his first real writings were born—in the foxholes between shellings.

Some of the profits from magazine sales to *Collier's, Esquire,* and *The Saturday Evening Post* were sent home to be used to encourage new writers.

In 1948 Salinger had won a contract with the prestigious New Yorker magazine, with stories about heartache—the frustrating search for peace and undiscriminating, non-sexual love in a world where childhood innocence was sadly perverted by adulthood and sincerity corroded by fame. But the critics agreed—somehow his stories held hope for mankind.

The author talked of making it big in movies until Hollywood in 1950 altered his short story, "Uncle Wiggily in Connecticut," into "My Foolish Heart." He has rejected all offers since then from filmmakers, television and stage groups—even book clubs—and he blocks all attempts by editors to publish unpolished stories of his early career.

With his only novel, the tragicomic *Catcher* (1951), which speaks out—shouts out—against social and academic conformity, Salinger became an instant hero to students all over the world. The book—about Holden Caulfield, a sensitive 16-year-old who flees school in pursuit of meaningful contacts only to find a world riddled with phoniness— affected the vernacular of a generation and has been banned by some school boards for its obscenity and apparent support of rebellion.

Overwhelming reaction to *Catcher* had not eased by 1953, when Salinger, then 34 and deeply involved in Zen Buddhism, bought an un-winterized saltbox house in Cornish, New Hampshire, where he was happy to pump his own water and could quench his thirst for 1930s movies at showings by the nearby Dartmouth Film Society.

Outgoing, he invited acquaintances for yoga sittings and befriended high school students, jeeping them to basketball games, and entertaining them at record parties over Cokes and his favorite tune, "It Was Just One of Those Things."

"All of my best friends are children," he once said. One afternoon in 1953 he gave an unprecedented interview to a 16-year-old girl for the high school page of the local paper. The day after it was given prominence on the editorial page and flashed across the country, Salinger severed relations with the students and build a high fence around his house, claiming he needed isolation to keep his creativity intact. Few people have seen him since.

Also in 1953, *Nine Stories*, all he wished preserved from his first 29 short stories, was printed in book form. Two years later he married English-born Claire Douglas, a popular, attractive Radcliffe graduate; they had two children, Margaret, born in 1955, and Matthew, born in 1960.

For the next 12 years Salinger lived for two families, his own and the fictional Glasses. Sustained by packed lunches, often spent more time with the latter, writing up to 18 hours a day (in a special concrete bunker 100 yards from the house) about the complex world of the introspective Glass family, nice people seeking religious peace in a cruel society, whose jugglings with Zen taught them every person was as important as the next, even the grotesque "Fat Lady."

Salinger got so lost in his work at times that it nearly involved him in automobile accidents. Edith Taylor, wife of an English teacher who closely followed Salinger's career, recalls the author "swaying all over the road in his jeep, having deep conversations and quarrels with himself."

The Glasses first appeared in sophisticated stories in *The New Yorker*, then were collected in the books *Franny and Zooey* (1961) and *Raise High the Roofbeam, Carpenters* and *Seymour: An Introduction* (1963).

The books, translated around the world, sold out immediately, and his enormous success, despite his not offering one word of publicity on his own behalf, became a contradiction, a joke, of American life.

Here was a man who, at the height of his fame, the target of every major reporter and PhD. candidate, kept a simple, unlocked mailbox with a stenciled name tag in front of his house.

No other writer since the Hemingway-Fitzgerald era aroused so much public and critical interest, pro and con. Everybody had an opinion on J. D. Salinger. But he has never responded to his critics.

Salinger's production remained meager because of the fanatical editing and polishing he employed to make his stories tight as violin strings; he was accused of agonizing for days over the choice of a solitary word.

With "Hapworth 16, 1924," a story in *The New Yorker* in 1965 about modern-day saint Seymour Glass, the career ended, although he once told a friend he intended to write a lengthy trilogy on the Glasses, a sort of "American Remembrance of Things Past."

*The New Yorker* thought enough of his drawing power to keep him on a huge annual retainer fee (rumored to be $30,000), while a publicity stunt in 1977 in *Esquire*—which printed a story laced with hints it was composed by The Great Recluse—reportedly received the heaviest response of any piece in the magazine history.

Salinger still keeps an agent, Dorothy Olding of Harold Ober Associates in New York, but she, like all his editors, is mum about his career.

Warren French, a Midwest professor who moved to Cornish after writing a book-length study of Salinger, says he's surprised Salinger has never tried to form his own movie company, ". . . but I guess that would involve working with other people."

Claire was awarded the children and the house when she was granted a divorce from Salinger in 1967, but the author built a new home across the road and remained close to his family, visiting them daily.

In the meantime, enough has trickled out about his personal life to suggest he inserted parts of his history and lifestyle into his fiction. Most of his characters, seemingly more real and believable than he in their parallel world, are puritanical figures, standing for ideals in cement shoes, who quit school, skip their weddings, and shoot themselves in the right temple rather than compromise.

Yet unlike the author, interestingly, most of them are extroverted windbags.

### "Don't Ever Tell Anybody Anything"

It wasn't until a full year after I first met Salinger—June 1979—that I nerved myself to follow him up that steep driveway.

What I found at the top was beautiful—a rambling, dark-wooden lodge, nearly a Swiss chalet, not unlike one Caulfield had pined for ("I'd build a little cabin in the woods with the dough I made, but not right in them because I'd want it to be sunny as hell all the time").

It was nestled up the side of a cliff at the edge of the woods in bright sunlight with enough windows for a greenhouse. There was no visible entrance from the long grass, but a concrete tunnel led conspicuously from a locked, two-car garage up the cliff, past a bird feeder and under a wide sun deck.

His dogs sniffed, but stopped barking as I scaled the least hazardous side of the rock and made it to the back of the Tyrolean structure, where I found wooden steps leading up to a set of heavy sliding glass doors. And I climbed, determination denying my nervousness.

Hands visored to my eyes, I squinted through the glass . . . into a living room so old-fashioned and tattered I expected to see ghosts. A hanging light set the depressing atmosphere, and around it were several old, worn couches and easy chairs, a bookcase and thin, patterned red rug that were dwarfed in the spacious room.

A movie screen on the far wall was pulled halfway down to the floorboards, which were obviously older than the house. Sunshine, as it was in the Glass apartment, was unkind to the room. Disarray was the theme, with large metal spools of movie film, books, and *National Geographics* scattered about.

A large fireplace was clotted with crumpled writing paper and garbage.

But the dominant force was framed photographs, black and white, brown and yellow, spilling over the fireplace mantel and onto end tables. They were mostly group shots of his children and ex-wife, who had recently sold their old house and moved to the West Coast, and I couldn't keep the words of critic Arthur Mizener out of my head:

"The fact that the Glass family is closely knit is important to the feelings Salinger cares most about. The essential reality for him subsists in personal relations, when people, however agonizingly, love one another."

You could almost smell the mustiness through the glass. The room was surprising for a man wealthy from royalties: *Catcher* alone reportedly still sells 250,000 copies a year.

The owner was at ease in a chair facing another set of glass doors—the room was circled with them—watching a portable TV and writing on a pad. I knew he'd be home. He leaves only for necessities or if there happens to be a fire, I had learned in the interim.

Each weekday he drives to the nearest settlement, Windsor, Vermont (pop. 4,000), his lifeline to the world for a quarter of a century, and makes three hurried stops: the post office, Grand Union supermarket, and the Windsor Newsstand (he stopped buying his *New York Times* at Brooks Beauty and Health Aids after I passed my note through the clerk there).

He was said to treat the newsstand employees "politely and gently" and the women "gallantly." He even offered his name as reference to a teenage clerk seeking employment elsewhere.

On the street, unrecognized by most, he is a lonely, almost pitiful figure, with fright, not spring, in his walk (a very unmilitary walk), rushing as if he is on Mars and his air isn't going to last him home. If you see him before he sees you, and he's been your boyhood idol, you want to go home and cry a little.

"People want to get close to him," an official of the Windsor Chamber of Commerce said, "but he wears his privacy like a balloon. You're afraid if you get beyond superficial conversation, it'll burst."

A retired Cornish neighbor believes, "Everybody wants to be like Salinger and he wants to be like everybody else."

"He used to live in here," said a waitress at Nap's Lunch. "The kids listened like disciples to every word he said. They still read his stuff, but now he might as well be a writer who lives 2,000 miles away."

Not everyone approves of Salinger's lifestyle, but most so fear his opinion of them that they demand their comments remain anonymous. "He's speaking to me again," sighed a retired English teacher, blamed by Salinger for putting a *Time* magazine reporter on his trail years ago.

The indefatigable reporters who still make the long trek up here each year get no help from the *Windsor Chronicle*, the weekly tabloid that has, according to publisher Nancy Walker, an established policy "to respect the man's privacy" and has never done a story about him.

Salinger's voice has been heard publicly only once in the last 14 years: *The New York Times* reported a 1974 telephone call from him protesting the efforts of a San Francisco group to publish an unauthorized collection of his stories.

It has said the only letters he answers are from a prisoner at Sing Sing.

Salinger spotted me at the glass and stepped around a sleeping German shepherd before impatiently kicking out a 2-by-4 that held the clear doors shut. He had aged in the year since I'd seen him: The lines in his forehead and cheeks were deeper. He wore faded blue jeans, tennis shoes and a white shirt, the sleeves rolled up to the bony elbows. He still looked like he had a headache.

I thanked him for having helped me into a more realistic frame of mind.

"You look much better now," he said from that slow face. He smiled after I smiled, but he stood round-shouldered in the door as if protecting his depressing room.

"Are you still reporting?"

I nodded.

"You tried to bully me last time, " he said. "You tried to use me for the betterment of your career. The only advice I can give is to read others, get what you can out of a book and make your own interpretation of what the author is saying.

"Don't get hung up on the critics and that madness. Blend in your experiences, without writing facts, and use your creativity. Plan your stories and don't make rash decisions. Then, when it's finished, you're in your own stew . . ."

As he lectured, head and hands animated, he looked like he was beginning to enjoy himself, but suddenly he stopped in the middle of sentence and waited for me to talk. J. D. Salinger, Windbag? It had a certain ring to it.

As I looked out onto the sunlit reality of green hills and vales, I was enveloped in a feeling of freedom and openness. How could there be anything to conceal out there? "I'm sorry if I bothered you before," I said.

"If you'd had written beforehand, I would have saved you the bother of a long trip."

"I did. Five times. Didn't you get the tape of music relating to your career?"

"Tape?" he emptied his face of expression. "I might have. It was probably with the other stuff."

"Your writing seems to form attachments in its readers," I said.

"But I can't be held responsible," he shot out. "There are no legal obligations. I have nothing to answer for." His works were written for enjoyment and entertainment, he said with an overkill of emphasis, not for study and psychoanalysis.

"You haven't really given an explanation to your fans why you ran from them, then stopped publishing."

He raised his eyebrows. "Being a public writer interferes with my right to a private life. I write for myself.

"Don't you want to share your feelings?"

"No, that's wrong." He pointed his finger like a gun. "That's were writers get in trouble." He didn't have to be standing inside for the last paragraph of *Catcher* to haunt him: "I'm sorry if I told so many people about it. It's funny. Don't ever tell anybody anything. If you do, you start missing everybody."

Before leaving, I invited him to come with me for a drink one night. "Thanks, but no." He smiled, almost mischievously, with the actor's flair. "I'm busy these days."

The door closed and Jerome David Salinger, the closet sentimentalist, retreated again. Not to a small town in New England or even into his lovely cabin, but to the safety of his own mind.

**Postscript, January 2006**

Twenty-five years later, I still have mixed feelings about my Salinger piece.

It was an intensely personal journey and I believe I was driven partly to fill an emotional hole left by the empty relationship I had with my father. I am sorry that I exploited Salinger's privacy, but on the other hand, after talking with him, I felt some obligation to the many fans he had rebuffed and even to Salinger, to let him vent his side of the story, his frustration. After my visits with him, I dropped my desire to become a fiction writer, but more recently, I have had five nonfiction books published on fear and stress, perhaps ironic since Salinger once asked me if I was under psychiatric care.

# The Catcher in the Driveway

RON ROSENBAUM

F or more than forty years, J. D. Salinger has lived in self-exile behind a Wall of Silence, an enigma in a celebrity culture. Now, by allowing the reissue of his 1965 short story, "Hapworth 16, 1924," is the last private person in America trying to tell us something?

There is no name on the mailbox at the bottom of the driveway. It's the only mailbox on the route with no name. The house above the driveway is screened by a slope of trees, several of which brandish glaring neon-pink NO TRESPASSING signs. Signs that, in addition to specifying NO HUNTING, TRAPPING, FISHING in big black capitals, proceed further to emphasize the sweeping metaphysical inclusiveness of the prohibition by adding OR TRESPASSING OF *ANY* kind.

Just being here, at the bottom of the driveway, just beyond the verge of the property line, feels like a trespass of *some* kind. This is not just private property. It is the property of the most private man in America, perhaps the *last* private person in America. The silence surrounding this place is not just any silence. It is the work of a lifetime. It is the work of renunciation and determination and expensive litigation. It is a silence of self-exile, cunning, and contemplation. In its own powerful, invisible way, the silence is in itself an eloquent work of art. It is the Great Wall of Silence J. D. Salinger has built around himself.

It is not a passive silence; it's a palpable, provocative silence. It's the kind of silence people make pilgrimages to witness, to challenge. It's a silence we both respect and resent, a lure and a reproof. Something draws us to it, makes us interrogate it, test it.

There's a line in *Mao II,* Don DeLillo's novel about a Salinger-like reclusive writer who wonders: Why are so many so obsessed with my invisibility, my hiddenness, my absence?

"When a writer doesn't show his face," he answers himself, "he becomes a local symptom of God's famous reluctance to appear."

The silence of a writer is not the *same* as the silence of God, but there's something analogous: an awe-inspiring creator, someone we believe has some answers of some kind, refusing to respond to us, hiding his face, withholding his creation. The problem, the rare phenomenon of the unavailable, invisible, indifferent writer (indifferent to our questions, indifferent to the publicity-industrial complex so many serve), is the literary equivalent of the problem of theodicy, the specialized subdiscipline of theology that addresses the problem of the apparent silent indifference of God to the hell of human suffering.

And when a writer won't break his silence, we think of ways to break into it. We think of knocking on his door or leaving messages in his mailbox.

S.'s two mailboxes beckoned to me as I stood at the bottom of his driveway.

The gray metal U.S. Postal Service box was shut with a rusty hasp. But next to it stood a forest-green, open-ended mailbox with the logo of a local paper, West Lebanon's *Valley News,* on it. Empty, except that stuck in the back was a single piece of printed matter that looked as if it had been orphaned there for some time. Someone else's message for S.? It turned out to be a junk-mail flyer, perhaps the single most misdirected piece of junk mail in America.

GET ON TARGET! the flyer shrieked in hyperventilating three-inch-high type. It was a junk-mail flyer advertising customized promotional junk-mail flyers—meta junk mail. LET US HELP YOU ADVERTISE YOUR BUSINESS! it urged J. D. Salinger.

America's self-promotional culture reaching out to target the last private person left.

It made me think twice about leaving a letter there, a message for S. It made me think more than twice about what I might say, or whether I should just depart and leave his silence in silence.

I knew I had to consider my next move carefully, because I could end up doing something I might regret for a long time.

### The Season when the Silent Speak

The night before I set out for New Hampshire, I heard a strange tale about J. D. Salinger's Wall: the Fake Wounds Story. It came up after I'd mentioned my fascination with S.'s Wall in a talk I'd given at Harvard's Nieman Fellows house. From the ace reporters in my audience, I told them about my concept for the expedition: I would be heading up to Cornish, the tiny, hilly hamlet eighteen miles south of Hanover that has been S.'s place of silent retreat for the past forty-four years. Not to disturb S, not to knock on his door or wait on his doorstep. No, I told them, what I most wanted to do was gaze at S.'s *wall*. This was at least partially true. If S. *were* to emerge from behind the wall and engage me in a discussion about "the sound of one hand clapping," I would not decline. But I did not expect this would happen. My idea was that S's Wall itself—not just the physical wall of wood or stone I'd heard he'd built around his house but the metaphysical Wall, the Wall of Silence he'd built around himself, around his work—was in a way his most powerful, most eloquent, perhaps his most lasting work of art. I explained my notion of the Party of Silence: how writers like Salinger and Thomas Pynchon and William Wharton and to some extent Don DeLillo (less silent than publicity shy) constituted a small but powerful minority caucus in American culture. They are less a party than a loose-knit group of kindred spirits whose varieties of conscious silence range from writing but not publishing (S.) to publishing but not appearing (Pynchon) to publishing under a pseudonym to avoid publicity (Wharton) to publishing but not actively publicizing himself (DeLillo). Their varieties of reticence and concealment and self-effacement cumulatively constitute a provocative dissent from the culture of self-promotion that has swept contemporary publishing, a reproof to the roaring "white noise" (a DeLillo-novel title) of the publicity-industrial complex that dominates contemporary celebrity culture.

And suddenly this season, it seemed that the silent—in their own idiosyncratic gestural ways—had begun to speak! In January, a report stunned the literary world to the effect that S. had made a small but significant reversal, a slight opening, if not a breach, in the Wall. He had inexplicably, quixotically granted permission to a small-press publisher (Orchises Press in Alexandria, Virginia, which specializes in little-known contemporary poets) to issue a hardcover edition of his last published story, "Hapworth 6, 1924," which had first appeared in the June 19, 1965, issue of *The New Yorker* and survived mainly in faded nth-generation photocopies.

This was a surprising and puzzling reversal because S. had declined for three decades to permit the story to be issued in book form (as he had his other long *New Yorker* stories like "Franny" and "Zooey"). And he'd made it his practice to unleash from behind his wall attack-dog legal assaults on unauthorized publication of other uncanonical works (early uncollected short stories; personal letters a biographer found in university archives). He'd even succeeded in suppressing quotations from already published works: Late last year, his agents forced a non-profit Web site run by a fan of *The Catcher in the Rye* to cease offering inspirational quotations from the novel to other fans.

The "Hapworth" development wasn't earth-shattering on the face of it: S. wasn't releasing the rumored novel or novels he's been working on for the last three decades—the ones that, according to some reports, will continue to gather dust in a safe somewhere until (at least) after his death. He wasn't going to tour behind the "Hapworth" story or visit Oprah's Book Club. But against the background of the Wall, the monolithic, uncompromising Wall of Silence he'd erected around himself, the decision seemed to portend something more than the mere reprint of a magazine story.

S. turned seventy-eight this year; he'd been off for decades on what many supposed was some kind of spiritual quest, seeking something that demanded isolation and silence, a quest that had to be shielded by the Wall. Had he decided to compromise the strictness of his silence because of his awareness of mortality—the onrushing, unbreakable silence to come? Or had his quest at last produced some *answer* he wanted to begin to communicate? Was there something buried in the "Hapworth" story, some clue, some key to his silence, that he wanted to remind us of? Since it was S., now more mythic presence than real person, the speculations were tinged with a kind of millennial urgency—the promised return of a prophet.

What gave the Salinger announcement additional impact was that it came close upon the disclosure that his fellow pillar of the Party of Silence, Thomas Pynchon, was about to publish a new novel, *Mason & Dixon*, his first in seven years. And Pynchon would be followed, later this year, by a much-anticipated new DeLillo novel, *Underworld*.

Pynchon's silence had been a different sort of silence from S.'s, more moderate in one respect: Unlike S., he'd never ceased to publish out of principle. But more extreme than S.'s in another respect: S. had, in the postwar era, cut quite a public figure in the New York literary world—dining at the Stork Club with his British publishers, playing poker with writers and editors, lunching with urbane New Yorker wits like S. J. Perelman—before he suddenly exiled himself, silenced himself as a public persona, retreated behind his Wall, and stopped publishing, if not writing.

Pynchon, on the other hand, had almost from the very beginning refused to play the literary game: He'd *always* been an absence rather than a presence. He's been a stealth writer from the moment the publicity-industrial complex first tried to fix him on its radar screen. Legend has it that Pynchon was living in Mexico at the time his remarkable debut novel, *V.*, was about to appear in 1963 and that when he discovered that *Time* magazine had sent someone down there to photograph the new sensation, "he just got on a bus and disappeared," as one of his associates told me. Ever since, for thirty years, he's been a wraith, a rumor with no known address. (At least with Salinger, we knew what state, what town, he lived in.)

Pynchon's legendary invisibility had been so complete for so long that back in 1976 one imaginative author (John Calvin Batchelor) had even written an extremely clever mock-scholarly essay arguing the half-serious conjecture that Thomas Pynchon *was* J. D. Salinger, a Salinger who had been evading (or protecting) his Wall of Silence by publishing under cover of the Pynchon pseudonym. Others have suggested that the man behind the pseudonym William Wharton was actually Salinger incognito.

The accumulation of comic exotic speculations about Salinger and Pynchon is testimony in a way to the compelling hold their forms of silence still have over us. In a publicity-mad, celebrity-crazed culture, they have become in effect the Madonna and Michael Jackson of Silence, celebrities for their reticence and their renunciation of celebrity, for their Bartleby the Scrivener—like great refusal, the resounding echo of their silent "I would prefer not to." You can gauge the continuing totemic power of Salinger's name in the zeitgeist-sensitive film *Jerry Maguire*, in which Tom Cruise compares the unadorned reticence of the cover of his idealistic "Mission Statement" (the critique of go-go materialism that gets him fired from his sports-marketing agency) to the purity of the cover of *The Catcher in the Rye*.

Of course, within the Party of Silence, there is not one silence but many varieties and degrees of reticence. Literary history has given us *burning silence*, perhaps the most extreme and heartbreaking case being Nikolai Gogol's feeding the second part of his comic masterpiece *Dead Souls* into the flames of a wood-burning stove in the throes of a spiritual crisis or nervous breakdown. There is the *silence of low self-esteem:* Emily Dickinson's not believing her works were truly worthy of ever appearing. There is the *enforced silence* of censorship, the *internal silence* of crippling writer's block. But the silence one confronts in S.'s driveway is the silence whose power is most compelling: the deliberate silence that represents some kind of spiritual renunciation, what the Trappist writer Thomas Merton called *elected silence.* "The withheld work of art," someone says in a DeLillo novel, "is the only eloquence left."

### Trying the Patience of a Saint

To return to the Fake Wounds Story: Just as I'd hoped, one of the Nieman Fellows approached me after my talk with a fascinating story about S. He had a friend, he said, who, as a youth, had made the Pilgrimage to Salinger's House, a journey that is the closest thing a secular literary culture has to a religious ritual, a rite of passage. It is a pilgrimage S.—much to his regret, one must suppose—seemed to encourage with a famous passage in *The Catcher in the Rye* in which Holden Caulfield describes the powerful connection he feels with writers whose work he loves and how that kind of connection makes him want to call the writer up. He doesn't say *look* the writer up, but few pilgrims make that distinction because few have his phone number anyway. (I have a number for him. I just haven't used it.)

The Pilgrimage to S.'s House, to the shadow of his Wall, has itself become part of American literary myth, most prominently in W. P. Kinsella's *Shoeless Joe,* in which an Iowa farmer sets off for New Hampshire with a plan to kidnap J. D. Salinger and take him to a baseball game because a Voice has given him the mission to "ease his pain." The Fake Wounds Story turned out to be a kind of inadvertently parodic inversion of the ease-his-pain injunction. That night in my hotel room in Cambridge, I was able to track down the guy that the Nieman Fellow had told me about, the one who'd made the fake-wounds pilgrimage.

The way he told it, back in the sixties, when they were teenagers, he and a couple of similarly Salinger-obsessed buddies had hatched what they thought was a fiendishly clever plan to lure Salinger out from behind his Wall. The plan was to drive to Cornish and locate the Salinger house, at which point he planned to tear up his clothes and cover his head and body with ketchup to simulate blood—to make it look as if he'd been badly beaten up. They'd screech up the driveway to the walls of S.'s house, toss the "victim" out of the car, roar off, and leave him there moaning. The idea was that S. would then *have* to emerge—he couldn't resist the cry for help of a man who might be bleeding to death on his doorstep. S. would have to come out from behind his Wall, take the fellow in, and ease *his* pain.

In a slapdash way, it was a plan to try the patience of a saint, because embedded in it was an ethical/spiritual dilemma: The ketchup-smeared kid would not be just another feckless adolescent fan or a doorstepping journalist but a suffering human being in need of help. Could S. refuse?

And so they did it—smeared the ketchup, dumped the body out right in front of the wall. The kid began moaning in pain from his fake wounds and waiting to see whether S. would appear to help heal them.

A brief digression might be in order here on S.'s Wall, the theories of its origins and true purpose, including its possible genesis in the Girl Reporter Betrayal Story. A digression I make in the spirit of Thisbe's plaintive apostrophe in the Mechanicals' play in *A Midsummer Night's Dream,* the one that she addresses to the actor playing "Wall": *"O Wall, full often hast thou heard my moans."*

The most convincing account of the first appearance of S.'s Wall can be found in the only serious Salinger biography in existence, *In Search of J. D. Salinger,* by Ian Hamilton. It's a book whose tortured history is in a way monument to, and victim of, S.'s silence, one that bears real wounds, gaping holes in it from its encounter, its painful collision, with the Wall.

Hamilton, the respected British biographer of Robert Lowell and himself a poet, set out to write a life of S., knowing it was unlikely S. would cooperate. But Hamilton could not have expected the veritable war S. eventually waged against his book, a war to force Hamilton to rip out from his manuscript quotations and paraphrases from some private letters of S.'s he'd located.

Still, the wounded version of the Hamilton book that survived S.'s legal attack contains some surprising material, none more so than his account of the origin of the Wall.

According to Hamilton's chronology, S. moved to Cornish in January 1953. Then thirty-four, he was a success both critically and commercially from the 1951 publication of *The Catcher in the Rye* but not yet a cult figure. His hegira to the mountain fastness of the North must have helped contribute to the cult—he was no longer a New York writer, however special; he was now the Man on the Mountaintop. In fact, the property occupies a hilltop, albeit one that is almost invariably referred to as a hilltop "with a view of five states" (perhaps because of the implicit spiritual resonance of *states*).

Most accounts agree that S.'s retreat had *something* to do with the spiritual transformation he was undergoing. An increasing preoccupation with Eastern spiritual disciplines—particularly Hindu Vedantic philosophy, with its emphasis on karma and reincarnation, and Zen Buddhism, with its stress on the abandonment of ego in order to experience personal detachment and the oneness of creation —began showing up in his short stories in the early fifties. But Hamilton reveals that S.'s moving to Cornish didn't initially mean embracing a solitary spiritual life. At least at first, S. led a very active social life, both with adult neighbors in Cornish and (more curiously) with a crowd of high school youths in Windsor, the larger town across a covered bridge in Vermont. According to Hamilton, who tracked down some of S.'s high school pals, "He used to be a ball of fun," as one of them put it. "He was forever entertaining the high school kids—he bought us meals and drinks. He was very interested in the basketball and football games. . . . After the Spa [an after-school hangout], we used to pile into his jeep and go up to his house. It was always open house up there." "We all looked up to him," recalled another, "especially the renegades."

But then came the Betrayal, the original media sin. Apparently, one of the Windsor High School students asked S. for an interview for the high school page of a local paper. He gave her the interview, but the paper, the *Claremont Daily Eagle,* ran it like a scoop. According to a *Life* magazine account of the episode quoted by Hamilton, " 'The next time a carload of them drove up to Salinger's home, he did not seem to be at home . . . .' When they tried again, they found the house 'totally hidden behind a solid, impenetrable, man-tall, woven wood fence.' " Interviews interfere with his mission, S. told a photographer at the time. No more "until I've completed what I set out to do."

The Era of the Wall had begun. For S. within his Wall, it was a period of increased preoccupation with spiritual questions, signaled in the famous epigraph about silence he added that year to the hardcover edition of his first short-story collection, *Nine Stories:*

> *We know the sound of two hands clapping.*
> *But what is the sound of one hand clapping?*
> *—A Zen koan*

It all added to the mystique: What was going on behind the Wall, what kind of silent quest? The Wall excluded the world but lured it, too, inspiring quests of its own, wild speculations. In one of his later stories, S.'s narrator/alter ego speaks of the rumors that he spent "six months of the year in a Buddhist monastery and the other six in a mental institution."

There were many indications of rural normality as well: There was marriage to a young Englishwoman, Claire Douglas; there were children, Matt and Peggy; there was a yearlong live-in liaison with a young writer, Joyce Maynard; and then another marriage. The man wasn't a complete hermit or a monk. But there was a growing sense that the Wall that kept the world out had somehow succeeded in imprisoning S., walling him in. In DeLillo's novel about the Salinger-like novelist, there's an implicit parallel between a poet held hostage by terrorists in some basement in Beirut and the novelist held hostage in his little room, hostage to the terror of celebrity—or to the terrifying magnitude of his own vision of perfection.

**In Which S.'s Healing Philosophy is Disclosed**
At the very least, it seemed increasingly to wall in his work. In the dozen years after he built the wall in 1953, he published just four short stories; then came "Hapworth" and thirty-two years of silence. There was a growing sense among readers and critics that he was walling himself in imaginatively as well, writing with increasing obsessiveness about the insular inwardness of the Glass family (the Corleones of the sensitive lit set), a big New York family whose seven children are haunted and tormented in various ways by the enigmatic spirituality—and mysterious suicide—of the firstborn, Seymour. Guru, poet, avatar, former child prodigy and quiz-kid celebrity, Seymour, we learn in the "Hapworth" story (which takes the bizarre form of a twenty-thousand-word-long letter from an impossibly precocious seven-year-old Seymour writing home from summer camp), is himself haunted by visions of his past lives—his previous incarnational "appearances," as he calls them. And by a premonition of his own death, the gunshot suicide described cryptically in "A Perfect Day for Bananafish"—a story, a suicide, that has launched a thousand term papers and dissertations, all attempting to explain why Seymour silenced himself.

Was S. committing slow artistic suicide within the Wall, silencing himself within the Glass house of his Glass-family chronicle? Or had he achieved some strange new level of spiritual or artistic transcendence—writing that no longer required the ego validation of publication or readers, at least within his lifetime? Or—horrible thought—was he writing now only for God's eye and planning to pull a Gogol: feed the work to the flames before he died?

Those of us who cared rushed to rustle up faded Xeroxes of the "Hapworth" story and search it for clues, once the announcement was made of S.'s decision to permit the story a life beyond the Wall again.

At one point in "Hapworth"—S.'s most hermetic and self-referential work—little Seymour Glass seems to offer some signals about the silence of his creator.

In speaking of the karmic homework he needs to do, Seymour mentions the need to "move as silently as possible" and then cites an Eastern sage, Tsiang Samdup (in a way that presumes we are, of course, familiar with his authority), on Silence: "Silence! Go forth, but tell no man," the estimable Samdup enjoins us, according to little Seymour. Which hints at what S. might be doing: continuing to *go forth* with his writing but *telling no man*—not publishing what he's written. Until perhaps he's well on his way to the next incarnation.

The "Hapworth" story also offers us a tantalizing preview of the *next* never-seen Salinger story—the one he may have written but shown only to God, or perhaps the one he's been writing and revising, unable to finish. For all we know, it might be the story that silenced him. We know about this story, or we think we do, because seven-year-old Seymour in "Hapworth" foresees both the event that occasions it and the story that his brother Buddy, Salinger's alter ego, will write about the event. Is it just an accident that this story, the story that may have silenced S., is a story about a Temptation and a Fall into Celebrity? About the sudden celebrity that the Glass-family children fall into as wunderkind stars of a radio quiz show called *It's a Wise Child.* An exposure to publicity that would leave them all scarred and wounded in various ways. The putative post-"Hapworth" story can be seen as an allegory of the wounds S. himself experienced in his sudden transformation into a wunderkind celebrity.

Wounds, yes: Let us return again to the Fake Wounds Story, in which a possibly wounded S. inside his wall is confronted by a fraudulently wounded seeker moaning outside the wall. What happened, the somewhat chagrined fake-wounds victim told me, was that soon after he was dumped off, ketchup-smeared, moaning, the lights came on in the house behind the wall "as if someone was watching." And then, after a while, the lights went off. Then nothing. Silence. No one came out. Eventually, his friends returned, and they all slunk off. They didn't come away from it thinking S. was cruel or heartless. Rather, they got the feeling that the fake-wounds thing had been tried before: that it had become a regular *routine* for seekers to bear wounds, both real and false, to the wall. That S. had somehow developed the ability to diagnose the difference between blood and ketchup, between real pain and its simulation. This jibes somewhat with the story Jonathan Schwartz, the writer and radio personality, told me about a woman he knew who'd made the pilgrimage with her five-year-old child. She'd gone as far as knocking on S.'s door, and when he wouldn't let her in, she told him she had a tired, ailing child in her car. At that point, S. became enormously solicitous, invited them both in, and fed and played with the child for hours while they all watched the Marx brothers' *Monkey Business* and an episode of *I Love Lucy*.

Saint Francis of Assisi or Michael Jackson? The saint and the strangely reclusive celebrity both draw the wounded. The Fake Wounds Story has stayed with me because it seems to explain the powerful attraction of the Wall, the compelling seductiveness of the silence a writer like S. surrounds himself with. The power that lures us, either in person or metaphorically, to S.'s Wall is a feeling that the silence betokens some special knowledge, some wisdom, the penetration of some unutterable mystery beyond words, beyond speech, expressible only in silence. The Wall he's built is, metaphorically, a place where we can bring our *real* wounds to be examined, healed—the wounds, the holes in our soul, the empty places eaten away by a sense of inauthenticity, by the ravages of celebrity culture.

Which brings me to the rather extraordinary discovery I made about S. as a healer in the course of pursuing various inquiries about the Man Behind the Wall—something I believe has never been reported before. It's a revelation I was led to very indirectly by a chain of random connections and one that contradicts the conventional wisdom of an S. utterly in thrall to Eastern religious disciplines. While it's true that Eastern disciplines have their appeal for him, in fact the healing discipline that, for a time, at least, most appealed to him, one he also expounded upon to others, is a far more down-home, Western system of healing: homeopathy. Yes, homeopathy, the heretical alternative system of diagnosis and healing invented by the German physician Samuel Hahnemann in the late eighteenth century, one long dismissed by mainstream medicine, one taken up again by new-age healers, one reportedly still relied upon by the British Royal Family, among others.

Why homeopathy? Part of the appeal might lie in the way the German Romanticism of Hahnemann's healing system offered a bridge between the physical and the metaphysical, transcended the dualism of mind and body that S.'s child avatars like Teddy in *Nine Stories* and Seymour in "Hapworth" railed against. Homeopathy is all about the interpenetrating resonance of the two realms. Setting aside the question of its scientific validity, one can find a metaphoric poetry in homeopathy's attempt to explain itself that I'd suggest would resonate with S.'s solitary absent presence.

Old Samuel Hahnemann believed in treating similars with similars: that an infinitesimal dose of what was making you ill could make you better. If, for instance, you were vomiting, homeopathy prescribed tiny doses of nausea-inducing herbs. More peculiarly and controversially, Hahnemann believed that the more he diluted his remedies in distilled water, the more powerful they became. This has led critics to claim that at their "highest potency," i.e., their greatest dilution, his homeopathic remedies were diluted to the point of *invisibility* and that homeopathic doctors were essentially prescribing nothing *but* distilled water to their patients. To which homeopathic defenders poetically reply, It's not the presence of the curative herb in the water but the "potentizing" imprint the once-present, now-absent dose has left on the molecular-level configuration of the fluid. A memory of an encounter, now somehow inscribed in water.

I'm not defending the science, just admiring the poetry of a healing system in which absence and memory have more power than presence—and suggesting that somewhere in this homeopathic rhetoric there is a metaphor for S.'s own absence and invisibility in our culture: that the *withdrawal* of his presence has left his memory, his influence, perhaps even his healing power *more* potent than an undiluted presence would be. That his silence is a kind of homeopathic remedy for the disease of noise we all suffer from.

I learned some other surprising things about S. in the course of my inquiries. I learned that in addition to the Glass-family chronicle, he has also written a screenplay, a draft of some kind, in which his faithful Glass-family narrator and alter ego, Buddy, is forced to confront criticism of the increasingly murky and mystical turn S.'s later Seymour-obsessed Glass-family stories have taken. (I'd pay to see that.) I've also heard, though I'm less sure of this, that he may have written some film scripts under a pseudonym for European producers.

I learned that he's not a Howard Hughes–like recluse, that he has traveled here and abroad, that he's tuned in to the culture around him, hasn't walled himself off from it.

And finally, I learned what his favorite junk food is. I learned this from a friend who happened to find herself standing behind S. at a deli counter where he's a regular. S. was complaining about the way his *soppressata,* a rustic salami, was sliced (he likes it "thinly sliced and layered," like the prose in his early New Yorker stories), a concern that may be a tribute to his late father, Sol, a meat and cheese importer. I asked my friend to speak to the deli clerk and found out the astonishing fact that S.'s favorite junk food is (I swear) doughnut holes! The pastry equivalent of the sound of one hand clapping.

But of all these revelations, the one about homeopathy strikes me as the most powerful truth about who S. is: if not a healer then an investigator of illness in the largest sense of the word, a literary diagnostician of the sickness, or slickness unto death, we suffer from as individuals and as a culture.

His remedy? I learned that S. had a particular interest in a homeopathic remedy called lycopodium, a variety of club moss, diluted to near invisibility, of course. A quick check of the homeopathic literature produced the fascinating disclosure that there is among Hahnemann disciples something known as "the lycopodium personality." Described by one British practitioner as "diffident, conscientious, meticulous but self-conscious . . . [lycopodians] *dislike public appearances* [italics mine] and may take offense easily . . . ."

I had an uncanny feeling that in reading the homeopathic literature about the lycopodium personality, I was glimpsing at one remove the way S. diagnoses his own persona. And perhaps a clue to his decision to release the "Hapworth" story. A medicine for melancholy from Dr. S., a tiny but highly potentized dose of his presence injected afresh into the bloodstream of the culture, an infinitesimal opening in the Wall around himself, in the hope of evoking, in homeopathic fashion, a Presence, a memory of an Absence—lycopodium for the soul, ours and his.

### The Catcher in the Driveway

As I crossed the border from Massachusetts to New Hampshire, heading northwest on a wintry-bright, sudden-thaw late-February morning, I found myself haunted by several questions about my pilgrimage to S.'s Wall.

First, would I find the place at all? Not having the address, I was depending on the kindness of strangers to guide me there, although I'd heard that the flinty New Hampshire townspeople in Cornish were not known for their kindness to strangers seeking S. Of course, in a way I almost hoped I *wouldn't* be able to find the place: It would mean that S.'s neighbors had, in effect, built a wall *around* the Wall.

I took the exit off Route 89 at West Lebanon and headed south toward Cornish on a rural route that clung to the banks of the ice-bound Connecticut River, having no idea what to do once I reached Cornish.

After the recent *New York* magazine story disclosing Pynchon's location, or at least his neighborhood, S. may be the last private person left in America. I wanted to find the place, but I *feared* finding it—feared that (even if I would never publish the address or the directions there)

I might pose a threat, however symbolic, to that last preserve of privacy, an endangered species of privacy now nearly extinct. I feared also the questions I'd have to face if I did find it, questions about myself, what I'd do facing S.'s Wall, whether I'd intrude. Interrogating S.'s silence, facing his Wall, would inevitably entail interrogating, facing, a side of myself I might not want to see.

But, as fate would have it, a half hour after arriving in Cornish, I found myself at the bottom of S.'s driveway, gazing up at the NO TRES-PASSING signs, considering my next step and the ethical, literary, philosophical dilemmas it posed.

I found this place fast—not because it is easy to find but because I was lucky. That it was blind luck was something I confirmed in the two days I spent in Cornish afterward, testing the townspeople and the wall around the Wall; asking them to lead me to S.'s place and getting turned down. Some told me they didn't know the way; some told me they didn't know who S. was; some told me they wouldn't tell me if they did know; some told me they did know but wouldn't tell me; some told me, "The gentleman likes his privacy" or variations of that sentiment. At one general store, a guy told me that college students from Dartmouth still came regularly looking for it, but "folks don't tell" and he wouldn't. At another general store, I was told, with a disapproving sneer, "We don't give out that information."

So there *was* a wall around the Wall in S.'s adopted hometown. But not an impregnable wall.

In the parking lot of one of the general stores, after being sent off with a discouraging, disparaging "folks don't tell," I chanced upon an elderly couple in an aging pickup truck. I told them, "My boss sent me up here to find J. D. Salinger's house, you know, just the house, not to bother him. Any chance you could help me?" The old fellow in the pickup-truck cab started giving me elaborate directions that ended vaguely: "Follow the road to the top of the hill; then it kind of gets complicated to describe. You'd better just ask some people when you get up there."

That didn't sound too promising to me, asking people around there. But I was able, with some difficulty, to persuade the guy to let me follow him in my car as he drove to the place. And so we set off. I'm going to cover my tracks at this point. Let's just say that after a long drive and a long stretch of road that a sudden thaw had turned into hubcap-deep mud, the truck stopped at a driveway featuring the only mailbox on the route that had *no name* on it.

I got out of my car and went up to the cab of the truck.

"Is this it?" I asked the ancient one.

"This is it," he said, gesturing up a driveway that slanted up a wooded slope to a house heavily screened by trees—a house on a hill that, even from below, one could see, could well offer the proverbial "view of five states."

"You're sure this is it?" I said.

He nodded and waited, watching, I think protectively, to see what I'd do. He seemed to satisfy himself that I had no plans for an actual intrusion and drove off.

Of course, it is marginally possible that he was part of S.'s roving disinformation squad, specifically detailed to mislead strangers in town seeking S., directing them to a designated false S. address. But that sounded more Pynchonesque in its paranoia than Salingeresque.

I looked for other signs. The driveway slanting up the slope to the tree-screened house matched others' descriptions. The existence of a second, older building on the property matched accounts of S.'s building a new structure in the late sixties after a divorce. I didn't see a physical wall, but I later learned that when S. built the new structure on his property, the old wall was replaced by the now-tall stand of trees that screened and guarded the place. I was pretty confident this was the place. The orphaned GET ON TARGET! junk-mail flyer in the Valley News mailbox seemed ironic, poetic confirmation.

Assuming this was S.'s abode, assuming I had the right target in sight, what were my options? I could:

(1) Violate the NO TRESPASSING sign, violate my own previously

established ground rules, violate S.'s peace by going up the driveway and knocking on the door. But I just couldn't do that. I remembered the hunted, haunted, trespassed-and-violated look on S.'s face when a paparazzo caught him by surprise nearly ten years ago. Don DeLillo told me it was the sight of this terrified photo that inspired him to write *Mao II,* his meditation on a reclusive writer and the terror of celebrity. I felt bad enough just being here, felt that my presence outside his driveway was already a kind of karmic violation I would have to pay for with several unpleasant future lives. I could not take that step. I would not knock on his door.

(2) Wait here long enough and hope to find S. coming or going. Which would amount to staking him out, or "doorstepping" him, as the Brittab phrase has it. I couldn't do that.

(3) Just soak in the silence surrounding S.'s abode. Pay my silent respects to the Wall and go. When I'd confided to Jonathan Schwartz my misgivings about actually going up to S.'s place, he'd dismissed my hesitation. He had thought of it often, he said. He would not hesitate to do it, "just to breathe the same oxygen." So I breathed in the spring-like oxygen and tuned in to the sounds of S.'s silence, tuned in to the sound of a rushing rivulet of thaw-melted snow burbling down the slope from S.'s house to the road. A distant bird cry. The deep, soulful soughing of the wind through S.'s trees.

A man passed by, walking a dog.

"This is the Salinger house, isn't it?" I said.

He smiled in a friendly way but said, "I can't answer that."

I listened to the silence. S.'s silent presence is like an unvoiced koan, a trick question that forces one to question oneself. I meditated upon S.'s silence, upon the absence of it in my life, upon all the other absences in my life. I began to feel very sad; I began to feel S.'s sadness, his sorrow and pity for a world filled with unenlightened souls like mine.

But then I thought about the famous Fat Lady passage in *Franny and Zooey.* You recall: the one in which Franny, the oversensitive, spiritually obsessed youngest sister of the departed guru Seymour, is suffering a nervous breakdown because she can't take the insensitive and hypo-critical chitchat of the benighted souls that surround her in her tony college. She wants to withdraw from the world, find a pure com-munion with Jesus through incessant prayer, prayer so incessant that after a while it becomes the pure, silent language of the heart.

Zooey, one of Franny's brothers, brings her out of the spiritual crisis by reminding her of the Fat Lady. When they were all quiz-kid celebri-ties and got tired of performing for the unseen multitude of geeks and rubes in their audience, the sainted Seymour would tell them to do it "for the Fat Lady." And each of them would think of some overweight woman out there in the radio audience, maybe swatting flies on her porch while listening to the show. Don't look *down* on such people; do the show out of *love* for the Fat Lady, as Seymour urged them). "But I'll tell you a terrible secret," Zooey tells Franny. "*There isn't anyone out there who isn't Seymour's Fat Lady. . . . Don't you know who that Fat Lady really is? . . .* It's Christ Himself. Christ Himself, buddy."

A beautiful sentiment: Love every soul on the planet, however alien, for being an embodiment of godhood. But hasn't S. *rejected* that senti-ment in withdrawing from the world, in disdaining contact with the perhaps foolish fans who love his work, in fleeing from the inept, exces-sive ways in which the world expresses its love for a writer? Isn't S., like Franny, spurning the Fat Lady? Aren't I, in some way, the Fat Lady on his doorstep? Shouldn't S. love me, welcome me, like the Fat Lady?

I listened to the Wall of Silence. And decided just listening wouldn't be enough. I decided on a fourth option. I would write S. a letter and leave it in one of his mailboxes.

Easy to say, but after all this time, after all these years, what did I have to say to S.? What one thing would *you* say, dear reader, given a chance to communicate with the strange, silent, spiritual artist behind that Wall, the last private person in America?

I decided I needed to think about it overnight. I checked into a nearby country inn (where the proprietor said S. had held an anniver-sary party with his third wife a couple of years back).

Back at the inn, I checked my answering machine in New York to find an anguished message from Jonathan Schwartz about a just-published attack on S.—well, on "Hapworth," but one that extended to S.'s entire Glass-family oeuvre—by a major critic. Jonathan was sure that S. would see the attack; he thinks of S. as *very* tuned in to the literary world despite the impression of spiritual detachment. (He reminded me that when his friend and her five-year-old watched *Monkey Business* with S., the woman noticed stacks of *New Yorkers* and *New York Times*'s in S.'s house. Jonathan believes that many are misled by S.'s unworldly spiritual preoccupations and miss out on the mordant comic observations of worldliness his best work displays.) He was afraid the attack would embitter S. and convince him to alter his plans for letting "Hapworth" (and perhaps himself) out into the world again.

I suddenly had an image of S. as Punxsutawney Phil, the well-known groundhog of Groundhog Day. Of S. poking his ever-so-sensitive, twitching nose outside his burrow of silence, seeing his Shadow—sniffing the hostility—and deciding that it wasn't worth it. Returning to Silence forever.

I decided that maybe what I needed to do in the message I was drafting was—in my own ego-bound way—to try to "ease his pain." A kind of homeopathic remedy: a message from a single stranger to a man who feared the great mass of strangers. I say "ego-bound" because the method I chose could not be said to be free of self-serving vanity. I think that at the core of every pilgrimage to S. is the belief of each pilgrim that in his heart he *understands* the object of the pilgrimage better than anyone else—and the concomitant hope that S. will *recognize* that, validate that. In some way, he will acknowledge that *you*, you out of all of them, have penetrated to the heart of the Mystery: At last, I've found someone who *knows* me.

This plays into my own special vanity about my talent for literary exegesis. And so I started composing a letter on a yellow legal pad that began on an "ease his pain" note but shifted, I'll admit, rather rapidly, to a plea for Recognition.

*Dear Mr. Salinger,* I began. *I hope you won't mind if I pass along this appreciation of your "Hapworth" story.* [I was planning to include in the envelope an explicatory essay on "Hapworth" I'd published recently in *The New York Observer.*] *I thought you might get a chuckle out of my conjecture in there about the sound of one hand clapping. . . .*

This is where my very un-Zen-like vanity announces itself. It was more than a "conjecture": I thought I'd *nailed* that supposedly unanswerable one-hand-clapping koan. See, I once had a conversation about it with a fellow who'd spent seven years in a Zen monastery. He told me what he claimed was the spiritually "correct" answer to the question—that is, the answer an enlightened person would *spontaneously* come to if he was *truly* enlightened.

When asked by a master, What is the sound of one hand clapping? the enlightened initiate would just *know* not to reply in words but, in solemn silence, to raise just one hand from his side and wave it toward the center of his chest *as if* it were meeting the other hand for a clap. The sound of one hand clapping is the sound of that silent wave, the sound of an absence, the absence of the noise ordinarily made by the collision of two hands. The sound of one hand clapping is the silence one tunes *in* to in that absence, the resonant silence of the rest of creation, the vast Oneness of Being one absorbs in the absence of that narrowing clap.

That koan about the sound of one hand clapping appears, of course, as the epigraph at the opening of S.'s first collection, *Nine Stories.* My exegetical triumph was the discovery that if you turn to the first page of the text and begin reading "A Perfect Day for Bananafish," the famous story of Seymour Glass's suicide, you will find a rather astonishing image, a secret, surprising image of the sound of one hand clapping embedded right there. It's there in the description of Seymour's wife, Muriel, drying the lacquer on her nails in their Florida beachfront hotel room. It's there in S.'s description of Muriel waving one hand, "her left—the wet—hand back and forth through the air," to dry her nails. Making the gesture of one hand clapping. I'm confident I'm the only one who has truly understood it. In my handwritten note to S., I said, You'll note the way I expressed my admiration for your ability in that image "to insinuate the sound, the spiritual gesture, of Silence into the cacophonous din of our cosmetic culture."

I concluded by telling S. I was writing a story praising the art, the example, of his silence and that if he *had* anything to communicate (e.g., *Yes, Ron, you alone have understood me*), I would be honored to hear from him.

Was my message a product of mixed motives, both selfless and selfish? Yes, it was. But I never claimed to be as spiritually advanced as S. And I *have* shown restraint; I haven't used the telephone number I have for him.

The next morning, early, I drove back to S.'s driveway. Found the Sunday paper nestled in a U-shaped fold in the *Valley News* mailbox. I put my note and my "Hapworth"/one-hand-clapping essay in an envelope and slipped it into the fold. Stayed a moment to appreciate the silence, then drove off to have breakfast at a Denny's in nearby West Lebanon.

I could have left town then. Perhaps I *should* have left town then. But instead, I decided to go back. The way I rationalized my return was that I was going back only to see if the letter had at least been taken in with the Sunday paper. And in fact, when I arrived back, the paper was gone, and so was the envelope with my letter. Mission accomplished.

Again, I should have gone then. But there was a magnetism to the place. To S.'s invisible Wall. To the echoing silence that seemed to emanate from S.'s abode. If it *was* S.'s place. As long as S. remained invisible up there at the end of the driveway behind the NO TRES-PASSING signs and the no-name mailbox, it didn't really matter if it was or it wasn't. I could be paying tribute to S.'s silent invisibility *anywhere* he was invisible.

But I thought I would make one final gesture before heading home, one final tribute to S.'s silent presence or absence. I thought I would make the sound of one hand clapping. And so, facing up to the house,

I made the silent one-handed wave. I tuned in to the resonant, silent sound of creation that enveloped me and S., in to all five states of being. I was the Catcher in the Driveway.

And then, to my horror, I heard another sound—the sound of a car engine starting up, the sound of a car heading down the driveway toward me!

Would S. be at the wheel? My whole life passed before me in review. I had fantasized S. reading my letter and my appreciation of Muriel's one-handed wave and silently saying to himself, "At last. Someone who truly understands me and my work."

But I hadn't imagined S. finding me on his doorstep, looking like a doorstepper.

The car reached the bottom of the driveway. I was positioned next to my car, about twenty feet to the right. Because of the light, I couldn't see if there were two figures or one in the front seat or what they looked like.

The car paused at the bottom of the driveway. Seemed to take in my presence. And—if it could ever be said it was possible for a *car* to look furious—*this* car looked furious. Then roared off to the left, in the opposite direction from me, spraying mud.

In the silence left behind, I felt terrible. I felt a wave of remorse strike me. I had wanted to be known to S. as a serious seeker, someone who understood him and his silence, someone who respected his silent privacy—but perhaps someone he might *want* to speak to (because of my exegetical insights, of course). But now I felt that, inevitably, it *looked* to S. as if I were a doorstepper. I felt my intrusive driveway presence might inadvertently change S.'s mind about releasing "Hapworth," about releasing anything—that I might have thus ineradicably altered the course of literary history. If S. was Punxsutawney Phil, *I* was his Shadow. He'd retreat into his burrow; his wintry silence would never end.

I waved after the car. With one hand. Feeling devastated. For God's sake, reader, don't try to follow my path. My only consolation is to hope to hell I had the wrong house.

**Postscript**

The publication of *Gone,* Renate Adler's memoir of *The New Yorker,* brought with it a startling deal that seemed far more significant than the question of who stabbed whom in the back alleys of West Forty-third Street. According to Adler, Salinger told her that the real reason he'd stopped publishing in the magazine was that he was too solicitous of the modesty of *New Yorker* editor William Shawn to ask him to read (much less publish) the kind of writing Salinger had been doing, writing that involved sex. Was he being serious? Actually, I hope so: I'd love to read Salinger on sex. He is, after all, the writer who managed to turn an inventory of a woman's medicine cabinet into a veritable Arabian Nights' fantasy. And it's more hopeful than the "ethic of silence" Adler said some of Shawn's writers adopted, whereby it was somehow a spiritually superiour thing not to write.

It was in part to combat the almost universal negativity that had been projected upon Salinger's silence (as terminally eccentric, as vanity, even as pathology) that I'd initially undertaken this story. I wanted to make the case that his silence, whatever its source, had become something more than a negation, that it's become a kind of positive statement or at least a heroic critique of the publicity-industrial complex from which he'd withdrawn.

Yet I still feel conflicted about the story. I'm not sure whether it's possible to pay tribute to a writer's silence by going up to but not over his wall, without intruding on it. I'd argue that a story *about* these conflicts and doubts was worth doing: I was a surrogate for a public both respectful of and drawn to test Salinger's silence. And besides, shouldn't he love me like he loves "the Fat Lady"?

# PART II:

## CRITICS AND CRANKS

# Threads of Innocence

Book Review of *Nine Stories*

EUDORA WELTY

J. D. Salinger's writing is original, first rate, serious and beautiful. Here are nine of his stories, and one further reason that they are so interesting and so powerful seen all together, is that they are paradoxes. From the outside, they are often very funny: inside, they are about heartbreak, and convey it; they can do this because they are pure. The whole nine have an enchanting ease about them, a deceptively loose-appearing texture, a freshness and liveliness which might bid fair to disarm the reader, as he begins, say, the remarkable "For Esme with Love and Squalor." Nothing could be further from what Mr. Salinger is about to do to him.

The stories concern children a good deal of the time, but they are God's children. Mr. Salinger's work deals with innocence, and starts with innocence: from there it can penetrate a full range of relationships, follow the spirit's private adventure, inquire into grave problems gravely—into life and death and human vulnerability and into the occasional mystical experience where age does not, after a point, any longer apply. Mr. Salinger's world—urban, suburban, family, mostly of the Eastern seaboard—is never a clue to the way he will treat it: he seems to write without preconception of shackling things.

He has the equipment of a born writer to begin with—his sensitive eye, his incredibly good ear, and something I can think of no word for but grace. There is not a trace of sentimentality about his work, although it is full of children that are bound to be adored. He pronounces no judgments, he is simply gifted with having them, and with having them passionately.

The material of these stories is quite different, again, from his subject. Death, war, the flaws in human relationships, the crazy inability to make plain to others what is most transparent and plain to ourselves and nearest our hearts; the lack or loss of a way to offer our passionate feeling, belief, in their full generosity; the ruthless cruelty of conventional social judgments and behavior; the persistent longing—reaching sometimes to fantasy—to return to some state of purity and grace; these subjects lie somewhere near the core of J. D. Salinger's work.

They all pertain to the lack of something in the world, and it might be said that what Mr. Salinger has written about so far is the absence of love. Owing to that absence comes the spoilation of innocence, or else the triumph in death of innocence over the outrage and corruption that lie in wait for it.

The feeling may arise from these warm, uneven stories (no writer worth his salt is even, or can be) that Mr. Salinger has never, here, *directly* touched upon what he has the most to say about: love. Love averts itself in pity, laughter, or a gesture or vision of finality possibly too easy or simple in stories that are neither easy nor simple in any degree.

Mr. Salinger is a very serious artist, and it is likely that what he has to say will find many forms as time goes by—interesting forms, too. His novel, *The Catcher in the Rye*, was good and extremely moving, although—for this reader—all its virtues can be had in a short story by the same author, where they are somehow more at home.

What this reader loves about Mr. Salinger's stories is that they honor what is unique and precious in each person on earth. Their author has the courage—it is more like the earned right and privilege—to experiment at the risk of not being understood. Best of all, he has a loving heart.

# The Love Song
# of J. D. Salinger

ARTHUR MIZENER

A few months ago I gave lecture in the Middle West on F. Scott Fitzgerald, before about as intelligent undergraduate audience as you are likely to find. When I finished, the first question from the floor was about J. D. Salinger. This humbling non-sequitur is too familiar to be any surprise, for Salinger is probably the most avidly read author of any serious pretensions in his generation. There are good reasons why he should be, for though his work has certain limitations—both of subject matter and of technique—it is, within these limitations, the most interesting fiction that has come along for some time.

Salinger has been writing since he was fifteen and is evidently a dedicated—not to say obsessed—writer, but the relatively small amount of work he has produced in a career of nearly twenty years suggests that he has a hard time writing. Moreover, there is in his work a very high incidence of emotional collapse and even violent death. One of the sharpest implications of his work, in short, is that perceptive people have difficulty remaining operative, or even surviving, in our world; a great deal of his most brilliant wit, like so much of James Thurber's, is close to desperation. There are good and even historical reasons in

American culture for this state of mind, as I shall try to suggest, but they make the difficulty Salinger himself apparently faces no less disturbing to contemplate.

His immediate appeal is that he speaks our language, or, to be exact, makes a kind of poetry out of the raw materials of our speech. His ear picks up with stunning exactness the new speech of many kinds of people: of the brutally conventional—"But my *gosh.* Honestly! I just can't stand to see somebody get away with absolute murder. It makes my blood boil"; of the earnestly ignorant—"They got their *pores* open the whole time. That's their *nature* for Chrissake. See what I mean"; of the Army—"This here's officers' quarters, Mac." His people are wholly present in devastating dramatic immediacy, in everything they say.

What is more, Salinger uses with great skill the very American device of conveying meaning by describing object, gesture, action. He can create this kind of poetry on the simplest occasion, as for instance when an ordinary girl is waiting for a long-distance telephone call:

> She read an article in a woman's pocket-size magazine called "Sex is Fun—or Hell." She washed her comb and brush. She took the spot out of the skirt of her beige suit. She moved the button on her Saks blouse. She tweezed out two freshly surfaced hairs in her mole. When the operator finally rang her room, she was sitting on the window seat and had almost finished putting lacquer on the nails of her left hand.

But if Salinger is a poet in this sense, he is also a poet in the only sense that he himself would take seriously: he's a man with his own special insight into the meaning of experience. "A good horse," as his characters the Glass children learned from Lo Po, "can be picked out by its general build and appearance. But a superlative horse—one that raises no dust and leaves no tracks—is something evanescent and fleeting, elusive as thin air."

An inescapable, intense awareness of this "poetry that flows through things, all things," marks every one of Salinger's significant characters.

As Vincent Caulfield in "This Sandwich Has No Mayonnaise" (1945) remarks of his brother Holden, such people cannot "do anything but listen hectically to the maladjusted little apparatus [they wear] for a heart." That is what makes Holden worry all through *The Catcher in the Rye* about what the Central Park ducks do in the winter and constantly recall with delight that, when they played checkers, old Jane would never move her kings out of the back row.

## "A Dash Man—Not a Miler"

Obviously Salinger did not burst on the world with these powers of observation and this sense of experience fully developed. He had, in fact, rather more trouble than most writers in discovering his own way of feeling and the best mode of expression for it. His first published stories, which appeared mainly in the *Saturday Evening Post* and *Collier's* in the early forties, will quickly destroy any romantic notions one may have had about the value of the unpublished stories he wrote even earlier, by flashlight under the bedclothes after "Lights," when he was a student at Valley Forge Military Academy. The first published stories deal, in a mechanical and over-ingenious way, with the superficial interests of magazine readers of the time. In "The Hang of It" (1941), for example, a father tells us about his comically inept soldier son who keeps insisting that he will get the hang of soldiering. At the end we find out that the speaker is also the boy's commanding officer. This is intended to make what had at first appeared the boy's stupidity seem pathetic anxiety, but the events of the story are almost entirely farce and do not support the intention.

These trivial stories are nevertheless interesting. They show us Salinger's preoccupation with close personal relations, particularly family relations. They make clear his marked preference for first-person narration and interior monologue. And they show the related difficulty he has in saying what he wants to and at the same time constructing a "well made" plot. In 1945 he was saying, "I am a dash man and not a miler, and it is probable that I will never write a novel." Perhaps that judgment was right, for *The Catcher in the Rye*, despite its brilliance of observation and the virtuosity with which Salinger keeps Holden Caulfield's monologue going for the length of a novel, is primarily concerned neither with the working out of a plot nor the development of a character. It is a lyric monologue in which the complex feelings of an essentially static character are gradually revealed. For all Salinger's skill, *The Catcher in the Rye* has a claustrophobic and, at the same time, random quality.

The second stage of Salinger's career runs from 1943, when he published his first mature story, "The Varioni Brothers" in the *Post*, to about 1948. In this period his powers of observation became much sharper and he began to understand much better what he wanted to say. His plots, if they still cramped him, were not completely irrelevant, though it was still true—as it is today—that he was at his best in meditations like "Boy in France" (1945) and in the monologues of plotted stories like "Last Day of the Last Furlough" (1944). His material was still a little conventional—the vicissitudes of Gershwin-like songwriters, cruise-ship romances, soldiers going overseas. But his characteristic feelings about experience were beginning to come through. They are there in the beautifully revealed devotion of the letter from Babe Gladwaller's sister Mattie, aged ten, that Babe reads in his foxhole in "Boy in France." They are there when Sonny Varioni, the talented, bored, ambitious song-writer, realizes that he hears the music for the first time in his life when he reads his dead brother's book.

The best work of this second period is the group of independent but related stories about the Gladwaller and the Caulfield families, who are closely connected by the friendship of Babe Gladwaller and Vincent Caulfield. These stories appeared in four different magazines over a period of three years. The first four of them are mainly concerned with Babe and Vincent. Then, beginning in late 1945 with "I'm Crazy," Salinger began to focus on Holden Caulfield. Much of the family detail from the first four stories is kept in the two stories about Holden, but there are important changes, and, with only slight revisions, these two stories became chapters in *The Catcher in the Rye*. I think it is a fairly good guess that, after writing *The Catcher in the Rye*, which was published in 1951, Salinger decided that most of the things he had been working out in the Gladwaller-Caulfield stories could be more clearly realized if he started afresh without some of the awkward commitments of these stories.

In any event, in 1948 he began the third period of his career with the publication of "A Perfect Day for Bananafish" in *The New Yorker*. This is, in order of publication anyway, the first of his stories about the Glass family, of which there have so far been seven, all but one of them in *The New Yorker*. It is anybody's guess, of course, whether Salinger had the whole, still unfinished history of the Glass family in mind when he wrote "A Perfect Day for Bananafish" nearly ten years ago, but my guess is that, much as William Faulkner has apparently always had at least the main outlines of the McCaslin family history in mind, Salinger has known about all the Glasses from the beginning. For one thing, the order in which the stories have appeared (and probably were written) has little relation to the chronological order of events in the family history, yet all the minute particulars of the Glass family history are consistent. What we are told about Seymour Glass in 1948 in the first story fits precisely, both in fact and in implication, with what we have learned about him and the rest of the family since. Salinger's conception of the Glass children's situation has become richer during these nine years, but neither the facts nor the essential nature of that situation has changed.

**The Glass Family**

Because the details about the Glass family are scattered and because a reasonable knowledge of them is necessary for an understanding of Salinger's best work, it may help to set down in outline what we so far know about them. The parents Les Glass (Jewish) and Bessie Gallagher Glass (a fat Irish Rose, her youngest son lovingly calls her), were successful Pantages Circuit vaudevillians in the 'twenties. By the 'forties

Les glass was "hustling talent for a motion picture studio in Los Angeles." In the 'fifties they are living with their two youngest children in New York, in "an old but, categorically, not unfashionable apartment house in the East Seventies." They have had seven children.

The oldest, Seymour, was born in February 1917, entered Columbia at the age of fifteen, and took a Ph.D. in English. In 1940 he and his brother Buddy reluctantly gave up the room they had shared in the Glasses' apartment since 1929 and moved into an apartment of their own near 79$^{th}$ and Madison. Seymour taught English for a year or two before entering the service. While he was stationed at Fort Monmouth, he met a girl named Muriel Fedder, whom he married on June 4, 1942. When he returned from the service, he was—as he had promised Muriel and her mother he would be—psychoanalyzed, presumably by what Buddy calls one of those "*summa-cum-laude* Thinker[s] and intellectual men's-room attendant[s]" so greatly admired by people like Muriel's mother. Possibly as a result, Seymour one day deliberately drove the Fedders' car into a tree and it was decided that he and Muriel should take a vacation in Florida, at the place where they had spent their honeymoon. There, in room 507 of a fashionable beach hotel, on the afternoon of March 18, 1948, Seymour made his second, successful attempt to commit suicide by putting a bullet from an Ortgies calibre 7.65 through his right temple.

The second child, Buddy (whose given name is, I think, Webb), was born in 1919, as was Jerome David Salinger. Buddy is the writer of the family, and it is sometimes difficult to distinguish his voice from Salinger's. "*The Great Gatsby*," he says, "... was my 'Tom Sawyer' when I was twelve." Buddy never finished college (nor did Salinger, who tried three). He entered the service early in 1942 and, when he got out, became "a writer in residence." In 1955 he was teaching "at a girls' junior college in upper New York state where he lived alone in a small, unwinterized, unelectrified house about a quarter of a mile away from a rather popular ski run."

The next child and first girl in the family is Boo Boo Glass. "Her joke of a name aside, her general unprettiness aside, she is—in terms of

permanently memorable, immoderately perceptive, small-area faces—
a stunning and final girl." She appears to be—we do not know a great
deal about her yet—more successfully reconciled to the world than the
rest of the Glass children. Boo Boo was a Wave, stationed in Brooklyn.
During the war she met "a very resolute-looking young man" named
Tannenbaum, whom she later married. The Tannenbaums live in Tuck-
ahoe and have a summer place in New England. By 1955 they had
three children, the oldest of whom is Lionel, the central character in
"Down at the Dinghy," which was published in *Harper's* in 1949.

Boo Boo was followed by twins, Waker and Walt. Waker spent the
war in a conscientious objectors' camp in Maryland and by 1955 had
become a Catholic priest: "If you tell Waker it looks like *rain*, his eyes
all fill up." Walt entered the service in the spring of 1941 and by May
of 1942 was in the Pacific. In Japan, late in the autumn of 1945, a
Japanese stove he was packing as a souvenir for his commanding officer
exploded and killed him.

The sixth child, Zachary Martin Glass, known in the family as
Zooey, was born in 1929. Zooey's face is close to being "a wholly beautiful face" or, as Boo Boo says, he looks like "the blue-eyed Jewish-Irish
Mohican scout who died in your arms at the roulette table at Monte
Carlo." After college he became a television actor, though his mother
very much wanted him to take his Ph.D. in Mathematics or Greek, as
he easily could have. By 1952 he was playing leads.

The youngest child is a girl named Frances, born in 1934. Like Zooey
she is extraordinarily beautiful. In the summer of 1954, between her
junior and senior years in college, she played summer stock. Zooey, an
enthusiastically unrelenting critic, says she was very good, and Franny
clearly loves the theater. In her junior year she became interested in a boy
named Lane Coutell—interested enough to sleep with him. But in
November of 1955 she was plunged into a spiritual crisis—"I'm sick of
ego, ego, ego. My own and everybody else's. I'm sick of everybody that
wants to get somewhere, do something distinguished and all, be somebody interesting. It's disgusting—it is, it *is*. I don't care what anybody

says." After three difficult days at home, she is saved from collapse by her brother Zooey, who possibly saves himself at the same time.

Over a period of nearly eighteen years, beginning in 1927, one or more of the Glass children was performing, under the name of Black, on a famous radio quiz show known—"with perhaps typical Coast-to-Coast irony"—as "It's a Wise Child." Their educations were paid for by these performances.

## Suspended Explanation

This is the barest outline of what we know about the Glass family. Even so, the fullness of these details and their exactness are striking evidence of the imaginative intensity with which they have been conceived. They also make it possible for Salinger, for the first time, to use consistently the technique he is most happy with and to convey directly the feelings he cares most about.

For example, they provide the fullest opportunity for the kind of surprise an author can get from delayed or implied explanation, which writers of monologues like Salinger and Faulkner usually substitute for narrative suspense—an awkward and artificial device in a monologue. In Faulkner, one has to reconstruct the genealogy of the McCaslin family from dozens of scattered allusions before one fully understands any particular McCaslin story. In the same way one has to reconstruct the history of the Glass family.

Salinger uses suspended explanation much less extravagantly than Faulkner, but he has nonetheless confused some readers. Some of them, for instance, seem to have thought (until the matter was fully explained in "Zooey" in 1957) that the heroine of "Franny" (1955) was so badly upset during her football weekend with Lane Coutell not because she was in a spiritual crisis but because she was pregnant. There is no real reason for a careful reader to make this mistake about "Franny." In that story, Franny describes a length the idea of prayer in *The Way of a Pilgrim*, the little book she carries with her everywhere; and at the end of the story her lips are moving in the Jesus Prayer the Pilgrim recommends. Nevertheless, a good many readers apparently did misunderstand

"Franny." Some even seem to have doubts about who pushed whom into the empty swimming pool at the end of "Teddy," where, for much the same dramatic reasons that are at work in "Franny," Salinger depends on our understanding of Teddy's attitude to make us understand that it is Teddy who dies.

This kind of surprise is one of the most effective devices available to a writer like Salinger, and he uses it with great skill. He always plays fair; any careful reader knows what is going on. But we are frequently astonished and delighted when we catch our first glimpse of the precise connections between what had before seemed unconnected events. It must be some time, for instance, before a reader discovers that the Walt whom the drunken Eloise is talking about in "Uncle Wiggly in Connecticut" (1948) is Walt Glass, whose family connections did not begin to emerge in any detail until "Raise High the Roofbeam, Carpenters" (1955). But when the reader makes this discovery, a fascinating and important aspect of the Glass family falls into place for him. Walt was Bessie Glass's "only truly lighthearted son"; as such he shows us an important aspect of Salinger's sense of human possibilities.

The fact that the Glass family is large and closely knit is also important to the feelings Salinger cares most about. The essential reality for him subsists in personal relations, when people, however agonizingly, love one another. "I say," remarks Buddy Glass as he begins to tell us the story "Zooey," "that my current offering isn't a mystical story, or a religiously mystifying story, at all. *I* say it is a compound, or multiple, love story, pure and complicated."

This is true of all Salinger's mature stories. Their subject is the power to love, pure and—in children and the childlike—simple, but in aware people, pure and complicated. Salinger's constant allusions to the Bhagavad Gita, Sri Ramakrishna, Chuang-tzu, and the rest are only efforts to find alternate ways of expressing what his stories are about. This power to love can be realized—and represented—most fully in complicated personal relations like those of the Glasses.

Salinger's conception of these relations is an impressive—and certainly unconscious—evidence of the way he fits into a major tradition of American literature, what might be called the effort to define The Good American. For this tradition, American experience creates a dilemma by encouraging the individual man to cultivate his perception to the limit according to his own lights and at the same time committing him to a society on which the majority has firmly imposed a well-meaning but imperceptive and uniform attitude. People in this tradition of our cultural history have a highly developed, personal sense of their experience. At the same time, they have a strong conviction—even if a bitter conviction like Henry Adams'—that no man can survive in isolation and that the only community they have to love is the American community to which they have been committed by a lifetime's involvement. Such people cannot escape knowing that The Good American must be a member of a particularly demanding and not very perceptive community and simultaneously a supremely aware man, because they themselves live partly in the world of ordinary American experience and partly in what may perhaps fairly be called the transcendental world of extraordinary American experience.

The Glass children stand in this way at the center of our dilemma as, with less clarity of perception and less intensity of feeling, large numbers of Americans do. Like Thoreau and Henry Adams, Huck Finn and Ike McCaslin, Ishmael and Jay Gatsby, the Glass children are well aware of where they stand—committed involved, torn.

"I'd enjoy [doing a movie in France], yes," says Zooey. "*God*, yes. But I'd hate like hell to leave New York. If you must know, I hate any kind of so-called creative type who gets on any kind of ship. I don't give a goddam what his reasons are. I was *born* here. I went to *school* here. I've been *run over* here—*twice*, and on the same damned *street*. I have no business acting in Europe, for God's sake."

This sounds like the speaker in Allen Tate's "Ode to the Confederate Dead," except that the voice is wholly Northern and urban and is—for all its desperateness—less despairing.

## The Extra Dimension

It is the effort to convey their full sense of this situation that leads the Glass children to talk the way they do. For this extra dimension of understanding they use the everyday urban speech Salinger has been listening to all his life. The Glass children must speak the language of the place where they were born, went to school, were run over; it is their native language, the only one wholly theirs, just as the place itself is. But they need to express in this language an understanding of their experience which, if possessed to some degree by many Americans, is wholly clear to only a few of them.

An effort to resolve a similar conflict of feelings affects most of the writers of this tradition, with the result that they too develop odd, brilliant styles. Salinger's style most obviously resembles those of Mark Twain, Lardner, and Hemingway, who prided themselves on using homely American speech with great accuracy, but were saying things with it that few homely Americans are wholly conscious of.

Like Twain and Lardner, Salinger depends more than most prose writers on the fine shading of his style to convey his meaning. That is why he is at his best when one of his characters is speaking. When Buddy Glass writes his brother Zooey about Zooey's unprofitable love of Greek, he says, "Of course, you can go to Athens. Sunny *old* Athens." When Zooey wants to get out of the bathtub, he says to his mother, "I'm getting out of here in about three seconds, Bessie! I'm giving you fair warning. Let's not wear out our welcome, buddy." Each of these clichés is made absurd by the special quality of the Glass child's feeling, but it is at the same time what holds him, for all his special insight, in contact with the perception of ordinary people.

This perception is at its purest in children, whose wonderful directness fascinates Salinger. But he respects it wherever he finds it, whether in "the very corny boy" who gave Franny the gold swizzle stick she cannot bear to throw away, or in Zooey's producer LeSage, who delights in scripts that are down-to-earth, simple, and untrue, but believes with beautiful innocence that his "tired, bosomy, Persian-looking blonde [wife is] a dead ringer [for] the late Carole Lombard, in the movies." As Bill Gorton in *The Sun Also Rises* says of Cohn, "The funny thing is, he's nice, too. I like him. But he's just so awful."

The Glass family's most treasured jokes hover close to this reluctant sympathy with people like LeSage. For instance, at the end of Buddy's trip to Florida after Seymour's suicide, when he had wept nearly all the way, he heard a woman back of him in the plane saying, "with all of Back Bay Boston and most of Harvard Square in her voice, . . . and the next *morning*, mind you, they took a pint of pus out of that lovely young body of hers.' " As a result, when he got off the plane and Muriel "the Bereaved Widow came toward me all in Bergdorf Goodman black, I had the Wrong Expression on my face. I was grinning." It is this delicately balanced perception that gives the Glass children their special quality.

But if it makes them remarkable, it is also a quite terrible burden. "Smart men," as Dick Diver said a long time ago about Abe North in *Tender Is the Night*, "play close to the line because they have to—some of them can't stand it, so they quit." Like Abe North, Seymour, the most gifted of the Glass children, kills himself. He knows that, in spite of—because of—the unusual depth and intensity of his perception of experience, he needs to be a part of the daily life of the ordinary world. He tries, by psychoanalysis and marriage, to become part of Muriel Fedder's world. This commitment is not merely an intellectual need; it is a desperate emotional necessity for him: "How I love and need her undiscriminating heart," he says of Muriel. But Seymour finds it impossible to live simultaneously the life of his own discriminating heart and Muriel's life, with its "primal urge to play house permanently, . . . to go up to the desk clerk in some very posh hotel and ask if her Husband has picked up the mail yet, . . . to shop for maternity clothes, . . . [to have] her own Christmas-tree ornaments to unbox annually." He is torn apart by two incompatible worlds of feeling.

This, then, is the hard thing—not to find out "what it [is] all about," which the Glass children have known from very early, but "how to live it." Knowing what it is all about, in fact, is the burden.

"Those two bastards," says Zooey of Seymour and Buddy, who had taught Franny and him what wisdom is, "got us nice and early and made us into freaks with freakish standards, that's all. We're the Tattooed Lady, and we're never going to have a minute's peace, the rest of our lives, till everybody else is tattooed, too. . . . The minute I'm in a room with somebody who has the usual number of ears, I either turn into a goddam *seer* or a human hatpin. The Prince of Bores."

This, Zooey knows, is not a failure of love—he would not be concerned with his own freakishness if love failed—but a distortion of it. As his mother says to him:

> *If you [take to somebody] then you do all the talking and nobody can even get a word in edgewise. If you don't like somebody—which is most of the time—then you just sit around like death itself and let the person talk themselves into a hole. I've seen you do it. . . . You do,"* she said, *without accusation in her voice. "Neither you nor Buddy knows how to talk to people you don't like." She thought it over. "Don't love, really,"* she amended.*

"Which is most of the time" because apart from children and the occasionally simple adult, the world is made up of people who are innocently imperceptive and emotionally dead.

## The Power to Love

Of the drastic limitations of such people, Salinger has a terrifyingly lucid perception. His stories are filled with undergraduates "giving the impression of having at least three lighted cigarettes in each hand"; young teachers "who come . . . in, in [their] little button-down-collar shirts[s] and striped tie[s], and start . . . knocking Turgenev for about half an hour . . . [and] if you get into an argument with them, all they do is get this terribly *benign* expression"; parents who say, "I'll exquisite day *you*, buddy, if you don't get down off that bag this minute. And I mean it." Such people, as Teddy in the story which bears his name says of his parents, "love their reasons for loving us almost as much as they love us, and most of the time more."

Nevertheless the power to love can exist in unimaginative people, and when it does, as the Glass children know they ought to know, nothing else really counts. Bessie Glass "often seem[s] to be an impenetrable mass of prejudices, clichés, and bromides"; these are a continual irritation to her children: Franny is driven nearly frantic by Bessie's insistence on nice cups of chicken soup when Franny is suffering something like a crisis of the soul. But Zooey is right when he points out to her that she is "missing out of every single goddam religious action that's going on around this house. You don't even have sense enough to *drink* when somebody brings you a cup of consecrated chicken soup—which is the only kind of chicken soup Bessie ever brings anybody around this madhouse."

Even if the acts of such people are not consecrated by love, they must not be hated. "What I don't like," Zooey says to Franny, ". . . is the way you talk about all these people. I mean you don't just despise what they represent—you despise them. It's too damned personal, Franny."

What Zooey knows he must learn to do in order to survive is to love even what he calls the "fishy" people—because they are all the Fat Lady for whom Seymour told him to shine his shoes before going on the air, even though the audience could not see his feet.

"This terribly clear, clear picture of the Fat Lady formed in my mind," he tells Franny. "I had her sitting on this porch all day, swatting flies, with her radio going full-blast from morning till night. I figured the heat was terrible and she probably had cancer and—I don't know. Anyway, it seemed goddam clear why Seymour wanted me to shine my shoes when I went on the air. It made *sense.*"

"It makes sense because the highest standard of performance a man's own understanding can set for him must ultimately be embodied—however mystically—in the ordinary, suffering members of the community of his fellows. Otherwise there can be no solution to the dilemma the Glass children are caught in. Zooey puts this conviction in the highest possible terms:

*I'll tell you a terrible secret . . . [he says to Franny]. Are you listening to me? There isn't anyone out there who isn't Seymour's Fat Lady. . . . Don't you know that? Don't you know that goddam secret yet? And don't you know—listen to me, now—don't you know who that Fat Lady really is? . . . Ah, buddy. Ah, buddy. It's Christ Himself. Christ Himself, buddy.*

What Salinger has seen in American life is the extraordinary tension it sets up between our passion to understand and evaluate our experience for ourselves, and our need to belong to a community that is unusually energetic in imposing its understanding and values on its individual members. Whatever one may think of Salinger's answer to the problem, this view of American life is important; it has a long and distinguished history. But Salinger's achievement is not that he has grasped an abstract idea of American experience, important as that idea my be in itself; it is that he has seen this idea working in the actual life of our times, in our habitual activities, in the very turns of our speech, and has found a way to make us see it there, too.

# J. D. Salinger:
## "Everybody's Favorite"

ALFRED KAZIN

The publication of his two well-known stories from *The New Yorker* in book form, *Franny and Zooey*, brings home the fact that, for one reason or another, J. D. Salinger now figures in American writing as a special case. After all, there are not many writers who could bring out a book composed of two stories—both of which have already been read and argued over and analyzed to death by the enormous public of sophisticated people which radiates from *The New Yorker* to every English department in the land.

In one form or another, as a fellow novelist commented unlovingly, Salinger is "everybody's favorite." He is certainly a favorite of *The New Yorker*, which in 1959 published another long story around the Glass family called "Seymour: An Introduction" (almost 30,000 words), and thus give the impression of stretching and remaking itself to Salinger's latest stories, which have been appearing, like visits from outer space, at two-year intervals. But above all, he is a favorite with that audience of students, student intellectuals, instructors and generally literary, sensitive and sophisticated young people who respond to him with a consciousness that he speaks for them and virtually *to* them, in a language that is peculiarly honest and their own, with a vision of things that captures their most secret judgments of the world. The only thing that Salinger does not do for this audience is to meet with them. Holden Caulfield said in *The Catcher in the Rye* that "What really knocks me out is a book that, when you're all done reading it, you wish the author that wrote it was a terrific friend of yours and you could call him up on the phone whenever you felt like it." It is well for him that all the people in this country who now regard J. D. Salinger as a "terrific friend" do not call him up and reach him.

A fundamental reason for Salinger's appeal (like that of Hemingway in the short stories that made *him* famous) is that he has exciting professional mastery of a peculiarly charged and dramatic medium, the American short story. At a time when so much American fiction has been discursive in tone, careless in language, lacking in edge and force—when else would it have been possible for crudities like the Beat novelists to be taken seriously?—Salinger has done an honest and stimulating professional job in a medium which, when it is expertly handled, projects emotion like a cry from the stage and in form can be as intense as a lyric poem. A short story which is not handled with necessary concentration and wit is like a play which does not engage its audience; a story does not exist unless it hits its mark with terrific impact. It is a constant projection of meanings at an audience, and it is a performance minutely made up of the only possible language, as a poem is. In America, at least, where, on the whole, the best stories are the most professional stories and so are published in the most famous magazines, second-rate stories belong in the same limbo with unsuccessful musical comedies; unless you hit the bull's-eye, you don't score.

This does not mean that the best-known stories are first-rate pieces of literature any more than that so many triumphant musical comedies are additions to the world's drama; it means only that a story has communicated itself with entire vividness to its editor and its audience. The profundity that may exist in a short story by Chekhov or Tolstoy also depends upon the author's immediate success in conveying his purpose.

Even in the medieval tale, which Tolstoy in his greatest stories seems to recapture in tone and spirit, the final comment on human existence follows from the deliberate artlessness of tone that the author has managed to capture like a speech in a play.

What makes Salinger's stories particularly exciting is his intense, his almost compulsive need to fill in each inch of his canvas, each moment of his scene. Many great novels owe their grandeur to a leisurely sense of suggestion, to the imitation of life as a boundless road or flowing river, to the very relaxation of that intensity which Poe thought was the aesthetic perfection of a poem or a story. But whatever the professional superficiality of the short story in American hands, which have molded and polished it so as to reach, dazzle and on occasion deceive the reader, a writer like Salinger, by working so hard to keep his tiny scene alive, keeps everything humming.

Someday there will be learned theses on *The Use of the Ashtray in J. D. Salinger's Stories*; no other writer has made so much of Americans lighting up, reaching for the ashtray, setting up the ashtray with one hand while with the other they reach for a ringing telephone. Ours is a society complicated with many appliances, and Salinger always tells you what his characters are doing with each of their hands. In one long stretch of "Zooey," he describes the young man sitting in a bathtub, reading a long letter from his brother and smoking; he manages to describe every exertion made and every sensation felt in that bathtub by the young man whose knees made "dry islands." Then the young man's mother comes into the bathroom; he draws he shower curtains around the tub, she rearranges the medicine cabinet, and while they talk (in full), everything they do is described. Everything, that is, within Salinger's purpose in getting at such detail, which is not the loose, shuffling catalogue of the old-fashioned naturalists, who had the illusion of reproducing the whole world, but the tension of a dramatist or theater director making a fuss about a character's walking just so.

For Salinger, the expert performer and director (brother Buddy Glass, who is supposed to be narrating "Zooey," speaks of "directing" it and calls the story itself a "prose home movie",) gesture is the essence of the medium. A short story does not offer room enough for the development of character; it can present only character itself, by gesture. And Salinger is remarkable, I would say he is almost frenetically proficient, in getting us, at the opening of "Franny," to *see* college boys waiting on a rain platform to greet their dates arriving for a big football weekend. They rush out to the train, "most of them giving the impression of having at least three lighted cigarettes in each hand." He knows exactly how Franny Glass would be greeted by Lane Coutell: "It was a station-platform kiss—spontaneous enough to begin with, but rather inhibited in the follow-through, and with something of a forehead-bumping aspect."

And even better is his description of the boy at a good restaurant, taking a first sip of his martini and then looking "around the room with an almost palpable sense of well-being at finding himself (he must have been sure no one could dispute) in the right place with an unimpeachably right-looking girl." Salinger knows how to prepare us with this gesture for the later insensitivity of a boy who is exactly one of those up-to-date and anxiously sophisticated people whom Franny Glass, pure in heart, must learn to tolerate, and even to love, in what she regards as an unbearably shallow culture.

But apart from this, which is the theme of *Franny and Zooey*, the gesture itself is recognized by the reader not only as a compliment to himself but as a sign that Salinger is working all the time, not merely working to get the reader to see, but working to make his scene itself hum with life and creative observation. I don't know how much this appearance of intensity on the part of Salinger, of constant as well as full overage, is due to *New Yorker* editorial nudging, since its famous alertness to repetitions of words and vagueness of diction tends to give an external look of freshness and movement to prose. Salinger not only works very hard indeed over each story, but he obviously writes to and for some particular editorial mind he identifies with *The New Yorker*; look up the stories he used to write for the *Saturday Evening Post* and

*Cosmopolitan*, and you will see that just as married people get to look alike by reproducing each other's facial expressions, so a story by Salinger and a passage of commentary in *The New Yorker* now tend to resemble each other.

But whatever the enormous influence of any magazine on whose who write regularly for it, Salinger's emphasis of certain words and syllables in American speech and his own compulsiveness in bearing down hard on certain details (almost as if he wanted to make the furniture, like the gestures of certain people, tell *everything* about the people who use them) do give his stories the intensity of observation that is fundamental to his success. Lane Coutell, sitting in that restaurant with Franny and talking about a college paper on Flaubert he is horribly well satisfied with, says, "I think the emphasis I put on *why* he was so neurotically attached to the *mot juste* wasn't too bad. I mean in the light of what we know today. Not just psychoanalysis and all that crap, but certainly to a certain extent. You know what I mean. I'm no Freudian man or anything like that, but certain things you can't just pass over as capital-F Freudian and let them go at that. I mean to a certain extent I think I was perfectly justified to point out that none of the really good boys—Tolstoy, Dostoevski, Shakespeare, for Chrissake— were such goddam word-squeezers. They just *wrote*. Know what I mean?" What strikes me about this mimicry is not merely that it is so clever, but that it is also so relentless. In everything that this sophisticated ass. Lane Coutell, says, one recognizes that he is and will be wrong. Salinger disapproves of him in the deepest possible way; he is a spiritual enemy.

Of course, it is a vision of things that lies behind Salinger's expert manner. There is always one behind every manner. The language of fiction, whatever it may accomplish as representation, ultimately conveys an author's imitation of things; makes us hear, not in a statement, but in the ensemble of his realized efforts, his quintessential commentary on the nature of existence. However, the most deliberate the language of the writer, as it must be in a short story, the more the write must convey his judgment of things in one highlighted dramatic action as is done on the stage.

At the end of "Franny," the young girl collapses in the ladies' room of the restaurant where she had been lunching with her cool boy friend. This conveys her spiritual desperation in his company, for Lane typifies a society where "Everything everybody does is so—I don't know— not *wrong*, or even mean, or even stupid necessarily. But just so tiny and meaningless and—sad-making." Her brother Zooey (Zachary Glass), at the end of the long second story, calls her up from another telephone number in the same apartment and somehow reaches to the heart of her problem and gives her peace by reminding her that the "Fat Lady they used to picture somnolently listening to them when they were quiz kids on the radio—the ugly, lazy, even disgusting-looking Fat Lady, who more and more typifies unattractive and selfish humanity in our day—can be loved after all, for she, too, is Jesus Christ.

In each story, the climax bears a burden of meaning that it would not have to bear in a novel; besides being stagy, the stories are related in a way that connects both of them into a single chronicle. This, to quote the title of a little religious pamphlet often mentioned in it, might be called *The Way of a Pilgrim*. Both Franny and Zooey Glass are, indeed, pilgrims seeking their way in a society typified by the Fat Lay, and even by Lane Coutell's meaningless patter of sophistication. No wonder Franny cries out to her unhearing escort: "I'm sick of just liking people. I wish to God I could meet somebody I could respect." The Glasses (mother Irish, father Jewish) are ex-vaudevillians whose children were all, as infant prodigies performers on a radio quiz program called "It's a Wise Child." Now, though engaged in normally sophisticated enterprises (Franny goes to a fashionable women's college, Zooey is a television actor, Buddy a college instructor), they have retained their intellectual precocity—and, indeed, their precocious charm—and have translated, as it were, their awareness of themselves as special beings into a conviction that they alone can do justice to their search for the true way.

The oldest and most brilliant of the children, Seymour, shot himself in 1948 in Florida; this was the climax of Salinger's perhaps most famous story, "A Perfect Day for Bananafish." And it is from Seymour's old room in the Glass apartment that Zooey calls up his sister, Franny, on a phone that is normally never used, that is still listed in the name of Seymour Glass, and that has been kept up by Buddy (who does not want a phone in his country retreat) and by Zooey in order to perpetuate Seymour's name and to symbolize his continuing influence on them as a teacher and guide. It is from reading over again, in Seymour's old room, various religious sayings from the world's literature that Seymour had copied out on a piece of beaverboard nailed to the back of a door that Zooey is inspired to make the phone call to Franny that ends with the revelation that the horrible Fat Lady is really Jesus Christ.

This final episode, both in the cuteness of its invention and in the cuteness of speech so often attributed to Seymour, who is regarded in his own family as a kind of guru, or sage, helps us to understand Salinger's wide popularity. I am sorry to have to use the word "cute" in respect to Salinger, but there is absolutely no other word that for me so accurately typifies the self-conscious charm and prankishness of his own writing and his extraordinary cherishing of his favorite Glass characters.

Holden Caulfield is also cute in *The Catcher in the Rye*, cute in his little-boy suffering for his dead brother, Allie, and cute in his tenderness for his sister, "old Phoebe." But we expect that boys of that age may be cute—that is, consciously appealing and consciously clever. To be these things is almost their only resource in a world where parents and schoolmasters have all the power and the experience. Cuteness, for an adolescent, is to turn the normal self-pity of children, which arises from their relative weakness, into a relative advantage vis-à-vis the adult world. It becomes a role boys can play in the absence of other advantages, and *The Catcher in the Rye* is so full of Holden's cute speech and cute innocence and cute lovingness for his own family that one must be an absolute monster not to like it.

And on a higher level, but with the same conscious winsomeness, the same conscious mournfulness and intellectual loneliness and lovingness (though not for his wife), Seymour Glass is cute when he sits on the beach with a little girl telling her a parable of "bananafish"—ordinary-looking fish when "they swim into a hole where there's a lot of bananas," but after that they're so fat they can't get out of the hole again. . . . They die." His wife, meanwhile busy in their room on the long-distance phone to her mother in New York, makes it abundantly clear in the hilariously accurate cadences and substance of her conversation why her husband finds it more natural to talk to a four-year-old girl on the beach than to her. Among other things, Seymour expects not to be understood outside the Glass family. But agonizing as this situation is, the brilliantly entertaining texture of "A Perfect Day for Bananafish" depends on Seymour Glass's conscious cleverness as well as on his conscious suffering— even his conscious cleverness *about* the suffering of "ordinary-looking" fish who get so bloated eating too many bananas in a "hole" they shouldn't have been attracted to in the first place.

In the same way, not only does the entertaining surface of *Franny and Zooey* depend on the conscious appealingness and youthfulness and generosity and sensitivity of Seymour's brother and sister, but Salinger himself, in describing these two, so obviously feels such boundless affection for them that you finally get the sense of all these child prodigies and child entertainers being tied round and round with veils of self-love in a culture which they—and Salinger—just despise. Despise, above all, for its intellectual pretentiousness. Yet this is the society, typified by the Fat Lady (symbolically, they pictured her as their audience), whom they must now force themselves to think of as Jesus Christ, and whom, as Christ Himself, they can now at last learn to love.

For myself, I must confess that the spiritual transformation that so many people associate with the very sight of the word "love" on the

printed page does not move me as it should. In what has been considered Salinger's best story, "For Esme—with Love and Squalor,"
Sergeant X in the American Army of Occupation in Germany is saved
from a hopeless breakdown by the beautiful magnanimity and remembrance of an aristocratic young English girl. We are prepared from this
climax or visitation by an earlier scene in which the sergeant comes
upon a book by Goebbels in which a Nazi woman had written, "Dear
God, life is hell." Under this, persuaded at last of his common suffering
even with a Nazi, X writes down, from *The Brothers Karamazov*:
"Fathers and teachers, I ponder 'What is hell?' I maintain that it is the
suffering of being unable to love."

But the love that Father Zossima in Dostoevsky's novel speaks for is
surely love for the world, for God's creation itself, for all that precedes
us and supports us, that will outlast us and that alone helps us to
explain ourselves to ourselves. It is the love that D. H. Lawrence,
another religious novelist, spoke of as "the sympathetic bond" and that
in one form or another lies behind all the great novels as a primary
interest in everyone and everything alive with us on this common
earth. The love that Salinger's horribly precocious Glass characters
speak of is love for certain people only—forgiveness is for the rest;
finally, through Seymour Glasses's indoctrination of his brothers and
sisters in so many different (and pretentiously assembled) religious
teachings, it is love of certain ideas. So what is ultimate in their love is
the love of their own moral and intellectual excellence, of their chastity
and purity in a world full of bananafish swollen with too much food.
It is the love that they have for themselves as an idea.

The worst they can say about our society is that they are too sensitive to live in it. They are the special case in whose name society is
condemned. And what makes them so is that they are young, precocious, sensitive, different. In Salinger's work, the two estates—the
world and the cutely sensitive young—never really touch at all.
Holden Caulfield condemns parents and schools because he knows
that they are incapable of understanding him; Zooey and Franny and

Buddy (like Seymour before them) know that the great mass of prosperous spiritual savages in our society will never understand them.

This may be true, but to think so can lead to a violation of art. Huckleberry Finn, so often cited as a parallel to the hero of *The Catcher in the Rye*, was two years younger than Holden, but the reason he was not afraid of an adult's world is that he had respect for it. He had never even seen very much of it until he got on that raft with a runaway Negro slave he came to love and was able to save. It was still all God's creation, and inspired him with wonder. But Holden and, even more, the Glass children are beaten before they start; beaten in order not to start. They do not trust anything or anyone but themselves and their great idea. And what troubles me about this is not what it reflects of their theology but what it does to Salinger's art.

Frank O'Connor once said of this special métier, the short story, that it is "the art form that deals with the individual when there is no longer a society to absorb him, and when he is compelled to exist, as it were, by his own inner light." This is the condition on which Salinger's work rests, and I should be sorry to seem unsympathetic toward it. It is an American fact, as one can see from the relative lack in our literature of the ripe and fully developed social novel in which the individual and society are in concrete and constant relationship with each other. But whatever this lack, which in one sense is as marked in the novels of Scott Fitzgerald as it is in Salinger's emphasis upon the short story, it is a fact that when Fitzgerald describes a character's voice, it is because he really loves—in the creative sense, is full interested in—this character. When Salinger describes a character's voice, it is to tell us that the man is a phony. He has, to borrow a phrase from his own work, a "categorical aversion" to whole classes and types of our society. The "sympathetic bond" that Lawrence spoke of has been broken. People stink in our nostrils. We are mad with captious observation of one another. As a friend of mine once said about the novels of Mary McCarthy, trying to say with absolute justice what it was that shocked her so much in them, "The heroine is always right and everyone else is wrong." Salinger is a far more accomplished and objective writer of fiction than Mary McCarthy, but I would say that in his work the Glass children alone are right and everyone else is wrong.

And it is finally this condition, not just the famous alienation of Americans from a society like our own, that explains the popularity of Salinger's work. Salinger's vast public I am convinced, is based not merely on the vast number of young people who recognize their emotional problems in his fiction and their frustrated rebellions in the sophisticated language he manipulates so skillfully. It is based perhaps even more on the vast number who have been released by our society to think of themselves as endlessly sensitive, spiritually alone, gifted, and whose suffering lies in the narrowing of their consciousness to themselves, in the withdrawal of their curiosity from a society which they think they understand all too well, in the drying up of their hope, their trust, and their wonder at the great world itself. The worst of American sophistication today is that it is so bored, so full of categorical aversion to things that writers should never take for granted and never close their eyes to.

The fact that Salinger's work is particularly directed against the "well-fed sunburned" people at the summer theater, at the "section men" in colleges parroting the latest fashionable literary formulas, at the "three-martini" men—this, indeed, is what is wrong. He hates them. They are no longer people, but symbols, like the Fat Lady. No wonder that Zooey tells his sister: Love them, love them all, love them anyway! But the problem is not one of spiritual pride or of guilt; it is that in the tearing of the "sympathetic bond" it is not love that goes, but the deepest possibilities of literary art.

# Anxious Days
# for the Glass Family

JOHN UPDIKE

Quite suddenly, as things go in the middle period of J. D. Salinger, his later, longer stories are descending from the clouds of old *New Yorkers* and assuming incarnations between hard covers. "Raise High the Roof Beam, Carpenters," became available last year in "Stories from *The New Yorker* 1950–1960," and now "Franny" and "Zooey" have a book to themselves. These two stories—the first medium-short, the second novella- length—are contiguous in time, and have as their common subject Franny's spiritual crisis.

In the first story, she arrives by train from a Smith-like college to spend the week-end of the Yale game at what must be Princeton. She and her date, Lane Coutell, go to a restaurant where it develops that she is not only unenthusiastic but downright ill. She attempts to explain herself while her friend brags about a superbly obnoxious term paper and eats frogs' legs. Finally, she faints, and is last seen lying in the manager's office silently praying at the ceiling.

In the second story, Franny has returned to her home, a large apartment in the East Seventies. It is the Monday following her unhappy Saturday. Only Franny's mother, Bessie, and her youngest brother,

Zooey, are home. While Franny lies sleeplessly on the living-room sofa, her mother communicates, in an interminably rendered conversation, her concern and affection to Zooey, who then, after an even longer conversation with Franny, manages to gather from the haunted atmosphere of the apartment the crucial word of consolation. Franny, "as if all of what little or much wisdom there is in the world were suddenly hers," smiles at the ceiling and falls asleep.

Few writers since Joyce would risk such a wealth of words upon events that are purely internal and deeds that are purely talk. We live in a world, however, where the decisive deed may invite the holocaust, and Salinger's conviction that our inner lives greatly matter peculiarly qualifies him to sing of an America where, for most of us, there seems little to do but to feel. Introversion, perhaps, has been forced upon history; an age of nuance, of ambiguous gestures and psychological jockeying on a national and private scale, is upon us, and Salinger's intense attention to gesture and intonation help make him, among his contemporaries, a uniquely relevant literary artist. As Hemingway sought the words for things in motion, Salinger seeks the words for things transmuted into human subjectivity. His fiction, in its rather grim bravado, its humor, its morbidity, its wry but persistent hopefulness, matches the shape and tint of present American life. It pays the price, however, of becoming dangerously convoluted and static. A sense of composition is not among Salinger's strengths, and even these two stories, so apparently complementary, distinctly jangle as components of one book.

The Franny of "Franny" and the Franny of "Zooey" are not the same person. The heroine of "Franny" is a pretty college girl passing through a plausible moment of disgust. She has discovered—one feels rather recently—a certain ugliness in the hungry human ego and a certain fatuity in her college environment. She is attempting to find her way out with the help of a religious book, *The Way of a Pilgrim*, which was mentioned by a professor. She got the book out of the college library. Her family, glimpsed briefly in the P. S. of a letter she has written, appear to be standard upper-middle gentry. Their name is nowhere given as Glass; Franny never mentions any brothers. Her boy friend is crass and self-centered but not entirely unsympathetic; he clumsily does try to "get through" to Franny, with a love whose physical bias has become painfully inappropriate. Finally, there is a suggestion—perhaps inadvertent—that the girl may be pregnant.

The Franny of "Zooey," on the other hand, is Franny Glass, the youngest of the seven famous Glass children, all of whom have been in turn wondrously brilliant performers on a radio quiz program, *It's a Wise Child.* Their parents, a distinctly unstandard combination of Jewish and Irish, are an old vaudeville team. From infancy on, Franny has been saturated by her two oldest brothers, Seymour and Buddy, in the religious wisdom of the East. *The Way of a Pilgrim,* far from being newly encountered at college, comes from Seymour's desk, where it has been for years.

One wonders how a girl raised in a home where Buddhism and crisis theology were table talk could have postponed her own crisis so long and, when it came, be so disarmed by it. At any rate, there is no question of her being pregnant; the very idea seems a violation of the awesome Glass ethereality. Lane Coutell, who for all his faults was at least a considerable man in the first Franny's universe, is now just one of the remote millions coarse and foolish enough to be born outside the Glass family.

The more Salinger writes about them, the more the seven Glass children melt indistinguishably together in an impossible radiance of personal beauty and intelligence. Franny is described thus: "Her skin was lovely, and her features were delicate and most distinctive. Her eyes were very nearly the same quite astonishing shade of blue as Zooey's but were set farther apart, as a sister's eyes no doubt should be." Of Zooey, we are assured he has a "somewhat preposterous ability to quote, instantaneously and, usually verbatim, almost anything he had ever read, or even listened to, with genuine interest." The purpose of such sentences is surely not to particularize imaginary people but to instill in the reader a mood of blind worship, tinged with envy.

In "Raise High the Roof Beam, Carpenters" (the first and best of the Glass pieces: a magic and hilarious prose-poem with an enchanting end effect of mysterious clarity), Seymour defines sentimentality as giving "to a thing more tenderness than God gives to it." This seems to me the nub of the trouble: Salinger loves the Glasses more than God loves them. He loves them too exclusively. Their invention has become a hermitage for him. He loves them to the detriment of artistic moderation. "Zooey" is just too long; there are too many cigarettes, too many goddams, too much verbal ado about not quite enough.

The author never rests from circling his creations, patting them fondly, slyly applauding. He robs the reader of the initiative upon which love must be given. Even in "Franny," which is, strictly, pre-Glass, the writer seems less an unimpassioned observer than a spying beau vindictively feasting upon every detail of poor Lane Coutell's gaucherie. Indeed, this impression of a second male being present is so strong that it amounts to a social shock when the author accompanies Franny into the ladies' room of the restaurant.

"Franny," nevertheless, takes place in what is recognizably our world; in "Zooey" we move into a dream world whose zealously animated details only emphasize an essential unreality. When Zooey says to Franny, "Yes, I have an ulcer, for Chrissake. This is Kaliyuga, buddy, the Iron Age," disbelief falls on the "buddy" as much as on "Kaliyuga," and the explanatory "the Iron Age" clinches our suspicion that a lecturer has usurped the writing stand. Not the least dismaying development of the Glass stories is the vehement editorializing on the obvious—television scripts are not generally good, not all section men are geniuses. Of course, the Glasses condemn the world only to condescend to it, to forgive it, in the end. Yet the pettishness of the condemnation diminishes the gallantry of the condescension.

Perhaps these are hard words; they are made hard to write by the extravagant self- consciousness of Salinger's later prose, wherein most of the objections one might raise are already raised. On the flap of this book jacket, he confesses, "There is a real-enough danger, I suppose, that sooner or later I'll bog down, perhaps disappear entirely, in my own methods, locutions, and mannerisms. On the whole, though, I'm very hopeful." Let me say, I am glad he is hopeful. I am one of those—to do some confessing of my own—for whom Salinger's work dawned as something of a revelation. I expect that further revelations are to come.

The Glass saga, as he has sketched it out, potentially contains great fiction. When all reservations have been entered, in the correctly unctuous and apprehensive tone, about the direction he has taken, it remains to acknowledge that it is a direction, and that the refusal to rest content, the willingness to risk excess on behalf of one's obsessions, is what distinguishes artists from entertainers, and what makes some artists adventurers on behalf of us all.

# J. D. Salinger's Closed Circuit

MARY MCCARTHY

Who is to inherit the mantle of Papa Hemingway? Who, if not, J. D. Salinger? Holden Caulfield in *The Catcher in the Rye* has a brother in Hollywood who thinks *A Farewell to Arms* is terrific. Holden does not see how his brother, who is *his* favorite writer, can like a phony book like that. But the very image of the hero as pitiless phony-detector comes from Hemingway. In *Across the River and Into the Trees*, the colonel gets a message on his private radar that a pock-marked writer he darkly spies across the room at Harry's Bar in Venice has "outlived his talents"—apparently some sort of crime. "I think he has the same pits on his heart and in his soul," confides the heroine, in her careful foreign English. That was Sinclair Lewis.

Like Hemingway, Salinger sees the world in terms of allies and enemies. He has a good deal of natural style, a cruel ear, a dislike of ideas (the enemy's intelligence system), a toilsome simplicity, and a ventrilo-quist's knack of disguising his voice. The artless dialect written by Holden is an artful ventriloquial trick of Salinger's like the deliberate, halting English of Hemingway's waiters, fishermen, and peasants—anyone who speaks it is a good guy, a friend of the author's to be trusted.

*The Catcher in the Rye*, like Hemingway's books, is based on a scheme of exclusiveness. The characters are divided into those who belong to the club and those who don't—the clean marlin, on the one hand, and the scavenger sharks on the other. Those who don't belong are "born that way"—headmasters, philanthropists, roommates, teachers of history and English, football coaches, girls who like the Lunts. They cannot help the way they are, the way they talk; they are obeying a law of species—even the pimping elevator operator, the greedy prostitute, the bisexual teacher of English who makes an approach to Holden in the dark.

It's not anybody's fault if just about everybody is excluded from the club in the long run—everybody but Ring Lardner, Thomas Hardy, Gatsby, Isak Dinesen, and Holden's little sister Phoebe. In fact, it is a pretty sad situation, and there is a real adolescent sadness and lonely desperation in *The Catcher in the Rye*; the passages where Holden, drunk and wild with grief, wanders like an errant pinball through New York at night are very good.

But did Salinger sympathize with Holden or vice versa? That remained dubious. Stephen Dedalus in a similar situation met Mr. Bloom, but the only "good" person Holden meets is his little sister—himself in miniature or in apotheosis, riding a big brown horse on a carousel and reaching for the gold ring. There is something false and sentimental here. Holden is supposed to be an outsider in his school, in the middleclass world, but he is really an insider with the track all to himself.

And now, ten years after *The Catcher in the Rye* we have *Franny and Zooey*. The event was commemorated by a cover story in *Time*; the book has been a best-seller since *before* publication.

Again the theme is the good people against the stupid phonies, and the good is still all in the family, like a family-owned "closed" corporation. The heroes are or were seven children (two are dead), the wonderful Glass kids of a radio quiz show called *It's a Wise Child*, half-Jewish, half-Irish, the progeny of a team of vaudevillians. These prodigies, nationally known and the subjects of many psychological studies, are now grown up: one is a writer-in-residence in a girls' junior college; one is a Jesuit priest; one is a housewife; one is a television actor (Zooey); and one is a student (Franny). They are all geniuses, but the greatest genius of them all was Seymour, who committed suicide on vacation in an early story of Salinger's called "A Perfect Day for Bananafish." Unlike the average genius, the Glass kids are good guys; they love each other and their parents and their cat and their goldfish, and they are expert phony-detectors. The dead sage Seymour has initiated them into Zen and other mystical cults.

During the course of the story, Franny has a little nervous breakdown, brought on by reading a small green religious book titled *The Way of the Pilgrim*, relating the quest for prayer of a simple Russian peasant. She is cured by her brother Zooey in two short séances between his professional television appointments; he recognizes the book (it was in Seymour's library, of course) and on his own inspiration, without help from his older brother Buddy or from the Jesuit, teaches her that Jesus, whom she has been sweating to find via the Jesus Prayer, is not some fishy guru but just the Fat Lady in the audience, the average ordinary humanity with varicose veins, the you and me the performer has to reach if the show is going to click.

### The Admissions Policy

This democratic commercial is "sincere" in the style of an advertising man's necktie. The Jesus Zooey sells his sister is the old Bruce Barton Jesus—the word made flesh, Madison Avenue's motto. The Fat Lady is not quite everybody, despite Zooey's fast sales patter. She is the kind of everybody the wonderful Glass kids tolerantly approve of. Jesus may be a television sponsor or a housewife or a television playwright or your Mother and Dad, but He (she?) cannot be an intellectual like Franny's horrible boyfriend, Lane, who has written a paper on Flaubert and talks about Flaubert's "testicularity," or like his friend Wally, who, as Franny says plaintively, "looks like somebody who spent the summer in Italy or someplace."

These fakes and phonies are the outsiders who ruin everything. Zooey feels the same way. "I hate any kind of so-called creative type who gets on any kind of ship. I don't give a goddam what his reasons are." Zooey likes it here. He likes people, as he says, who wear horrible neckties and funny, padded suits, but he does not mind a man who dresses well and owns a two-cabin cruiser so long as he belongs to the real, native, video-viewing America. The wonderful Glass family have three radios, four portable phonographs, and a TV in their wonderful living-room, and their wonderful, awesome medicine cabinet in the bathroom is full of sponsored products all of which have been loved by someone in the family.

The world of insiders, it would appear, has grown infinitely larger and more accommodating as Salinger has "matured." Where Holden Caulfield's club excluded just about everybody but his kid sister, Zooey's and Franny's secret society includes just about everybody but creative types and students and professors. Here exception is made, obviously, for the Glass family: Seymour, the poet and thinker, Buddy, the writer, and so on. They all have college degrees; the family bookshelves indicate a wide, democratic culture:

> Dracula *now stood next to* Elementary Pali, The Boy Allies at the Somme *stood next to* Bolts of Melody. The Scarab Murder Case *and* The Idiot *were together,* Nancy Drew and the Hidden Staircase *lay on top of* Fear and Trembling.

The Glass family librarian does not discriminate, in keeping with the times, and books are encouraged to "mix." In Seymour's old bedroom, however, which is kept as a sort of temple to his memory, quotations, hand-lettered from a select group of authors are displayed on the door: Marcus Aurelius, Issa, Tolstoy, Ring Lardner, Kafka, St. Francis de Sales, Mu Moon Kwan, etc. This honor roll is extremely institutional.

The broadening of the admissions policy—which is the Text of Zooey's sermon—is more a propaganda aim, though, than an accomplishment. No doubt the author and his mouthpiece (who is smoking a panatela) would like to spread a message of charity. "Indiscrimination," as Seymour says in another Salinger story, ". . . leads to heal and a kind of very real, enviable happiness." But this remark itself exhales an ineffable breath of gentle superiority. The club, for all it's pep talks, remains a closed corporation, since the function of the Fat Lady, when you come down to it, is to be what?—an audience for the Glass kids, while the function of the Great Teachers is to act as their coaches and prompters. And who are these wonder kids but Salinger himself, splitting and multiplying like the original amoeba?

### Bathroom Worship

In Hemingway's work there was never anybody but Hemingway in a series of disguises, but at least there was only one Papa per book. To be confronted with these seven faces of Salinger, all wise and lovable and simple, is to gaze into a terrifying narcissus pool. Salinger's world contains nothing but Salinger, his teachers, and his tolerantly cherished audience—humanity; outside are the phonies, vainly signaling to be let in, like the kids' Irish mother, Bessie, a home version of the Fat Lady, who keeps invading the bathroom while her handsome son Zooey is in the tub shaving.

The use of the bathroom as stage set—sixty-eight pages of "Zooey" are laid there—is all too revealing as a metaphor. The bathroom is the holy-of-holies of family life, the seat of privacy, the center of the cult of self-worship. What methodical attention Salinger pays to Zooey's routines of shaving and bathing and nail cleaning, as though these were rituals performed by a god on himself, priest and deity at the same time! The scene in the bathroom, with the mother seated on the toilet, smoking and talking, while her son behind the figured shower curtain reads, smokes, bathes, answers, is of a peculiar snickering indecency; it is worth noting, too, that this scene matches a shorter one in a public toilet in the story "Franny," a scene that by its strange suggestiveness misled many *New Yorker* readers into thinking that Franny was pregnant—that was why, they presumed, such significance was attached to her shutting herself up in a toilet in the ladies room, hanging her head and feeling sick.

These readers were not "in" on the fact that Franny was having a mystical experience. Sex is unimportant for Salinger; not the bed but the bathroom is the erotic center of the narcissus ego, and Zooey behind the shower curtain is taboo, even to the mother who bore him—behind the veil. The reader, however, is allowed an extended look.

A great deal of attention is paid, too, to the rituals of cigarette lighting and to the rites of drinking from a glass, as though these oral acts were sacred, epiphanies, in the same way, the family writings are treated by Salinger as sacred scriptures or the droppings of holy Birds, to be studied with care by the augurs, letters from Seymour, citations from his diary, a letter from Buddy, a letter from Franny, a letter from Boo Boo, a note written by Boo Boo in soap on a bathroom mirror (the last two are from another story "Raise High the Roof Beam, Carpenters").

These imprints of the Glass collective personality are preserved as though they were Veronica's veil in a relic case of well-wrought prose. And the eerie thing is, speaking of Veronica's veil, a popular subject for those paintings in which Christ's eyes are supposed to follow the spectator with a doubtless reproachful gaze, the reader has the sensation in his latest work of Salinger that the author is sadly watching him or listening to him read. That is, the ordinary relation is reversed, and instead of the reader reading Salinger, Salinger, that Man of Sorrows, is reading the reader.

At the same time, this quasi-religious volume is full of a kind of Broadway humor. The Glass family is like a Jewish family in a radio serial. Everyone is a "character." Mr. Glass with his tangerine is a character; Mrs. Glass in her hairnet and commodious wrapper with her cups of chicken broth is a character. The shower curtain, scarlet nylon with a design of canary-yellow sharps, clefs, and flats, is a character; the teeming medicine cabinet is a character. Every phonograph, every chair is a character. The family relationship, rough, genial, insulting, is a character.

In short, every single object possessed by the Glass communal ego is bent on lovably expressing the Glass personality—eccentric, homey, good-hearted. Not unlike "Abie's Irish Rose." And the family is its own best audience. Like Hemingway stooges, they have the disturbing faculty of laughing delightedly or smiling discreetly at each other's jokes. Again a closed circuit: the Glass family is the Fat Lady, who is Jesus. The Glass medicine cabinet is Jesus, and Seymour is his prophet.

Yet below this self-loving barbershop harmony a chord of terror is struck from time to time, like a judgment. Seymour's suicide suggests that Salinger guesses intermittently or fears intermittently that there may be something wrong somewhere. Why did he kill himself? Because he had married a phony, whom he worshiped for her "simplicity, her terrible honesty"? Or because he was so happy and the Fat Lady's world was so wonderful?

Or because he had been lying, his author had been lying, and it was all terrible, and he was a fake?

# Salinger Biography Is Blocked

ARNOLD LUBASCH

A biography of J. D. Salinger was blocked yesterday by a Federal appeals court in Manhattan that said the book unfairly used Mr. Salinger's unpublished letters.

Reversing a lower court decision, the appeals court ruled in favor of Mr. Salinger, who filed suit to prohibit the biography from using all material from the letters, which he wrote many years ago.

"We're delighted," said R. Andrew Boose, the attorney for Mr. Salinger. "We've told him of the decision, and he is also delighted."

**Publication Delayed Last Year**
The disputed biography, *J. D. Salinger: A Writing Life* by Ian Hamilton, was to be published late last year by Random House, but it was held up by the unusual court case.

A Random House spokesman said after the appeals court ruling yesterday, "We are not going to be able to comment until we've had a chance to study the opinion." The only further legal appeal for the publishing house is in the Supreme Court of the United States.

In its 24-page decision, the United States Court of Appeals for the

Second Circuit said the case focused on "whether the biographer of a renowned author has made 'fair use' of his subject's unpublished letters."

## The "Fair Use" Standard

According to legal scholars, the "fair use" standard is vague and open to wide interpretation.

Legal opinion on the appeal court's ruling was varied. Charles Rembar, a noted constitutional lawyer, had not seen the opinion. But from the language the court used in announcing the decision, he said, "then the conclusion is inescapable—the judgment had to follow, as the night the day."

But Floyd Abrams, another noted constitutional lawyer, expressed reservations. "It seems to me a deeply troubling limitation on the ability of a publisher to print a significant book," he said, "and of the public to learn about one of the most fascinating and important writers of our time."

Mr. Salinger wrote the letters to his friend and editor, Whit Burnett, and to several other people, including Ernest Hemingway.

"The biography," the appeals court said, "copies virtually all of the most interesting passages of the letters, including several highly expressive insights about writing and literary criticism."

In a footnote, the appeal court's decision cited a letter in which Mr. Salinger complained about an editor who praised one of his stories while rejecting it. "Like saying," he wrote, "she's a beautiful girl, except for her face."

Another letter criticized Wendell Willkie, the 1940 Presidential candidate, saying, "He looks to me like a guy who makes his wife keep a scrapbook for him."

The decision included another footnote referring to a 1943 letter in which "Salinger, distressed that Oona O'Neill, whom he had dated, had married Charlie Chaplin, expressed his disapproval of the marriage in this satirical invention of his imagination:

"I can see them at home evenings. Chaplin squatting grey and nude, atop his chiffonier, swinging his thyroid around his head by his bamboo cane, like a dead rat. Oona in an aquamarine gown, applauding madly from the bathroom."

"I'm facetious," the letter added, "but I'm sorry. Sorry for anyone with a profile as young and lovely as Oona's."

## One Judge Died

Judge Jon O. Newman wrote the decision, with the concurrence of Judge Roger J. Miner, for the three-judge panel that heard the appeal. The third member of the panel, Judge Walter R. Mansfield, died on January 7 while the case was under consideration.

In reversing a ruling that Judge Pierre N. Leval issued on November 5 in Federal District Court in Manhattan, the appeals court declared yesterday that the biography could not be published in its present form.

"The plaintiff J. D. Salinger," the appeals court noted, "is a highly regarded American novelist and short-story writer, best known for his novel *The Catcher in the Rye*. He has not published since 1965 and has chosen to shun all publicity and inquiry concerning his private life."

"The defendant Ian Hamilton is a well respected writer on literary topics," it continued. "He serves as literary critic of *The London Sunday Times* and has authored a biography of the poet Robert Lowell."

Mr. Hamilton, who wrote the biography despite Mr. Salinger's refusal to cooperate with him, made use of the unpublished Salinger letters, which were written between 1939 and 1961. The recipients or their representatives donated the letters to university libraries, where they were discovered by Mr. Hamilton.

## Salinger Obtained Copyright

When Mr. Salinger learned that the letters were being used in the biography, he registered them for copyright protection and objected to the biography's publication unless all of the material from the letters was deleted.

In response to Mr. Salinger's objection, the appeals court observed, Mr. Hamilton and Random House revised the original galleys of the biography by paraphrasing much of the material that had previously been quoted from the letters.

The appeals court continued, however, that Mr. Salinger identified 59 instances where the revised biography contained "passages that either quote from or closely paraphrase portions of the unpublished letters."

Mr. Salinger then sued the biographer and publisher, charging that the use of his letters involved copyright infringement and unfair competition.

Judge Leval of the lower court rejected Mr. Salinger's request for an injunction in the suit, ruling last November that the biography had made only minimal use of material that was entitled to copyright protection. But he temporarily held up publication to permit an appeal.

In the subsequent decision by the appeals court, Judge Newman noted that "the author of letters is entitled to a copyright in the letters, as with any other work of literary authorship."

### "The Heart of the Book"

Under the copyright law, the appeals court said, a publisher can make "fair use" of unpublished works. But it said the biography's extensive use of "close paraphrases" of the Salinger letters had gone beyond the permitted limits.

"The copied passages, if not the heart of the book," the opinion said, "are at least an important ingredient of the book as it now stands. To a large extent, they make the book worth reading."

Although Mr. Salinger has indicated that he would not publish his letters in his lifetime, the appeals court said he was entitled to protect his opportunity to sell them.

# Summer Reading;
# *Rises at Dawn, Writes, Then Retires*

Book Review of *In Search of J. D. Salinger* by Ian Hamilton

MORDECAI RICHLER

"What really knocks me out," says Holden Caulfield in *The Catcher in the Rye*, "is a book that, when you're all done reading it, you wish the author that wrote it was a terrific friend of yours and you could call him up on the phone whenever you felt like it." However, had Holden called his celebrated but reclusive creator, J. D. Salinger, the odds are he would have hung up on him. Mind you, that's certainly the 69-year-old author's prerogative. He is not obliged to chat with his many admirers or reporters from newsweeklies or gabby talk-show hosts or even to sit still for serious biographers, however well intentioned.

Ian Hamilton's *In Search of J. D. Salinger* raises many questions larger than the legal tangle that delayed the book's publication for two years, about which more later.

For openers, beyond a taste for gossip (a taste I admittedly share), I fail to understand what I take to be a burgeoning curiosity about writers' lives. I find the biographies of politicians, tycoons and other con men great fun because their art is their lives, but with a few exceptions (most recently Richard Ellmann's *Oscar Wilde*) the lives of writers strike me as boring. This, of course, is just as it should be because it is their fiction that is charged with incident and invention while their lives, in the nature of things, tend to be uneventful. I wouldn't go quite so far as the publisher Colin Haycraft, who wrote in *The London Sunday Telegraph*, "The world is a peculiar place, but it has nothing on the world of books. This is largely a fantasy world, in which the pecking order goes as follows: if you can't cope with life, write about it; if you can't write, publish."

But the truth is that most novelists start out by retreating into a cave with a ream of blank paper and when they totter out with a finished manuscript they are two, maybe three years older and have missed out on an awful lot. As a rule, embarrassingly little beyond the ordinary (marital messes, losing battles with booze and tobacco and the I.R.S., spats with other writers and publishers) has happened off the page. Take J. D. Salinger, for instance. According to a neighbor, he is said to rise at 5 or 6 A.M. in his home in Cornish, New Hampshire, and then walk "down the hill to his studio, a tiny concrete shelter with a translucent plastic roof," and spend 15 or 16 hours at his typewriter. Later he may watch one of his vast collection of 1940's movies. Hardly the stuff of drama.

The most prolix, unnecessary and trivial of the recent spill of literary biographies come in the new bastardized form of books-of-the-tape, or oral histories. A case in point is *Mailer: His Life and Times*, recorded by Peter Manso, wherein we learn from Arnold (Eppie) Epstein, who sailed through fifth grade with Norman, that the future novelist was not much taken with sports. "He was busy building his model airplanes, and built some of the best models any of us had ever seen. . . . Other kids made models, but Norman always did the best ones, and this more or less set him apart." A condition Mr. Mailer's mother appreciated much earlier: "Even in the first grade," she recalls, "his teacher recognized his talent and let him write whatever he wanted to." Which was undoubtedly dandy for Norman at the time, but does nothing to enlarge my understanding of his sadly underestimated novel *The Deer Park*.

Then, in a more recent book-of-the-tape, *The True Gen: An Intimate Portrait of Ernest Hemingway by Those Who Knew Him*, by Denis Brian (so to speak), there is a solemn discussion about whether Hemingway actually did it in that hospital in Italy with the nurse Agnes von Kurowsky Stanfield, the model for Catherine Barkley in *A Farewell to Arms*, or whether the old master was guilty of locker-room braggadocio. Henry Villard, who was in the hospital with Hemingway, says the most he witnessed of any hanky-panky between Ernest and Agnes was their brief hand-holding under the guise of her taking his temperature, but maybe Mr. Villard just didn't peek at the right time. Or he snoozed through it. Anyway, when he read *A Farewell to Arms* 11 years later he was "astonished and shocked" by "scandalously explicit love scenes" that "came across as personal experience." "Much of the novel covered the overwhelming Italian defeat by the Austrians at the battle of Caporetto. I knew Hemingway had not even been in Italy when that took place." A revelation, I reckon, that makes Hemingway as big a fibber as Tolstoy, who did not march into the sound of gunfire at Borodino.

The most prevalent form of literary biography does not set out to illuminate but to level. Usually these studies are written by professors who must publish for promotion, but sometimes they are the work of kin. In either case, they can be awfully picky. In Susan Cheever's *Home Before Dark*, a memoir of her father, she writes that though John Cheever liked to recount how his ancestor Ezekiel Cheever had arrived in Boston Harbor on the Arbella in 1630, her research had revealed that Ezekiel didn't actually arrive until 1637 on board the Hector. Worse news. Cheever's aristocratic New England background was largely his own invention.

Anticipating, perhaps, Cheever wrote in his journal in 1961: "I have been a storyteller since the beginning of my life, rearranging facts in order to make them more interesting and sometimes more significant."

In the opening pages of his book, Ian Hamilton writes, "I had it in mind to attempt not a conventional biography—that would have been

impossible—but a kind of Quest for Corvo, with Salinger as quarry."
The analogy won't wash. A. J. A. Symons' book *The Quest for Corvo*, a
fine and original work, happens to be about a literary scoundrel, Fred-
erick Rolfe, a bizarre character whose squalid life was more fascinating
than anything he wrote, while the obverse is true of J. D. Salinger, of
whom Mr. Hamilton justifiably observes, "The action, for [him], was
on the page."

There is another problem. Symons undertook his quest in 1925, 12
years after Rolfe's death, but Mr. Salinger, happily, is still among the
quick. At the risk of sounding stuffy, I think it indecently hasty to
undertake a biography-cum-critical study of a still working writer and
in highly questionable taste to pronounce him a perfect subject
because, in Mr. Hamilton's view, "he was, in any real-life sense, invisible, as good as dead." Invisible? Look here, we are talking about a
writer whose only published novel, *The Catcher in the Rye*, which first
appeared in 1951, was declared in 1968 to be one of America's 25
leading best sellers since the year 1895 and still sells something like a
quarter of a million copies annually worldwide.

Ian Hamilton, to be fair, is not a vulgarian: he has good credentials
as a biographer, poet and critic. In the first chapter of *In Search of J. D.
Salinger*, he declares that he will confine himself to the years the
author's life was in the public domain, that is to say, until 1965, when
he last published. But Mr. Salinger, in a court deposition made in an
attempt to restrain publication of Mr. Hamilton's book, revealed that
he has been hard at it all these years, still writing, and so he is far from
as good as dead. If and when he does publish again, he could astound
us as he once did with *The Catcher in the Rye*.

Ian Hamilton first read *The Catcher in the Rye* when he was 17
years old. Discouraged from undertaking this biography by Mr.
Salinger, Mr. Salinger's family and friends, he writes, "when I really
ask myself how this whole thing began, I have to confess that there was
more to it than mere literary whimsy. There was more to it than mere
scholarship. Although it will seem ludicrous, perhaps, to hear me say

so now, I think the sharpest spur was an infatuation, an infatuation that bowled me over at the age of seventeen and which it seems I never properly outgrew. Well, I've outgrown it now." Outgrown it, alas, by composing a biography that is at best unfriendly, at worst hostile. The 21-year-old Mr. Salinger's letters to Whit Burnett of *Story* magazine are described, for example, as "too garrulously self-promoting . . . mock-boastful, and, now and then, plain boastful." In January 1940, once Burnett had accepted the young writer's first story, we are told that for Mr. Salinger this was a way of showing Them.

"To judge from his letters . . . he was fairly buzzing with self-admiration and not at all disposed to keep quiet about it." But an examination of these letters, as quoted in the original version of "Salinger" but excised from the published book, shows no such thing. They are, in fact, exuberant, self-deprecating and charged with hope.

After Burnett had accepted Mr. Salinger's first short story, we learn in these letters, he wrote to the editor: "I'm twenty one. New York born, and I can draw a rejection slip with both hands tied behind me. Writing has been important to me since I was seventeen. I could show you a lot of nice faces I've stepped on to illustrate the point. Now that you've accepted the story I'll tell everyone to waste no pity on the unpublished short story writer, that his ego can cope with people and circumstance, that he is his own worst enemy. Oh, I'll be wisdom itself."

In another unpublished letter, to a friend who had written to congratulate him on his first publication, Mr. Salinger replied: "Truly, I'm unspeakably pleased that you liked my stories. I have of course an ardent admirer in myself, but mostly when I'm at work. When I'm finished with a piece, I'm embarrassed to look at it again, as though I were afraid I hadn't wiped its nose clean. Or to that effect."

The letters are also, as Mr. Salinger noted with hindsight in court, occasionally gauche or effusive. "It's very difficult," he said. "I wish . . . you could read letters you wrote 46 years ago. It's very painful reading."

Yes, possibly. But Mr. Salinger would have been better served if he had allowed his letters to be quoted rather than described so vindictively. On the other hand, Mr. Hamilton's hostility is understandable. He has been through a good deal. The first judge to hear the case ruled in the biographer's favor: "Hamilton's book cannot be dismissed as an act of commercial voyeurism or snooping into a private being's private life for commercial gain. It is a serious, well-researched history of a man who through his own literary accomplishments has become a figure of enormous public interest. This favors a finding of fair use."

But on January 29, 1987, the United States Court of Appeals for the Second Circuit reversed the earlier judgment. Mr. Hamilton could not quote from the letters he had discovered in the Firestone Library at Princeton University and elsewhere.

The bald facts about J. D. Salinger are as follows:

He was born into New York affluence of a sort in 1919. His father, Sol Salinger, was Jewish, a cheese importer, and his mother, Marie Jillich, was a Scottish-born gentile. At 17, he was enrolled in Valley Forge Military Academy, the model for Pencey Prep in *The Catcher in the Rye*. His first fiction was published in Story in 1940. He went on to publish other stories of no great distinction in *Collier's*, *The Saturday Evening Post*, and *Esquire*. He joined the Army in 1942, landed at Utah Beach with the 12th Infantry Regiment on June 6, 1944, and was involved in heavy fighting in the Hurtgen Forest. His first marriage, to a French doctor in 1945, lasted only eight months. In the late 1940's, Mr. Salinger's stories appeared in *Collier's*, *The Saturday Evening Post*, *Cosmopolitan*, and *Good Housekeeping*. But with the exception of one story ("A Slight Rebellion Off Madison"), which appeared in 1946, *The New Yorker* had not yet "taken him up." Then, in 1948, after several rejections, he finally gained acceptance from the magazine. His next two published stories in *The New Yorker* were "A Perfect Day for Bananafish" and "Uncle Wiggily in Connecticut." Three years later came *The Catcher in the Rye*, which was turned down by Harcourt, Brace before being published by Little, Brown. He retreated to a 90-acre estate in Cornish, New Hampshire, in 1953 and is still resident there. His second marriage, to Claire Douglas in 1954, ended in divorce in 1967. They have a son, Matthew, and a daughter, Margaret Ann.

J. D. Salinger's other books are *Nine Stories, Franny and Zooey,* and *Raise High the Roof Beam, Carpenters and Seymour: An Introduction.* He published his last story, "Hapworth 16, 1924," in *The New Yorker* in 1965. According to rumor, reported by Mr. Hamilton, he has since then completed at least two full-length manuscripts, which are locked in a safe. In its present unfortunately truncated form, Ian Hamilton's biography does not turn up much that is new and does turn up a good deal that is neither here nor there. We are told, for instance, that the name Holden Caulfield probably came from joining the name of a boyhood friend called Holden to that of the movie actress Joan Caulfield, on whom Mr. Salinger once had a crush. J. D., we also learn, was bad at arithmetic. "A private for most of his time at Valley Forge," Mr. Hamilton tells us, "he was promoted in time to appear as corporal in the yearbook. Academically, he did enough to graduate: 88 in English, 84 in German, 83 in French, and 79 in modern European history."

Mr. Hamilton's biography is tainted by a nastiness born of frustration perhaps, but hardly excused by it. Mr. Salinger is never given the benefit of a doubt. He is described as a "callow self-advancer." Aged 22, we are told, "the Salinger we were on the track of was surely getting less and less lovably Holden-ish each day. So far, our eavesdropping had yielded almost nothing in the way of human frailty or warmth. The first-person voice we'd been so pleased to come across had spent most of its time boasting or pushing its career." This vengeful book is also marred by Mr. Hamilton's coy, tiresome device of splitting himself in two, as it were, referring to Mr. Salinger's biographer in the third person. ("I was already thinking of 'him' as somehow separate from 'me.' ") This, in turn, allows the use of the royal we, as in the opening of chapter three: "We traveled back from Valley Forge to New York feeling triumphant. Look at what had been amassed, so far: Salinger's school records, some telling items of juvenilia. . . . And, sure enough, my companion now had a smug, workmanlike look about him. . . . He'd done his job. He had his Chapter I." But when the first version of his book was completed in 1985 Mr. Hamilton already had doubts. It was, he writes, all right, but "whatever its merits, the book had by no means solved the mystery of Salinger." He tells friends, "It isn't much. Don't get the idea that it's a biography, because it isn't. But it's not too bad."

Starting out with his sleuthing other self, Mr. Hamilton set himself admirable ground rules. He would not attempt to seek out Mr. Salinger's ex-wife, his children, his sister, or surprise his friends on the telephone. In 1961, a less fastidious Time researcher waylaid Mr. Salinger's sister Doris at Bloomingdale's, where she worked. Ms. Salinger told him, "I wouldn't do anything in the world my brother didn't approve of. I don't want to be rude, but you put me in a very difficult position. Why don't you leave us alone? Hundreds of people want to write stories about him."

Anything I might add to this cry from the heart would obviously be redundant.

# From Salinger, a New Dash of Mystery

## Book Review of "Hapworth 16, 1924"

MICHIKO KAKUTANI

So, at long last, we have news that the famously reclusive J. D. Salinger is bringing out another book, not a new story, but one called "Hapworth 16, 1924," which appeared in *The New Yorker* in the 1960's. Read in retrospect, that story continues—perhaps even completes—the saga of the Glass family, that band of precocious, high-strung whiz kids who have captivated Salinger fans for four decades. It also stands as a logical, if disappointing, culmination of Mr. Salinger's published work to date.

Why wait three decades to bring out this story in book form? And why choose the obscure Orchises Press in Alexandria, Virginia, to publish it? One can only speculate: that the author wanted to remind his readers of his existence, that he wanted to achieve a kind of closure by putting his last published story between book covers, that he wanted readers to reappraise the Glass family (and by extension his body of work) through a story that, within the Glass canon, is nothing less than revisionistic.

As with most things connected with Mr. Salinger, an air of mystery hovers about the publication of "Hapworth." His agent has not returned phone calls, and even bookstores say they do not know exactly when they will have copies of the book for sale, this month, perhaps, or March or April. In the meantime, the story can be found in the June 19, 1965, issue of *The New Yorker*—in the library stacks or on microfilm.

*The New Yorker* story, a novella really, takes the form of a nearly interminable letter ostensibly written from summer camp by the 7-year-old Seymour Glass. It is unlikely to be of any interest to anyone who has not closely followed the emotional peregrinations of the Glass family over the years, and for ardent Glass-ites, it is likely to prove a disillusioning, if perversely fascinating, experience, an experience that will forever change their perception of Seymour and his siblings.

Like Holden Caulfield, the Glass children are both avatars of adolescent angst and emblems of Mr. Salinger's own alienated stance toward the world. Bright, gregarious and entertaining (their parents are retired vaudevillians), the Glasses embody all the magic of their creator's early stories; they appeal to the reader to identify with their sensitivity, their braininess, their impatience with phonies, hypocrites and bores.

The Glasses' emotional translucence, their febrile charm, their spiritual yearning and nausea—all delivered in the wonderfully idiomatic voice of cosmopolitan New Yorkese—initially made them a glamorous mirror of our own youthful confusions. Yet there is a darker side to their estrangement as well: a tendency to condescend to the vulgar masses, a familial self-involvement that borders on the incestuous and an inability to relate to other people that, in Seymour's case at least, will have tragic consequences indeed.

Seymour, of course, was the oldest of the Glass children, who in the 1948 short story "A Perfect Day for Bananafish" (collected in *Nine Stories*) put a gun to his head and blew his brains out. In that story, Seymour appeared to be a sweet if somewhat disturbed young man, ill equipped to deal with the banal, grown-up world represented by his frivolous wife.

In subsequent stories, we learned, largely through the reminiscences of his brother Buddy—the family historian and Mr. Salinger's alter ego, who actually purports to have written "Bananafish" and "Raise High the Roof Beam, Carpenters" (1955)—that Seymour was regarded as the family saint and resident mystic. In "Seymour: An Introduction" (1959), Buddy described his brother as "our blue-striped unicorn, our double-lensed burning glass, our consultant genius, or portable conscience, our supercargo and our one full poet."

Seymour was the one who inculcated the younger Glasses in Eastern mysticism and Western philosophy and preached a Zen-like doctrine of acceptance. Seymour was the one who said that "all we do our whole lives is go from one little piece of Holy Ground to the next." Seymour was supposed to be the one who saw more.

It is something of a shock, then, to meet the Seymour presented in "Hapworth": an obnoxious child given to angry outbursts. "No single day passes," this Seymour writes, "that I do not listen to the heartless indifferences and stupidities passing from the counselors' lips without secretly wishing I could improve matters quite substantially by bashing a few culprits over the head with an excellent shovel or stout club!"

This Seymour confesses to lustful feelings about the camp matron ("I have looked forward with mounting pleasure to the possibility, all too slight for words, of her opening the door, quite unwittingly, in the raw"), condescends to his parents ("Jesus, you are a talented, cute, magnificent couple!") and boasts of his own talent ("the distinguished Edgar Semple having told Mr. Fraser that I have the makings of a splendid American poet, which is quite true in the last analysis").

For a child, Seymour makes requests for reading material that verge on the preposterous: among many other books, he asks for "the complete works again of Count Leo Tolstoy" and "any unbigoted or bigoted books on God or merely religion, as written by persons whose last names begin with any letter after H; to stay on the safe side, please include H itself, though I think I have mostly exhausted it."

Though Seymour and his siblings have always been renowned for their precocity, this hardly sounds like a 7-year-old, no matter how brilliant or advanced. After all, Buddy told us in an earlier story that when

Seymour was 8, he was writing poems like this: "John Keats/John Keats/John/Please put your scarf on."

Indeed, there are plenty of suggestions that Buddy—who introduces the Hapworth letter, saying he's typed "an exact copy" of Seymour's words—is actually the letter's author, distorting Seymour in much the same way that he once said he distorted Seymour in "Bananafish," impersonating a brother through an act of ventriloquism as Zooey did in the 1957 story "Zooey." It is never explained, for instance, why Seymour, once described as "the least prolific letter writer in the family," has penned such a ludicrously long epistle. Equally unexplained are the bizarre hints in the letter that Seymour can foretell the future, that he has predicted, at such a young age, his own untimely death and Buddy's dazzling future as a writer.

Why would Buddy Glass want to distort his brother's memory, tear down the myth of the saintly Seymour he has so carefully constructed in the past? No doubt one possible motive lies in the Glass siblings' resentment of Seymour's mentorship and sanctimonious love of perfection and their bitterness over his suicide, which left the "Whole Loving Family high and dry." Buddy, especially, has always had a deeply ambivalent relationship with his older brother, his professed love and adoration belying, in "Seymour: An Introduction" at least, envy, pique and simple weariness with being haunted by a ghost.

In the end, of course, Buddy is a fictional narrator, a mouthpiece for his creator, and so the larger question becomes, what light does "Hapworth" shed on Mr. Salinger's conception of the Glasses and the evolution of his art?

The first thing the reader notices, in looking back on the Glass stories, is that the tales have grown increasingly elliptical over the years, tidily crafted works like "Bananafish" and "Franny" giving way to the increasingly verbose "Zooey" and the shapeless, mock stream of consciousness employed in "Seymour" and "Hapworth." The second thing one notices is that the stories have also grown increasingly self-conscious and self-reflexive, much the way many of Philip Roth's later fictions have. This solipsism, in turn, makes the reader increasingly aware of the solipsism of the Glass family itself, underscoring the rarefied, self-enclosed air of all the stories they inhabit.

"Seymour," which teasingly conflates Buddy's and Mr. Salinger's identities, is filled with little gibes against critics with tin ears, defensive remarks about being a literary entertainer with "surface charms," and even allusions to rumors about being a recluse. "Hapworth" can similarly be read as a response of sorts to Mr. Salinger's critics, who in the years before its *New Yorker* publication took his Glass stories to task for being too cute, too self-involved, too smug.

In fact, with "Hapworth," Mr. Salinger seems to be giving critics a send-up of what he contends they want. Accused of writing only youthful characters, he has given us a 7-year-old narrator who talks like a peevish old man. Accused of never addressing the question of sexual love, he has given us a young boy who speaks like a lewd adult. Accused of loving his characters too much, he has given us a hero who's deeply distasteful. And accused of being too superficially charming, he has given us a nearly impenetrable narrative, filled with digressions, narcissistic asides and ridiculous shaggy-dog circumlocutions.

In doing so, however, Mr. Salinger has not only ratified his critics' accusations of solipsism, but also fulfilled his own fear that one day he might "disappear entirely, in my own methods, locutions, and mannerisms." This falling off in his work, perhaps, is a palpable consequence of Mr. Salinger's own Glass-like withdrawal from the public world: withdrawal feeding self-absorption and self-absorption feeding tetchy disdain.

The infinitely engaging author of *The Catcher in the Rye* (1951), the writer who captured the hearts of several generations with his sympathetic understanding, his ear for vernacular speech, his pitch-perfect knowledge of adolescence and, yes, his charm, has produced, with "Hapworth," a sour, implausible and, sad to say, completely charmless story.

# J. D. Salinger's Holden Caulfield, Aging Gracelessly

JONATHAN YARDLEY

Precisely how old I was when I first read *The Catcher in the Rye*, I cannot recall. When it was published, in 1951, I was 12 years old, and thus may have been a trifle young for it. Within the next two or three years, though, I was on a forced march through a couple of schools similar to Pencey Prep, from which J. D. Salinger's 16-year-old protagonist Holden Caulfield is dismissed as the novel begins, and I was an unhappy camper; what I had heard about *The Catcher in the Rye* surely convinced me that Caulfield was a kindred spirit.

By then *The Catcher in the Rye* was already well on the way to the status it has long enjoyed as an essential document of American adolescence—the novel that every high school English teacher reflexively puts on every summer reading list—but I couldn't see what all the excitement was about. I shared Caulfield's contempt for "phonies" as well as his sense of being different and his loneliness, but he seemed to me just about as phony as those he criticized as well as an unregenerate whiner and egotist. It was easy enough to identify with his adolescent angst, but his puerile attitudinizing was something else altogether.

That was then. This is half a century later. *The Catcher in the Rye* is now, you'll be told just about anywhere you ask, an "American classic," right up there with the book that was published the following year, Ernest Hemingway's *The Old Man and the Sea*. They are two of the most durable and beloved books in American literature and, by any reasonable critical standard, two of the worst. Rereading *The Catcher in the Rye* after all those years was almost literally a painful experience: The combination of Salinger's execrable prose and Caulfield's jejune narcissism produced effects comparable to mainlining castor oil.

Over that half-century I'd pretty much forgotten about *The Catcher in the Rye*, though scarcely about Salinger, whose celebrated reclusiveness has had the effect of keeping him in the public eye. He has published no books since *Raise High the Roof Beam, Carpenters and Seymour: An Introduction* in 1963, but plenty has been published about him, including Ian Hamilton's decidedly unauthorized biography, *In Search of J. D. Salinger* (1988); Joyce Maynard's self-serving account of her affair with him, *At Home in the World* (1998); and his daughter Margaret A. Salinger's (also self-serving) memoir, *Dream Catcher* (2000), not to mention reams of lit crit and fanzine fawning. Rumors repeatedly make their way across the land that Salinger is busily at his writing table, that his literary fecundity remains undiminished, that bank vaults in New England contain vast stores of unpublished Salingeriana, but to date all the speculation has come to naught, for which we should—though too many people won't—be grateful.

If there's an odder duck in American literature than Salinger, his or her name doesn't come quickly to mind. He started out conventionally enough—born in Manhattan in 1919, served (valiantly) in the infantry in Europe during World War II, wrote short stories that were published in respectable magazines, notably the *New Yorker*—but he seems to have been totally undone by the fame that *The Catcher in the Rye* inflicted upon him. For nearly four decades he has been a semi-hermit (he married for the third time about a decade and a half ago) in his New England fastness, spurning journalists and fending off adoring fans, practicing the Zen Buddhism that seems to have become an obsession with him.

It's weird, but it's also his business. If, Garbolike, he just vants to be alone, he's entitled. But whether calculated or not, his reclusiveness has created an aura that heightens, rather than diminishes, the mystique of *The Catcher in the Rye.* It isn't just a novel, it's a dispatch from an unknown, mysterious universe, which may help explain the phenomenal sales it enjoys to this day: about 250,000 copies a year, with total worldwide sales over—probably way over—10 million. The mass-market paperback I bought last summer is, incredibly, from the 42nd printing; for the astonishing price of $35,000 you can buy, online, a signed copy not of the first edition—a signed copy of *that,* we must assume, would be almost literally priceless—but of the 1951 Book-of-the-Month Club edition.

Viewed from the vantage point of half a century, the novel raises more questions than it answers. Why is a book about a spoiled rich kid kicked out of a fancy prep school so widely read by ordinary Americans, the overwhelming majority of whom have limited means and attend, or attended, public schools? Why is Holden Caulfield nearly universally seen as "a symbol of purity and sensitivity" (as *The Oxford Companion to American Literature* puts it) when he's merely self-regarding and callow? Why do English teachers, whose responsibility is to teach good writing, repeatedly and reflexively require students to read a book as badly written as this one?

That last question actually is easily answered: *The Catcher in the Rye* can be fobbed off on kids as a book about themselves. It is required reading as therapy, a way to encourage young people to bathe in the warm, soothing waters of resentment (all grown-ups are phonies) and self-pity without having to think a lucid thought. Like that other (albeit marginally better) novel about lachrymose preppies, John Knowles's *A Separate Peace* (1960), *The Catcher in the Rye* touches adolescents' emotional buttons without putting their minds to work. It's easy for them, which makes it easy for teacher.

What most struck me upon reading it for a second time was how sentimental—how outright squishy—it is. The novel is commonly represented as an expression of adolescent cynicism and rebellion—a James Dean movie in print—but from first page to last Salinger wants to have it both ways. Holden is a rebel and all that—"the most terrific liar you ever saw in your life," "probably the biggest sex maniac you ever saw"—but he's a softy at heart. He's always pitying people—"I felt sorry as hell for him, all of a sudden," "You had to feel a little sorry for the crazy sonuvabitch," "Real ugly girls have it tough. I feel so sorry for them sometimes"—and he is positively a saint when it comes to his little sister, Phoebe. He buys a record for her, "Little Shirley Beans," and in the course of moping around Manhattan he does something clumsy that gives him the chance to show what a good-hearted guy he really is:

*Then something terrible happened just as I got in the park. I dropped old Phoebe's record. It broke into about fifty pieces. It was in a big envelope and all, but it broke anyway. I damn near cried, it made me feel so terrible, but all I did was, I took the pieces out of the envelope and put them in my coat pocket. They weren't good for anything, but I didn't feel like just throwing them away. Then I went in the park. Boy, was it dark.*

Me, I damn near puked. That passage is flagrantly manipulative, a tug on the heartstrings aimed at bringing a tear to the eye. Ditto for Holden's brother, Allie: "He's dead now. He got leukemia and died when we were up in Maine, on July 18, 1946. You'd have liked him. He was two years younger than I was, but he was about fifty times as intelligent. He was terrifically intelligent. His teachers were always writing letters to my mother, telling her what a pleasure it was having a boy like Allie in their class. And they weren't just shooting the crap. They really meant it."

That's just easy exploitation of the reader's emotion. Give your protagonist a dead younger brother and a cute little sister—not to mention a revered older brother, D.B., a gifted writer who sounds a whole lot like J. D. Salinger himself—and the rest is strictly downhill. From first page to last, *The Catcher in the Rye* is an exercise in button-pushing, and the biggest button it pushes is the adolescent's uncertainty and insecurity as he or she perches precariously between childhood, which is remembered fondly and wistfully, and adulthood, which is the great phony unknown. Indeed a case can be made that *The Catcher in the Rye* created adolescence as we now know it, a condition that barely existed until Salinger defined it. He established whining rebellion as essential to adolescence and it has remained such ever since. It was a short leap indeed from *The Catcher in the Rye* to *The Blackboard Jungle* to *Rebel Without a Cause* to Valley Girls to the multibillion-dollar industry that adolescent angst is today.

The cheap sentimentality with which the novel is suffused reaches a climax of sorts when Holden's literary side comes to the fore. He flunks all his courses except English. "I'm quite illiterate," he says early in the book, "but I read a lot," which establishes the mixture of self-deprecation and self-congratulation that seems to appeal to so many readers. In one of the novel's more widely quoted passages he then says:

> *What really knocks me out is a book that, when you're all done reading it, you wish the author that wrote it was a terrific friend of yours and you could call him up on the phone whenever you felt like it. That doesn't happen much, though. I wouldn't mind calling this Isak Dinesen up. And Ring Lardner, except that D.B. told me he's dead.*

That Ring Lardner is one of Holden's favorite writers is a considerable, if wholly inadvertent, irony. Lardner was the master of the American vernacular who, as H. L. Mencken wrote, "set down common American with the utmost precision." Salinger, by contrast, can be seen straining at every turn to write the way an American teenager would speak, but he only produces an adult's unwitting parody of teen-speak. Unlike Lardner, Salinger has a tin ear. His characters forever say "ya" for "you," as in "ya know," which no American except perhaps a slap-stick comedian ever has said. Americans say "yuh know" or "y'know," but never "ya know."

The Catcher in the Rye is a maladroit, mawkish novel, but there can be no question about its popularity or influence. My own hunch is that the reason is the utter, innocent sincerity with which it was written. It may be manipulative, but it's not phony. A better, more cynical writer than Salinger easily could write a book about a troubled yet appealing teenager, but its artifice and insincerity would be self-evident and readers would reject it as false. Whatever its shortcomings, The Catcher in the Rye is from the heart—not Holden Caulfield's heart, but Jerome David Salinger's. He said everything he had to say in it, which may well be why he has said nothing else.

# PART III:

## DECONSTRUCTING JERRY

April 2002, revised February 2006

# A Brief Biography of J. D. Salinger

SARAH MORRILL

### Where was he born and all that David Copperfield type crap?

Jerome David Salinger was born in New York in 1919. His older sister's name is Doris. His father, Sol, was a Jew who was in the meat and cheese business. His relationship with his father was distant and he didn't even bother to attend his funeral. His mother, of whom he was very fond, was Irish Catholic. Being half Jewish was a source of enormous conflict for Salinger.

The cold relationship with his father, his conflict from being half Jewish, and especially his traumatic experiences in World War II, were negative aspects of his life which shaped his personality and his fiction.

*Let's stop right here.*

### Why do you want to know about Salinger?

When you read about the life of J. D. Salinger, ask yourself why you want to know about him. The answer to that question is more important than the details of his biography. Right?

Are you impressed by the literary value of his work? Are you especially intrigued by the fact he's a recluse? Do you feel as if you know him? That he understands you? Are you hoping that in real life he's like Buddy Glass? (He's not, but more about that later.)

It's not abnormal to be curious about an author who's made an impression upon you. A good friend of ours found out who John Updike's dentist is and seriously considered switching dentists just on the chance he might some day be sitting in the waiting room with him. And the life of Hemingway is a great read and it sheds some light on his fiction, but why do so many people want to know about Salinger?

He's a recluse, for one. People always want to know about recluses. What are they hiding? And if they're not hiding anything, what exactly is the nature of their psychopathology? It's intriguing. We wonder what it would be like to harbor such an eccentricity that only fame and money could buy. When he could be appearing on talk shows and enjoying the fame that most of us crave, he instead locks himself away and is the prison guard of his own cell. It was fascinating to read about Howard Hughes years ago. Here was a filthy rich man who saw no one but his trusted aides. He had a phobia of germs. He ate the same Baskin Robbins peach ice cream every night. He never cut his finger nails or cut his hair. Did he have an aide by his side 24 hours a day armed with a fly swatter? Who in the hell cares? *We* do. We are a nation of *People* magazine readers. (I, of course, have never bought a copy, but it's hard to put down while I'm in the grocery check-out line.)

In his biography of Salinger, Paul Alexander speculates that Salinger enjoyed, on some level, the attention that his reclusiveness generated. The mystique surrounding him has probably greatly increased his book sales. Alexander believes that every now and then when it seems interest is waning, Salinger will do or say something to get back in the public consciousness. He'll place a phone call to a reporter in San Francisco or he'll make an unexpected appearance in New York.

A recluse wanting attention? Alexander's evidence isn't too far-fetched and knowing what we do about Salinger, it's believable.

Salinger is a man of contradictions and though he's an extremist, he never was a purist. He has rigid rules of conduct that he frequently finds reason to break.

- He only eats organic food but when he's with his son, they sometimes go out for pizza.
- With his Buddhist beliefs, he scorned worldly desire, but he was vain about the attention his writing received and he pursued young women for sex.
- Salinger enjoyed aspects of Valley Forge Military School but portrayed it as a hell hole in his novel.
- Salinger was fond of the military but later had an aversion for it.
- Salinger admired Hemingway but parodied him and spoke critically of him.
- Salinger thought writers should never have their photographs appear with their work but he wouldn't have started his relationship with Joyce Maynard had he not seen her photograph alongside her magazine article.

So, yes, though Salinger is driven by a force to avoid human contact, he also yearns for attention, approval and love.

### Why is Salinger a recluse and how did it come about?

At an early age, Salinger was somewhat odd and stand-offish—not to a great degree, but it was noticeable and it drew comment. When called upon to be social, Salinger could appear to be warm and engaging as if he were a leading man in an old movie. He frequently would say the stock phrase, "I've heard so much about you!" He was never really awkward in manner or speech until his 70's when angrily confronting unwanted guests. During his school days he had no problem being the center of attention when amusing his classmates with well-told stories and jokes at other people's expense but when it was time to go out drinking, he usually chose to stay behind. A charming loner.

**What's the deal with his father?**

Salinger had early, inner conflict concerning his father. Sol, who was cold toward his son, constantly placed pressure on him to make money and to have a secure job with high social status. He also wanted him to some day take over the family business of importing and processing meat and cheese from Eastern Europe.

Salinger, as a young man, was sent to Poland by his father to see first hand that end of the meat business. Surprisingly, Salinger went willingly, but he was so disgusted by the slaughterhouses that after that, he firmly decided to embark on a different career path. His disgust for the meat business and his rejection of his father probably had a lot to do with his vegetarianism as an adult.

When his father died, Salinger didn't go to the funeral and barely made mention of the fact to his live-in girlfriend at the time, Joyce Maynard, and to his daughter, Peggy.

About the only positive thing we know about his father is that he's the source for the title of Salinger's most acclaimed short story. When they went to the beach, Sol used to hold Jerry by the waist in the water and tell him to look for "bananafish."

**What's the deal with being Jewish?**

Salinger also felt very conflicted about being half Jewish. (His mother was Irish Catholic.) This was a conflict of social status, not religion. Salinger wasn't sure how to define himself but he knew he was supposed to achieve social status. Being half Jewish drove him nuts.

It was not unusual in the 30's and 40's for people to be openly racist against Jews. The Ivy League colleges even had a policy not admit too many of them. To have high social status, you needed money, education, connections, and you had to be a gentile.

**What was his war experience?**

The greatest source of mental trauma for Salinger was his experiences in World War II. He entered the war with a special affection for the military but soon was right in the middle of some of the most intense, savage warfare of the century. He would see with his own eyes 50 of his fellow soldiers die in a day. Sometimes as many as 200. He landed at Utah Beach in an amphibious craft. Before nightfall, his counterintelligence group was able to advance two miles inland. For the next four months he saw some of the worst fighting of the war. In the first couple weeks, 75 percent of the soldiers in his unit died. After a few months, that figure jumped to 125 percent (his unit, the Twelfth Infantry Regiment, had a continual stream of replacements.) Salinger also witnessed some of the most costly blunders made by Allied generals.

After the liberation of Paris, Salinger checked himself into to the military hospital for going "Section 8." After a few weeks he was released and he eventually was discharged from the army. It took a bit of work on his part to get a discharge for other than psychiatric reasons but somehow he managed it. His daughter believes that he was one of the first American soldiers to see the horrors of the concentration camps. Though some of his fictional characters were in the army, Salinger has never written about or even discussed the horror of what he experienced. (In "Esme" there is an attempt.)

### How did he feel about the Viet Nam War?

During the Viet Nam War he expressed contempt for the military and caustically ridiculed a few young men who were about to register for the draft.

### What were his publisher problems?

All writers see rejection slips before they achieve success but Salinger's journey down that road seemed particularly rough. Paul Alexander's book chronicles this progression well. Instead of a sudden aversion toward editors and publishers, it was gradual and not as unjustified as one might think.

**What was he like as a student growing up?**

He lived on Manhattan's Upper West Side as a child and attended Valley Forge Military Academy in Pennsylvania. Before the military academy, he flunked out of a few private schools for not even trying to do the work. Attending the military academy was probably his idea. He probably wanted to get away from his family. His mother, not his father, took him to the entrance interview and he was matriculated in just a few days. Salinger was the manager of the fencing team, just as was Holden in *The Catcher in the Rye*. Unlike Holden, Salinger did well at the military academy and enjoyed it. Salinger was down right fond of the military until his experiences in World War II.

He briefly attended New York University where he "didn't apply himself." Later, he attended Ursinus College, a no-name college which he said he enjoyed. He seemed particularly proud that it wasn't an Ivy League school. Salinger had a strong dislike of Ivy League snobbery and being half Jewish gave him good reason.

At Columbia University he audited a writing class taught by Whit Burnett who was the editor of *Story* magazine. Burnett said Salinger sat in the back and stared out the window until the last half of the last semester. He then seemed to come alive. Salinger wrote a story, "The Young Folks," which Burnett decided to run in *Story* magazine which was a huge honor. Salinger respected Burnett and Burnett went out of his way to encourage Salinger. (How did Burnett see any genius in Salinger? If "The Young Folks" has any literary merit, I'd certainly like somebody to show me.)

Friends recall he was a loner and rather impressed with himself. He immodestly told many people that some day he would be a great writer. They also recall he was quite handsome.

**What did Salinger write?**

Salinger published 35 short stories in various publications, including many in the *Saturday Evening Post*, *Story*, and *Colliers* between 1940 and 1948, and *The New Yorker* from 1948 until 1965.

Thirteen of these stories were collected for his three books, *Nine Stories, Franny and Zooey,* and *Raise High the Roof Beam, Carpenters and Seymour: An Introduction.* These joined his short novel, *The Catcher in the Rye.* The remaining twenty-two stories were never officially published by Salinger outside their original magazine appearances. Six were collected in anthologies, however.

He suffered through ten years of rejection notices from *The New Yorker* before one of his stories, "A Perfect Day for Bananafish," was finally accepted. That story sailed through the approval process; the editors at *The New Yorker* were very impressed. After that, he seemed to become the great writer he is known as today.

Some critics believe his distinctive style was influenced by *The New Yorker.* Others say that *The New Yorker* gave him the freedom to write the way he wanted and allowed him to write about subjects that other magazines wouldn't touch. Salinger considered *The New Yorker* the only magazine that published serious fiction and he had the strong ambition to only be published there.

The fact that *The New Yorker* never printed author profiles appealed to Salinger and he adopted the opinion that the less known about the author, the more attention can be directed to the literature on the printed page. This, no doubt, accelerated his reclusion.

To fully appreciate what Salinger does with the story "The Laughing Man," you need to read Oliver LaFarge's award winning (though dated) novel titled *Laughing Boy.*

"Raise High the Roof Beam, Carpenters" is a fascinating story which is wonderfully constructed. Seymour inspires Buddy with the parable of the superlative horse yet Buddy, who's less enlightened, tells the story with one cute but annoying superlative after another.

*Franny and Zooey* can be a chore to get through but the ending makes it worth it. You know that book that Franny was obsessed with? It's a real book, and thanks to Salinger, it's still in print. It's *The Way of A Pilgrim.* You can learn all about the Jesus Prayer and how to pray incessantly. (Paul said to pray incessantly. Not just a lot, but incessantly. So how do you do that? If you eat, you'll be praying with your mouth full. It's like the sound of one hand clapping, a favorite Salinger koan.)

Franny was closely patterned after his wife, Claire. How closely? She still has the receipt for her copy of *The Way of A Pilgrim* which she bought from Brentano's Bookstore. (I wonder what that would fetch on eBay?) Some people say that Franny, as a young child, was patterned after Peggy.

*Franny and Zooey* has had a strong spiritual influence on many Christians we know—but gosh, it's one book that could have been a lot shorter. I know of nobody who has ever read it twice, though, at the time, critics liked it. (I now know hundreds of people who have read it more than once. After reading this line, they email me and set me straight. Thank you all for writing. Now please stop.)

The stories that generated the most mail for Salinger were "Franny," "Zooey and Teddy".

Since he started writing for *The New Yorker*, only one of his stories, "De Daumier-Smith's Blue Period," was rejected by them which is odd because it is one of his best. The rejection caught Salinger off guard and he was deeply disturbed by it.

Later, heads must have rolled at *The New Yorker*. Realizing they committed a colossal blunder, the word must have gone down to never turn down another submission from Salinger again, no matter what.

Salinger probably got wind of that and set himself to typing the long, meaningless story "Hapworth" as an act of revenge. Salinger, who was paid by the word, must have taken perverse delight with every keystroke.

**What has Salinger's love life been like?**

Salinger had a serious attraction to Oona O'Neill who later married Charlie Chaplin. Expecting to marry the young Oona himself, he was more than mildly embittered. Friends say he took it hard and that it took an unusually long time for him to move on. Some people believe he tried to have a literary success in Hollywood just to score a point against Chaplin.

His love letters were reported to be elaborate works of art. They were exceeding clever. Any female reading one would conclude the writer was highly educated, intelligent, creative and fun. His letters were passed around and they were so well written that they often scared off the recipient. On at least one occasion, Salinger was a ghost writer for another man who was trying to impress a woman. (It didn't work.)

He married a young girl he met in Europe, Sylvia, who he divorced soon after they came back to the states after the war. Some say the marriage was annulled. His daughter refers to Sylvia as his first wife. Once, in the '60s, Salinger got a letter from her and he tore it up without even opening it. Such extreme behavior is typical Salinger.

Salinger later married Claire Douglas who was a young woman attending Radcliffe. They had two children and lots of problems. Claire felt isolated in the house with the two children while Salinger spent all day and sometimes all night in his writing bunker. Claire is an intellectual woman who has written books and earned a Ph.D. According to Peggy, she was not a good mother.

Then he had a number of young girl friends. One of them was Joyce Maynard. She had written a magazine article and Salinger wrote her a fan letter on onion skin paper with a few words of advice on how to handle fame in her promising future. A correspondence ensued with plenty of parenthetical remarks on every page. She drove to Windsor and met him at a restaurant. On her second visit, she moved in. She was 19.

Was Salinger enthralled by her writing? It's doubtful. He probably wouldn't have started the correspondence with her if her fetching photo hadn't appeared on the magazine cover.

Maynard had difficulties with Salinger when it came to sex but they expected these difficulties would go away in time. They talked about having a baby and even picked out a name but month after month passed and she was still only able to engage in oral sex. (Do you really want to know all of this?) Salinger took her to a sex therapist but it didn't do any good so then he dumped her. Suddenly he just told her that things weren't working out and that he was probably too old to have any more children anyway so she should just gather up all her things and move out. Maynard was devastated.

Sometimes when Salinger saw a pretty, young woman on TV that he was especially attracted to, he wondered if she might be a big fan of his, big enough to want to meet him and maybe having a relationship with him. He wrote to several of them. Catherine Oxenburg was one. She didn't answer Salinger's letter. TV actress Elaine Joyce did and they soon met. She was in the show *Mr. Merlin* at the time. Like Maynard, she too moved with in with him for a while and their romantic relationship lasted on and off for about seven years. If she ever writes a book about Salinger, it will be interesting. Apparently attracted to writers, Elaine Joyce later married Neil Simon, who, as luck would have it, had a strong attraction for pretty, young actresses.

Salinger's third wife, if you count Sylvia, is a nurse 30 years his junior. Her name is Colleen and they're still married. Colleen is a simple, kind woman who likes to make tapestries and quilts. She's active in community affairs and by all accounts is a very nice, even-tempered person.

## Has Salinger ever been interviewed?

People who have seen and talked to Salinger recently say he seems normal. But of course, if they say anything else, he'll never speak to them again. Most reporters and fans who have talked to him say he's abnormally hostile.

Salinger once gave an interview to two schoolgirls for their school paper, and he has at least twice talked with people who politely approached him. But the so-called interviews to the press consisted mostly of, "I don't give interviews" spoken through a front door just slightly ajar.

According to Ian Hamilton, the schoolgirl article was played up as a "scoop" and it was then that he stopped socializing with the local teenagers. He was very upset by the article.

Yes, Salinger used to socialize with local teenagers. That is, he opened up his house and let them drop by, hang out, play his stereo, and throw impromptu parties. After the newspaper interview appeared, his teenage "friends" were no longer welcome at his house.

The press has behaved very badly in their pursuit of Salinger. He's made it very clear that he doesn't want to talk to the press or to anybody else about literary matters. Unfortunately, those who have made contact with Salinger appear to be among the most stupid people on Earth.

So don't visit his house. You could get arrested, but worse than that, it would be the wrong thing to do. Also, don't try contacting his son or his sister or other relatives. But you could read the book his daughter wrote. It's very good.

### What does Salinger do for entertainment?

On Wednesdays he used to go into town and eat lunch at a pub called Peter Christian's (which has been replaced by Zin's). Sometimes he ordered organic soup and other times he had a sandwich called "Peter's Mother's Favorite" which had turkey in it, among other things. And he would order extra pickles and chips.

He has an extensive collection of old movies which he plays on a reel to reel projector. He used to lend some of his films to the Dartmouth Film Society.

It might depress you to know that Salinger has always been an avid TV watcher. *Gilligan's Island, Leave it to Beaver, Peyton Place, Dynasty*, and obviously, *Mr. Merlin*. His favorite was, and maybe still is, *The Andy Griffith Show*. He watches TV while eating dinner off of a folding metal tray in his living room. There's now a satellite dish on his house which you can see from the public road at foot of his driveway.

### What do his children think of him?

Though they lived under the same roof, Salinger treated Matthew and Peggy differently so it's not a surprise that they feel differently about him. Matt adores his dad and sees him often. Peggy wrote a stingingly critical book about him and the two will probably never speak to each other again.

When Peggy was grown and was excited with the news that she was going to have a baby, Salinger didn't tell her he looked forward to being a grandfather. Instead, he told Peggy that he was disgusted by her pregnancy and that she should have an abortion. Salinger, the oddball that he is, looked upon pregnancy as something unclean and unnatural. That was confirmed by Peggy's mother. Salinger gave her a terrible time during her two pregnancies.

**What do his friends and family call him?**

Not J. D. Not Jerome. It's Jerry. When he was a boy, it was "Sonny."

**How can I contact Salinger?**

Well, you could befriend his son Matt by offering him a part in the next movie you're casting and then ask him to pass a note to his dad when he sees him in Cornish for Thanksgiving dinner. It wouldn't be the first time. But do you really want to contact a person who wants to be left alone? That's not nice. If you are curious about how to find J. D. Salinger's house in Cornish, New Hampshire, or if you would just like to know the best way to send him a letter, send me an email and convince me you're not a pest. Please do not actually try to see him and if you try to write him, keep in mind your chances of getting a response are quite slim.

There was a time when Salinger answered inquires if they happened to come from very young, very pretty women, but now that he's in his 80's and seriously hard of hearing, he's probably "outgrown" that behavior. (We sure hope so.)

**Where does Salinger live?**

Some biographers say he lives in the same red barn-like house he bought back in 1953 in Cornish, New Hampshire. But no, his divorced wife, Claire Douglas, got it in the settlement. J. D. moved to a similar place down Lang Road. The two properties are connected and are a part of the 450 acres that Salinger owns. They call this first house "The Red House." Claire moved to Norwich, Vermont and then to the Pacific Northwest. The house was rented out to a group of Dartmouth students and then it was later sold.

This first house was on about 100 acres. In the early '60s he found out that on some nearby pasture land there were plans to build a trailer park so he jumped in and bought the land, 450 acres.

Salinger wanted to buy a place near Essex or Ipswich or Gloucester, but he thought he couldn't afford it. This was before anybody knew what a great success *The Catcher in the Rye* would turn out to be. When he bought this first house, it didn't have running water or electricity. The main house is hidden by a fence and birch trees. He used to spend time on a vegetable garden there.

### What does he drive?

He used to drive an old jeep that had curtains in the side windows. He also used to drive a BMW and his wife's Rover. Everyone who's ever ridden with him says he drives too fast, almost like he's back in WWII dodging bullets.

### Where does he write?

His first house had a cement bunker for writing on his property which was about 100 yards away from the main, single story house. A stream flowed between the bunker and the main house. The roof was translucent green fiberglass. There was a wood stove which served as the source of heat but which he also used for cooking from time to time. There was an intercom that connected to the main house but it was only for emergencies since he absolutely hated to be interrupted. His wife, Claire, stayed all alone in the house while Salinger sometimes was in his bunker for as long as 16 hours. During the early days, their house didn't have a phone. The concrete blocks were painted green and they referred to it as "The Green House." Inside, a cot took up one side of a wall. On the opposite side was his desk and chair. His chair was actually a large car seat, believe it or not, large enough to sit on in the lotus position. The car seat was supported on wood and bricks to bring it closer to desk level. On the desk was a manual typewriter. Taped all over the place within reach of his writing position were small post-it-like notes. They were on the wall, his lamp, his typewriter, etc. Later, when he moved to his second house, he took the car seat with him for his new study which is now inside his house.

Sometime when he had writers block, he left Cornish for a week or two and checked himself into a resort hotel to do some writing there.

Later in life, Salinger stopped having long bouts of inspiration. He instead settled into a routine of rising early and knocking off work around 2 PM.

### Does he continue to write?

Salinger testified in court in 1986 that he does and he's told a couple of reporters who have barged in on him that he does, but is it true? That's hard to say. His daughter Margaret believes it's true. When Joyce Maynard was living with him, she said he entered his study and spent most of the day there but she never saw his writing nor the vault where he said he kept his written work. Maynard said that Salinger would rise early, eat breakfast and then enter his study to first mediate and then write.

It's true that Salinger is spending time alone in a room every day and he says he's writing but it's conceivable that all he's doing is mediating or reading or writing drivel or writing "All work and no play makes Jack a dull boy" à la Jack Nicholson in *The Shining*.

When asked once if this writing would be published posthumously, he was evasive. He said he's writing for himself. But his daughter said he once called her into his study to show off how he color coded his manuscripts. One color meant to publish it as-is after his death. Another color signified it could be released after his death but only after it was edited. And there were other colors for other conditions.

So, if he's been writing all these years, why is he in the process of publishing "Hapworth" in book form? That doesn't make any sense. "Hapworth" is garbage. If he's actually been writing, he would publish something else. The fact that publishing "Hapworth" doesn't make any sense might be the simple reason he wants to do it. And it could be a riddle which indicates when he expects to die. More on that later.

**What kind of clothes does Salinger wear?**

Sometimes pressed jeans or painters' pants but usually L.L. Bean kind of clothing when he's hanging around Cornish. He's always been fastidious. Sometimes he wears an English tailored wool jacket.

**Did his children inherit any of his talent?**

Yes. Peggy became a scholar, studied at Oxford and wrote a great book about her life with father. Matthew became an actor/producer. Yes, that Matt Salinger.

**What does Salinger eat?**

Mostly vegetarian with the exception of smoked salmon and lamb cooked at 150 degrees. In town, he sometimes orders salad, organic soup, turkey sandwiches and pizza. At home he eats frozen vegetables, usually peas. For a time he worked hard in his large garden and made an honest attempt to grow all the food he needed.

**Is Salinger a good writer?**

Good question, even if I do ask it myself. Does Salinger receive attention because he's a good writer or because he's a recluse? He's generally considered a major American author who would have been a best-selling author regardless of his personal idiosyncrasies but it's also true that he continues to sell an enormous amount of books each year due to the mystique.

He might be one of the best American writers of the 20th century. But a lot of the attention he gets is because of a peculiar cult-like draw he has over a lot of people. Norman Mailer and John Updike don't think he deserves all the attention he gets but Nabokov was in complete awe of "A Perfect Day for Bananafish. "

Mailer said that Salinger was "one of the best minds that ever remained in prep school."

Some say the only reason *The Catcher in the Rye* sold well initially was due to the selection by the Book of the Month Club but that opinion is not widely held.

The critics were mildly impressed with it but it slowly built a strong following, especially on college campuses.

**Why doesn't he have his portrait on the dust jackets of his books?**

Salinger was strange before the publication of *The Catcher in the Rye* but his reclusiveness and odd behavior took a dramatic upswing during its publication. He insisted that the cover be unadorned and that his portrait not appear on the dust cover. For a first time novelist, he placed extraordinary demands on his publishers.

Why didn't he want his picture on the cover? It could be that he was extending the attitude of *The New Yorker* that what really counted were the words on the page, not the personality that wrote them. Other writers from *The New Yorker* didn't shun publicity like this when they published their books but Salinger had a way of jumping into things as an extremist.

Salinger's fiction is character driven, not plot driven. He wrote with such authenticating detail that you feel like there really must have been the Glass family. When you close one of his books, you half expect to see the author listed as "Buddy Glass." The words "J. D. Salinger" wake us up from the dream like suspension of disbelief. To have put his picture or biographical information would have interfered with illusion he wanted us to at least partially believe, that the characters he made were real.

**How does he write?**

With a typewriter using just two fingers.

**What's his favorite movie?**

*39 Steps*, without a doubt. (He watches it over and over and it's practically an obsession.)

**Was Salinger ever a Scientologist?**

Sort of. He dabbled in it for a brief period of time and then abandoned it.

**Does he practice homeopathy?**

Yes, and this has been a strong interest he's held onto for years. He still spends quite a bit of time on it during a typical day.

**Is he an expert on Eastern philosophy and literature?**

He'd like you to think so, but his knowledge is about what you'd have if you minored in Eastern Thought at a state college.

**Were there any other sweet young things other than Joyce Maynard?**

Yes. Several. Once he traveled to Scotland to see one but concluded she was "too homely." She was a fan who wrote him a letter. Part of the attraction was due to the fact she lived in Scotland, the setting of *39 Steps*.

**Did he really once refer to Holden as a real person?**

His daughter says he talked about all of his characters as real people, not as characters in fiction. And he never mentioned the titles of his books. So yes, he probably did, when he was once quoted saying, "Holden wouldn't approve."

**Did Salinger really see Hemingway shoot the head off of a chicken?**

Probably not. We believe he saw Hemingway just once, at the Ritz, when Paris was liberated.

**Which house of his caught on fire?**

Both of them did. The first house fire originated in the closet and may have been set by his wife Claire. The fire at his second house did not do much damage. (Friends of Claire have contacted me to say that she in no way had anything to do with the fire but they weren't there either. Read Peggy's book and decide for yourself.)

**Salinger dislikes most people but who does he actually like?**

Judge Learned Hand and William Shawn and his jeep buddy during WWII whose name escapes me.

**What's up with "Hapworth 16, 1924?" And when is it going to be published?**

It was already published forty years ago in *The New Yorker*. Salinger arranged to have it reissued in book form by Orchises Press of Virginia but when it will be out is anybody's guess. The publisher at Orchises Press talked to reporters about it which probably made Salinger madder than hell. Indeed it is one more Salinger-made-mystery for us to ponder. It's a riddle and in a few more paragraphs I'll tell you what I make of it.

If you can't wait to see how awful "Hapworth" is, visit your local university library. Ask for the June 19th, 1965, issue of *The New Yorker*. If you want to photocopy it, bring a lot of quarters.

It is a long piece without any point and there hasn't been any serious reviewers who have been in the least bit positive (aside from an English professor I know but I suspect he would also [say] the emperor was fully clothed.) One wonders why Salinger wrote it. It reads like the product of a once talented man who now is suffering from mental illness.

Like Picasso's dog face sculpture in Chicago or Robert Graham's poop-shaped Quetzaquatl statue in San Jose or Bob Dylan's singing like Gabby Hayes, "Hapworth" isn't the real deal. It's intentionally poor work created by a famed artist who knows, sadly, that he can get away with it. And the joke is on us.

Students of Salinger will only want to read it to see how remarkably bad it is.

Salinger, who always wanted to be Seymour Glass (but settled, at least in his own mind, for being Buddy), seems to know him better now and has changed his mind. Salinger doesn't like him anymore and he doesn't want us to like him either. Seymour disillusions us with his own words and in a way, it's like a suicide.

Salinger keeps delaying the publication date of "Hapworth" and it's my belief, though I confess it sounds a trifle bizarre, that he's planning his own death to coincide with the date of publication. Nobody writes about suicide as much as Salinger without actively considering it himself. And this work looks like an act of literary suicide for Salinger as well as a character suicide for Seymour. I believe Salinger keeps delaying publication because he's not quite ready to die.

**How can I find out more about J. D. Salinger?**

The best secondary source we've read on Salinger's work is the one by Professor John Wenke. His biographical information is outdated (well, highly inaccurate, to tell you the truth) but his literary analysis is quite good.

Ian Hamilton, the respected poet, wrote a fairly good book called *In Search of J. D. Salinger*. Like us, the more Hamilton learned about Salinger, the less he cared to know. And not surprisingly, this is a well written book. The only problem with reading this first is that it might make your lose your appetite for more information.

There's a biography by Paul Alexander which is fairly good: *J. D. Salinger: A Biography*. A serious problem with this book is that it takes every interesting rumor about Salinger and prints it as fact. Alexander talked to a lot of people and did a great deal of research but I think he was careless with what he included. It is not the work of Woodward and Bernstein. Also, he reports about conversations between Salinger and Joyce Maynard and his version is rather different from Maynard's. What are his sources? The only other person present was Salinger himself and had Alexander communicated with Salinger, he would have put that on the dust jacket. Alexander's book is good at filling in gaps and showing how Salinger made gradual changes in his personality. Alexander is also good at linking Salinger's fiction with his personal life though Alexander doesn't quite understand all of Salinger's fiction. Literature is not his field. Read this book to gain an overall understanding but keep in mind it's the least accurate of the four.

Joyce Maynard's book, *At Home in the World*, is much, much better than the critics would have you believe. I was expecting to be disgusted by it but I wasn't. First of all, Maynard is an excellent writer. Second, she includes many unflattering facts about herself which she could have easily left out which makes her book rather credible. Third, her book actually sheds light on understanding Salinger and how his life and fiction are related. Maynard is not a likable person but this is a good book.

But the best book, by far, is the one by Salinger's daughter, Margaret (Peggy) Salinger. It's called *Dream Catcher: A Memoir*. It's also the one that's the most critical. It's especially good at explaining the context of WWII and the fact of his being half Jewish. This book goes beyond reporting facts. It's also a good source for confirming many of the questionable things Maynard wrote about. (Her chapter heading quotations are sometimes distracting and strangely off topic and there are sections where she seems to digress into interesting theories just to show off her expensive education, but these are small faults when you consider the book as a whole.)

Salinger is an odd, unhappy person and a genius. When you read his biography, you'll be glad you're not him. There's more to life than being a genius. Salinger knows this, and even says so in his writings, but it hasn't done him any good. In short, his books are wonderful but his life stinks.

## J. D. is not your Buddy

You know how in "A Perfect Day for Bananafish" Seymour screams at his wife for not bothering to learn German so she can read some of the books he recommends? That's how nuts and hostile Jerry Salinger is in real life. And remember the part where he kisses the bottom of the girl's foot? Well, Joyce Maynard can tell you about that. "Bananafish" is a good story for understanding Salinger—his attraction for young girls, his irrational, hostile temper, his brilliance, his belief that he just doesn't belong in the real world. Too smart, too sensitive, too crazy, and a bit of a pervert.

Salinger, too, commits suicide, but he's been doing it very slowly.

If you feel a powerful need to personally connect with Salinger, that might just be what he wanted. Read his biographies and you'll cure yourself of that desire. But there's another reason to read his biographies. You'll be able to see how his writing was like therapy. He tried to become Buddy Glass by creating him in fiction.

But it didn't work.

# Theft, Rumor, and Innuendo

Excerpt from *Salinger: A Biography*

PAUL ALEXANDER

### 1

By 1973, Salinger had become such a part of the literary landscape in America that when *Esquire* published an unsigned story entitled "For Rupert—With No Regrets," which contained numerous echoes of Salinger's work, intense speculation broke out in literary circles—even in the public at large—that Salinger had written the story, or that some other author had written it with the intention of making it appear as if Salinger had. Few readers guess who the author actually was.

"Lee Eisenberg, a young man for whom I imagined a great future, became editor of *Esquire*," said Gordon Lish, the magazine's fiction editor at the time. "Lee was under enormous pressure from the owners, who wanted to kill the magazine because it was selling so poorly on the newsstands. So one day Lee asked me if I had any stunt we could pull to boost newsstand sales. This was the days of my considerable drinking. I'd drink a bottle, sometimes two. I remember being really boozed up when this discussion took place. I also remember saying in a drifty way that I'd go home and try something that he must never tell anyone I was behind it. Then I went home, quite drunk, and within the space of two hours, I wrote 'For Rupert—With No Regrets.' I brought it in the next day and gave it to Eisenberg on the guarantee that my authorship should never be revealed. When we ran it in the magazine, which we did right away, there was no signature on the story. There was just a statement that the story had come in over the transom unsigned and it didn't matter where it came from."

Response to "For Rupert—With No Regrets" was overwhelming and unexpected. "There was an enormous amount of press coverage," said Lish. "The speculation was that either Updike or Cheever had written the story although many readers believed it *might* have been Salinger who wrote it. There was colossal interest from TV and radio. *Esquire* sold the magazine out. Two or three months later, I finally told an agent I wrote it because she made me believe I owed her. Within days, she was at a cocktail party telling people I had written the story. So I came into a great deal of criticism. The story of who the author really was broke on the front page of the *Wall Street Journal*. I heard from Salinger through that agent that what I had done was absurd and despicable. That needled me because I didn't think it was either. My feeling was that if Salinger was not going to write stories, someone had to write them for him."

## 2

It was a cold and rainy fall evening in Cornish some months later when Salinger picked up his telephone and called Lacey Fosburgh, a San Francisco-based correspondent for *The New York Times*. Along with the occasions in 1951 when he talked to William Maxwell for the *Book-of-the-Month Club News* and the lunch with Shirlie Blaney in 1953 that led to the article in the *Claremont Daily Eagle*, this was only the third time in his life Salinger had knowingly agreed to be interviewed by a reporter. On that night, as she answered her telephone, Fosburgh could not believe what good luck had brought her—the first interview Salinger had given in two decades.

"Some stories, my property, have been stolen," Salinger said to

Fosburgh after warning her that he would speak "only for a minute." "Someone's appropriated [the stories]. It's an illicit act. It's unfair. Suppose you had a coat you liked and somebody went into your closet and stole it. That's how I feel."

What Salinger was referring to was *The Complete Uncollected Short Stories of J. D. Salinger*, a volume that had been published two months earlier without his permission. First in San Francisco and then in New York, Chicago, and other big cities, wholesale booksellers, all identifying themselves as "John Greenberg from Berkeley, California," had been going into bookstores and selling a volume made up of stories Salinger had published in magazines and journals between 1940 and 1948, but which had not been included in *Nine Stories*. The retailers, who paid $1.50 a book, sold the volume for between $3 and $5. In September and October 1974, retailers sold over 25,000 copies of Salinger's *Complete Uncollected*. There was, of course, one problem: Salinger hadn't wanted the book published.

"It's irritating. It's really very irritating. I'm very upset about it," said Salinger, who had been tipped off about the scheme by Andreas Brown, the owner of Gotham Book Mart. Salinger was so angered by Brown's news that he filed a civil law suit in Federal District Court in San Francisco against "John Greenberg" and seventeen bookstores across the country. In the suit Salinger asked for $250,000 in punitive damages and an immediate junction against the book.

"I wrote [the stories] a long time ago," Salinger told Fosburgh, "and I never had any intention of publishing them. I wanted them to die a perfectly natural death. I'm not trying to hide the gaucheries of my youth. I just don't think they're worthy of publishing."

For her part, Fosburgh made the best of the situation and got Salinger to answer as many questions as possible. Naturally she asked him about his refusal to publish "There is a marvelous peace in not publishing," Salinger said. "It's peaceful. Still. Publishing is a terrible invasion of my privacy. I like to write. I live to write. But I write just for myself and my own pleasure." Then Salinger talked about how much he *was* writing. "I don't necessarily intend to publish posthumously, but I do like to write for myself," he said. "I pay for this kind of attitude. I'm known as a strange, aloof kind of man. But all I'm doing is trying to protect myself and my work."

The main issue on Salinger's mind as he spoke to Fosburgh was the pirated edition of his stories. "It's amazing some sort of law-and-order agency can't do something about this," he went on. "Why, if a dirty old mattress is stolen from your attic, they'll find it. But they're not even looking for their man"—the mysterious publisher. "I just want this all to stop," Salinger said as a way of wrapping up a telephone call that had gone on for almost half an hour. "It's intrusive. I've survived a lot of things, and I'll probably survive this." It was then that Salinger ended the conversation, hanging up the telephone.

On November 3, 1974, the editors at *The New York Times* decided Fosburgh's article about Salinger's call was so newsworthy they ran it on the front page. The *Times* article spurred intense media interest in Salinger, the pirated edition of his stories, and the lawsuit. "Through the years," *Newsweek* stated in a story the magazine ran as a follow-up to the *Times* piece, "Salinger has made news only with the rare publication of his works and with such scattered items as his wife's divorce from him in 1967, his rumored liaison with nineteen-year-old writer Joyce Maynard in 1973, and a suit his lawyers filed recently over an unauthorized volume of early Salinger stories. It was the latter event that prompted him to talk to *Times* reporter Lacey Fosburgh."

Because of this, the magazine sent Bill Roeder to Cornish to try to get an interview with Salinger. It was the same approach many other reporters and fans had begun to take.

"His house is a brown, modern-looking hilltop chalet with a sun deck facing across the Connecticut River into the mountains of Vermont," Roeder wrote in his article, which appeared in *Newsweek* on November 18. "The view is breathtaking." However, even that spectacular view paled after Roeder walked up to the house, knocked on the front door, and came face-to-face with Salinger, who answered his own door. "Salinger, tall, gaunt, and grey-haired at fifty-five, was dressed in a blue jump suit." Roeder reported. After he introduced himself to Salinger, the two men engaged in a brief chat. "His part of [the] conversation was reluctant—his hand never left the door-knob—but civil."

Was he still writing? Roeder asked.

"Of course I'm writing," Salinger said.

What kind of life did he live?

"I like to hang on to my privacy—my undocumented privacy," Salinger said before he added, "Is there anything more boring than a talking writer?"

After ten minutes, Roeder ended the strained, awkward exchange by thanking him for his time and extending his hand to shake Salinger's. Salinger reluctantly obliged, extending his own hand.

"This is not a friendly gesture," Salinger said. "I really don't appreciate your coming here."

## 3

In 1975, Harper and Row published a book called *A Fiction Writer's Handbook*, edited by Whit Burnett and his wife Hallie. At the end of the book, the publisher included a piece called "Epilogue: A Salute to Whit Burnett, 1899–1972." The piece was the introduction Salinger wrote for *Story Jubilee* that Burnett had refused to run. Since the publication of that anthology, Burnett had died; it seemed appropriate to print a memoir written by Salinger, who had become one of Burnett's most famous pupils. It's ironic that Salinger's beautiful and moving memoir of Burnett would appear in the rather mundane setting of a fiction writers' handbook, but there it was.

This, of course, was the first piece of writing by Salinger to appear in print since "Hapworth 16, 1924" had been published in *The New Yorker* on June 19, 1965—a fact further underscoring the irony of Salinger's memoir being printed in a fiction writers' handbook. A decade had passed and Salinger had not published any of those new Glass stories he had promised in the editorial note to *Raise High the Roof Beam, Carpenters and Seymour: An Introduction*—except for "Hapworth 16, 1924." Most of Salinger's critics and many of his fans had come to believe that, no matter what he said or implied, Salinger had stopped writing. His brief memoir about Burnett gave some minor indication that he had not.

Then, in that same year, 1975, Brendan Gill, who had written for *The New Yorker* for years, offered what he considered to be proof that Salinger *was* writing—an informal testimonial from William Shawn. "I had feared that the author's prolonged and obsessive scrutiny of the Glass psyches had led him to still his hand," Gill wrote in a book of his called *Here at The New Yorker*, "but Shawn has said that it is not so. Though Salinger's absence from the pages of the magazine is from week to week and from year to year an obscurely felt deprivation, the fact is that he goes on writing, and surely someday he will be willing to let us observe the consequences."

More innuendo, more rumor, but this was nothing compared to a theory about to be published that would make the rounds among the fans and admirers of Salinger—the most outrageous piece of gossip yet.

On April 22, 1976, the *Soho Weekly News* published an article by John Calvin Batchelor called "Thomas Pynchon Is Not Thomas Pynchon, or, This is the End of the Plot Which Has No Name." In his article Batchelor argued that Thomas Pynchon was not born on May 8, 1937 in Glen cove, Long Island, New York; did not matriculate at Cornell University; did not go into the Navy for two years; did not work for a time as an editorial writer for Boeing Aircraft Corporation; and did not write such works of fiction as "Entropy," "Low-Lands" and *V.* Instead, according to Batchelor, Pynchon was born on January 1, 1919 in New York City, matriculated at Ursinus College, joined the army, met Ernest Hemingway during the war, and wrote *The Catcher in the Rye* and *Franny and Zooey*. "Yes," Batchelor wrote, Thomas Pynchon "is Jerome David Salinger."

"What I am arguing," Batchelor continued, "is that J. D. Salinger, famous though he was, simply could not go on with either the Glass family, which had by 1959 become his weight to bear, or with his own nationally renowned reputation, which had become by 1959 chained to both Holden Caulfield's adolescence and Seymour Glass's art of penance. So then, out of paranoia or out of pique, J. D. Salinger dropped 'by J. D. Salinger' and picked up 'by Thomas Pynchon.' A *nom de plume* afforded Salinger the anonymity he had sought but failed to find as Caulfield's creator. It was the perfect cover."

The response to Batchelor's article was immediate. As one might expect, Batchelor received a number of letters, many of them unfriendly. As one might *not* have expected, Batchelor also received a letter from Thomas Pynchon. Written on MGM stationery and mailed from Pluma Road, Malibu, California, the letter said that he, Pynchon, had read the article, that some of it was true and that some of it was not (none of the interesting parts was true, he said), and that Batchelor should "keep trying." That letter and additional factors—he began to meet people who actually knew Pynchon—forced Batchelor to reassess his theory that Thomas Pynchon was J. D. Salinger, or rather that J. D. Salinger was Thomas Pynchon. "I am telling you right now," Batchelor wrote a year later on April 28, 1977, in the *Soho Weekly News*, "that some if not most of those manuscripts"—*V. The Crying of Lot 49, Gravity's Rainbow*—"have come from J. D. Salinger. I am telling you right now that parts of those manuscripts might have come from Donald Barthelme" (a *New Yorker* writer known for his postmodern short stories). "I'd like to think Salinger wrote almost everything. It's the romantic in me."

In the future, while he would never grant an interview of any kind (rumor has it that he once jumped out the window of a house and ran away because he heard Norman Mailer was on his way there to talk to him), and while he would never allow himself to be photographed in any way (he does not have a driver's license, it's said, because he refuses to have his photograph taken), Thomas Pynchon did finally surface enough so that people, even John Calvin Batchelor, had to admit that he did exist and that he had written all of the books credited to him. Pynchon would marry Melanie Jackson, the New York literary agent, with whom he would have a son. That son, as luck would have it, would even end up attending the same Manhattan prep school as Batchelor's son.

"I've come to accept that Pynchon wrote those books," Batchelor says. "What I came to accept was that, with Salinger and Pynchon, we are dealing with two eccentrics, not one. Sometimes it takes getting a perspective on a situation and that's what I've done in this case."

By 1976, as he remained a source of gossip within the literary community, Salinger had been divorced from Claire for almost a decade. In that time, Margaret had grown up and attended college, and Matthew had gone off to Phillips Exeter Academy. Salinger apparently continued to write regularly. He saw his children as often as he could. In fact, on one occasion in 1976, he went to Phillips Exeter to see Matthew perform in a play. It was ironic that Matthew, who routinely appeared in school plays, was toying with the idea of going into the profession of acting, just as his father had considered doing when he was Matthew's age. There was one difference. Whereas Sol was opposed to his son going into the arts, Salinger was supportive of Matthew's interest. In fact, if Matthew had decided to go into acting for a living, Salinger could not have been more pleased with that decision.

"In 1976, at Exeter I was in a school production of *Kennedy's Children* with Matt Salinger," says Becky Lish, Gordon Lish's daughter. "The play takes place in a bar, with four or five characters speaking monologues. There's a bartender who has no lines, or, if he does, only one or two. Matt played the bartender who doesn't speak. I remember his father came to the show. I remember at the time being surprised at how old he was—he was an older man. I think I had expected *my* father. Of course, as a high-school student I thought that what we were doing was fascinating and thrilling and I'm sure it was anything but to

Salinger. But there he was. In my memory I think he was sitting in the front row. We all thought it was neat that he was there and also just sort of strange. I mean, some of us, myself included, had decided to be shipped off to prep school based on some sort of fantasy that we could become Holden Caulfield."

# Eighty Years of Solitude

JOHN DUGDALE

J. D. Salinger turns 80 on New Year's Day, up in snowbound Cornish, New Hampshire, but the double celebration is unlikely to bear much resemblance to the convivial New England yules of Bing Crosby and Perry Como. Instead, an ordinary day is on the cards: a spot of yoga, some Zen meditation, reading favorite authors such as Kafka or Tolstoy, and hours tinkering with writing that will probably never be published.

In place of a fireside sing-song, Salinger (tall, white-haired, and deaf in one ear) and his third wife will probably watch a forties movie, after a frugal supper obeying weird dietary rules. But as a birthday treat, he might be allowed to indulge his craving for junk food—he reputedly loves doughnuts—and TV sitcoms. It's a safe bet that Jerry Salinger is a fan of Jerry Seinfeld, a fellow New York Jew who resembles him in his thirties and shares both his attraction to girl-women and his mordant view of grown-up humanity.

What also links Seinfeld and Salinger, of course, is that both decided to quit when they were ahead, differentiating the latter from other fifties writers who succumbed to severe writer's block, as if unable to adjust to the frenzied sixties. Ralph Ellison failed to complete a follow-up to *Invisible Man*, his pioneering 1952 exploration of black identity, although he lived on into the 1990s. *To Kill A Mockingbird* remains Harper Lee's only novel. Harold Brodkey took 32 years to finish *The Runaway Soul*. Just as the perfectionist film directors Stanley Kubrick and Terrence Malick (both prone to leave long gaps between films) have never actually abandoned cinema, so these writers continued to work towards a comeback. Salinger, in contrast, called a formal halt: no new fiction has appeared since "Hapworth Camp, 1924" was published in 1965.

Alone in renouncing publication, Salinger is also unique in belonging simultaneously to a second group—including Thomas Pynchon, Cormac McCarthy, and (until recently) Don DeLillo—who are ferociously insistent on privacy, never appearing in public and doing their best to foil biographers and profile writers. Salinger's last interview grudgingly accompanied the publication of *The Catcher In The Rye* in 1951.

As his work tailed off just when Pynchon's stories began to appear, the jokey theory that the newcomer was really a pseudonym for Salinger had a certain credibility. Certainly, Pynchon's quest for anonymity was shaped by the American press's hounding of the older writer; he fled to Mexico when his debut novel, *V*, appeared in 1963, having seen *Newsweek* and *Time* send rival teams of investigators up to New Hampshire two years earlier, exactly as if Salinger was a criminal fugitive in hiding ('We have found a lead that may finally open Mr. Salinger's closet of little girls', one of *Time*'s literary G -Men wired back).

Haunted by Salinger's example, Pynchon echoes his name in that of Richard Wharfinger, the paranoid Jacobean playwright who fascinates the heroine of his second novel, *The Crying Of Lot 49*. It's as if he can foresee, at 29, being the object of the same biographical detective work, the same betrayals by ex-friends, the same forbidden photos—the first image of him for 40 years was snatched in New York two years ago, just as Salinger was caught, aghast and angry, in a celebrated 1988 picture.

Seeing the latter photo ('like an execution . . . it's not a great leap of the imagination to think he's just been shot') inspired DeLillo to pen *Mao II*, in which the hero, Bill Gray, is a famous author-recluse who has spent years endlessly rewriting the same book. Pondering Salinger's impasse, however, led DeLillo to quit this brotherhood of silence. After a lifetime shunning the marketing process ('You become consumable, absorbed. Everything becomes a TV commercial in the end, everything is used up'), he astounded the U. S. book world last year by undertaking a conventional promotional tour to sell *Underworld*.

What's odd about Salinger's symbolic potency for Pynchon and DeLillo is that they are out-and-out literary novelists, following the same tactics as the giants of Modernism (Joyce's 'silence, exile and cunning') to prevent their opaque, multi-layered structures being simplified by crass biographical parallels or their own clumsy attempts to explain them.

Salinger, on the other hand, is a bestselling author whose longer fiction is instantly accessible and requires little critical unwrapping. In *The Catcher In The Rye*, Holden Caulfield runs away from boarding school to New York, finding everyone 'phoney'—except his kid sister Phoebe. In *Franny And Zooey*, student actress Franny Glass cracks up—finding everyone except her family 'phoney' and runs away from college to New York, where her brother therapeutically teaches her to see performance as a religious act. The dialogue in these stories is unrivalled, and millions of young readers across the world have found themselves mirrored in them since the fifties. But it's hard to see how arts page interviews, informal photos or unsanctioned biographical information could significantly distort their meaning.

Salinger nevertheless showed himself to be both a control freak and a publicist's nightmare from the very start of his career, opposed to proof and review copies of *The Catcher In The Rye* being sent out, hostile to his photo appearing on the jacket, testy when his editor gossiped to the press—and in London, just to ensure minimal publicity, when the novel came out in New York.

Already at loggerheads with publishers and agents, he later added reviewers, academics, journalists and biographers to his extensive list of enemies, taking on the outside world most dramatically in 1986 when he sought to block Ian Hamilton's biography, *In Search Of J. D. Salinger*, in the courts. More recently, his U. S. agent has banned websites from quoting from his work, forcing the closure of a site consisting of a fan's favorite passages from *Catcher*.

But the effect of such obsessively pursued control is, ironically, to boost the market value of defiance, encouraging Salinger's former lover Joyce Maynard to kiss and tell in her recent autobiography, *At Home In The World*, and turning that book into a literary sensation—when a more relaxed author could dismiss it as ancient history.

Wooed by letters from Salinger in spring 1972 after he saw a cover story by her in *The New York Times Magazine* (which used an alluringly kooky photo of her as its cover), Maynard eventually went to live with him in New Hampshire, giving up her studies at Yale and being inducted into a lifestyle centered on writing, meditation, homeopathy, an idiosyncratic diet, and—when his teenage children dropped in—hour after hour of junk television.

Sexual motives aside, Salinger clearly saw himself as acting as the catcher in the rye, saving a kid (exactly as Holden Caulfield describes the catcher's role) from 'going over the cliff'. For him, the virginal 18-year-old Maynard was a real-life Franny Glass: smart, troubled and still innocent and malleable enough to be rescued from shallowness and sickness.

Her account shows him trying to drive her away from serving the hated 'vultures' of journalism, publishing and academia ('You'll give up this business of delivering what everybody tells you to do'). The tension this causes is exacerbated by sexual problems; after nearly a year together, when a Daytona doctor fails to cure her vaginismus, Salinger bluntly asks her to fly home alone from Florida and move out.

At 53, between his second and third marriages, Maynard's Salinger resembles a male Miss Havisham, regressing to the time-warp of his salad days in the late forties and early fifties, before parenthood, before fame, before exile from Manhattan. Most nights he projects movies from that era, such as his favorite Hitchcock films, or they foxtrot to dance tunes played by the Lawrence Welk orchestra. She brings up feminism or Vietnam; he notes that the Duke of Windsor has died.

Twenty-five years on, however, Salinger's fictional world has never seemed more contemporary, ever since the Brat Pack made it okay again to take the exquisite moral crises of privileged kids seriously. Give or take a few drugs, the college students of Donna Tartt's *The Secret History* and Bret Easton Ellis's *Less Than Zero* enjoy a lifestyle little changed from that of Salinger's neurotic preppies in the immediate post-war period, as do the protagonists of Whit Stillman's films, *Metropolitan* and *The Last Days Of Disco*. Jay McInerney's *Story Of My Life* is overtly Salinger-derived, trumping his feat of ventriloquism in creating the voice of Holden Caulfield by imagining the journal of a spoilt 16-year-old girl.

And where the novel led, other media have followed: with American movies, TV series and rock music increasingly centering on under-25s, pop culture has become ever more Salingeresque, filled with pampered, precocious teenagers either prematurely assimilated into the brittle, phoney adult world (like Cher in *Clueless*) or trying to hang on to their innocence and idealism (like Dawson in *Dawson's Creek*). He almost certainly despises them, but his grandchildren are everywhere.

# The Holy Refusal

A Vedantic Interpretation of J. D. Salinger's *Silence*

DIPTI R. PATTANAIK

The silence of J. D. Salinger continues to be an enigma. That a successful writer should cease to publish at the height of his glory not only defeats our everyday notions about success, it also baffles the serious students of Salinger's work and life. His controversial biographer, Ian Hamilton, articulates the confusion quite aptly:

> *American intellectuals look with compassion on those eastern bloc writers who have been silenced by the state, but here, in their own culture, a greatly loved author had elected to silence himself. He had freedom of speech but what he had ended up wanting more than anything else, it seemed, was the freedom to be silent. And the power to silence—to silence anyone who wanted to find out why he had stopped speaking.*

Salinger's refusal to publish and shun public contact in life has encouraged adverse reactions from several critics. Warren French attributes his seclusion to "an inability to make the social adjustment expected of mature members of society" (33). James Lundquist is of the opinion that "his long silence as a writer and this insistence on personal privacy makes him a difficult writer to understand and to read with much sympathy" (31).

A more rigorous analysis of Salinger's refusal to publish his works and to make himself public can be found in Ihab Hassan's book, The Dismemberment of Orpheus. Here and in his article "Almost the Voice of Silence," Hassan seeks to find a place for Salinger in the literary tradition of silence which includes de Sade, the Dadaists, the surrealists and authors like Hemingway, Kafka, Camus, and Beckett. Silence in these authors as Hassan avers is used as a metaphor for all kinds of negative stances—anti-literature, alienation from reason and nature and creation of anti-language.

> *The writer behind Buddy, Salinger himself, gradually becomes as silent as an ideal reader. At first the silence is metaphoric, twisted and loving locquacious digressions, language shattered in its efforts to free itself of kitsch and sentimentality. In the end Salinger ceases to publish. Is this some form of holy refusal? (Hassan 251)*

Ihab Hassan and other sympathetic critics of Salinger seem to have found a philosophical basis for his silence. They try to establish that Salinger's silence is not merely an act of whimsy or a publicity stunt, but a conscious intellectual and spiritual stance worthy of sober critical attention. However, the silence of Salinger cannot be fully understood from the narrow perspective of Beckettian or Kafkaesque insubstantial imagination which believes in representing inauthentic consciousness through a cessation of language. Salinger's gesture of silence and withdrawal may be part of a larger effort to enact in life the values he hitherto problematized in art. Ultimately, in silence, his ideals of life and art coalesce.

Two of the most fundamental concerns of Salinger's career have been his search for "right living" as a human being and "right expression" as an artist. Moreover, he is one of the few modern writers whose art and life complement each other so well that one seems to be the extension of the other; Ian Hamilton records Leila Hadley remembering Salinger talking of Holden Caufield as a "real" person, his own Caulfieldian aversion to clichés and his measured speech habits and silence, like his own character Raymond Ford in "The Inverted Forest": "He did not speak much; he did not speak unless he had to speak" (Hamilton 126).

Right from the beginning, Salinger, like many of his fictional characters, had shown his disaffection for what David Riesman in "The Lonely Crowd" (1950) calls the "other-directed" life—the dominant competitive, egocentric, materialistic zeitgeist of twentieth century America. The pressure to conform to the success orientation and individualistic self-aggrandizement which formed the basis of the market society had driven him to the edge of sanity as it had done to the characters in his fiction. His early fiction was also recording his protest against the life in American cities which were full of people who had lost their authenticity and had turned into phonies. For example, "The Long Debut of Olios Tagged," published in *Story* (September–October 1942) is set in a New York "Society" and describes how Olios finally gets over her "grandness" and "phoniness." She has to undergo a series of shocks before recovering her authenticity.

Salinger was also conscious that art and mass media were conspiring to reinforce the wrong way of modern life by resorting to an inauthentic mode of expression. In many of his *New Yorker* stories Salinger chastized the modern film industry which celebrated sentimental indulgences not backed by any real feeling. He himself tried to write stories in which characters make the fight against verbal "phoniness" and "cliché" a mission of their lives. Somehow the verbal insincerity to him demonstrated the hollowness of the speaker. He made elaborate effort in his life (like joining writing schools) to cleanse his own art of any kind of excess and insincerity.

Early in his career Salinger became aware that the wide gulf between our secular and spiritual pursuits has created a great imbalance in modern life and art. He has also seen the role of the artist as being crucial in the process of synthesis which may redress this imbalance. Fortuitously, he encountered the ancient Eastern spiritual traditions of

Advaita Vedanta and Zen, (Hamilton 127–28) and mystical Catholicism, which not only prescribe a synthesis between spiritual and secular goals of life but also use the sacred and divine power of the "Word" to bring about such a synthesis. The teachings of Swami Vivekananda and Sri Ramakrishna which opened his eyes to the alternative mode of living, had made a plea to organise all human vocations around one central divine purpose. In fact, both Sri Ramakrishna and his chief disciple Swami Vivekananda had demonstrated how through renunciation of the fruits of work all human enterprise could be divinised. One of Salinger's acquaintances relates how he "intended devoting his life to one great work, and that work would be his life—there would be no separation" (Hamilton 125). Ian Hamilton rightly points out:

> *And yet for some years, Salinger has needed to set his gaze on some high purpose, and his dedication to his craft has often had a monkish tinge. Up until 1952, the order he aimed to belong to was an order based on "talent" as if it were the same thing as "enlightenment" and will seek in the curricula of holy men a way of dissolving what has all along been for him an irritating, hard to manage separation between art and life, that is to say, his art, his life. (126)*

Thus, the Eastern religions and mystic Catholicism provide some kind of an answer to his quest for "right living" and "right expression." A contemplative and renunciatory mode of living could spiritually counteract the dangers of the excessively materialistic and action-oriented life of twentieth century America; real art should try by whatever means to forge such a lifestyle, "do something beautiful" as Franny says. Salinger's art, especially the later fiction, is an attempt to dramatize his own version of right living. Ultimately his "silence" becomes the culminating gesture when his life becomes the message, a testament of the values his art hitherto professed.

Ian Hamilton's biography bears out the fact that after coming across the text of Sri Ramkrishna, Salinger had seriously considered undertaking the life of seclusion and withdrawal worthy of a monk. The Vedantic way of life which Sir Ramkrishna and Swami Vivekananda preached visualised two principal modes of living: the life of the householder and the life of the sannyasin. While the former led a civic life, the latter devoted his life completely to the prayer of God. Both ways of life had their different states of perfection. The householder reached his state of perfection by means of Karma-Yoga—a spiritual discipline which dedicated all the fruits of human action to God while the monk or the sannyasin found his salvation through Jnana Yoga—in complete renunciation of all human action except those for the greater benefit of the world and self-realization (Vivekananda 19-37).

The Bhagavad Gita describes how [the] yogi is called into his vocation mainly through one of four ways—the way of artih, after the total disgust with the uncertainties and suffering of the mundane world of sense-advancement, the way of artharthi, in pursuit of self-advancement, the way of jignasu, in quest of divine knowledge, and the best among the seekers, the way of the jnani, with the exclusive god-love and surrender of all actions:

*Chaturvidha bhajante mam janah. Sukrutinor juna Arto Jignasur-atharthi jnani cha bharatarshavh. (Jnanabijnana Yogah. Sloka-16)*

The dawn of genuine knowledge can mitigate the imperfections of worldly living and one can attain the state of equilibrium and calm detachment from joys and suffering—the state of Sthitaprajna. However, before arriving at the final stage of equanimity the seeker has to undergo a moral and spiritual discipline—sadhana which among other things requires a deliberate withdrawal from the sense-indulgences, elimination of lust, greed and the vainglorious ambition, curbing desire for success, indulgence in constant prayer, and surrender of the personal ego and whatever few works one may undertake to sustain one's physical being, to meditate on the idea of a personal God according to one's own propensities—Swadharma (Vivekananda 2:24–37).

Thus, silence is an important ingredient of such a spiritual discipline—as a sign of withdrawal from the whirlwind of material activity that fattens ego, of a quest for an awareness beyond the immediate and peripheral sense apprehensions and possibly of possession of a higher awareness which can only be transmitted to the initiated and may get trivialised by the everyday insincere use of the word. Sri Aurobindo, the modern mystic, articulates the need for a withdrawal into silence:

> *It is in the inner silence of the mind that true knowledge can come; for the ordinary activity of the mind only created surface ideals and representations which are not true knowledge. Speech is usually the expression of the superficial nature, therefore to throw oneself out too much in such speech wastes the energy and prevents the inward listening which brings the word of true knowledge. (Sri Aurobindo 653)*

A similar distrust of words can be discerned in Japanese culture which was shaped by the philosophy of Zen Buddhism, another Eastern religion to which Salinger was exposed quite early in his life. It is relevant to quote Masao Kunihiro here:

> *A corollary to the Japanese attitude towards language might be called the "aesthetic of silence":—making virtue of reticence and a vulgarity of verbalization or open expression of one's inner thoughts. This attitude can be traced to the Zen Buddhist idea that man is capable of arriving at the highest level of contemplative being only when he makes no attempt at verbalizations and discounts oral expression as the height of superficiality. (Kunihiro 13)*

It would be too presumptuous to conclude that the silence of J. D. Salinger is a proof of such Yogic awareness, because we do not have any means to ascertain the development of a writer's inner self. But since, in Salinger, art and life complement each other, we have to fall back upon his art to chart the gradual intensification of a spiritual quest in him.

Salinger's early fiction can be termed, in parlance of the Gita, the disaffection of an *artih*—a seeker in his early stages of the quest recoiling from the imperfections and uncertainties of the mundane world of sense apprehensions. In such a stage of spiritual journey, the seeker initially draws away from immediate outward action. Thomas Merton, the Catholic monk who turned to Zen Buddhism, articulates this attitude quite aptly:

> *A certain protest against the organized and dehumanizing routines of worldly life built around gain for its own sake. (Merton 15)*

*The Catcher in the Rye*, though it has a great deal of social realism in it, already shows the signs of the direction Salinger's fiction would take. Holden Caulfield graphically depicts his ambition of forsaking his social identity. He is like any other spiritual seeker quite tentative before finally jumping the threshold. He walks up Fifth Avenue again and again and has the spooky feeling that he is unable to get to the other side of the street: "Boy, it did scare me. You can't imagine. I started sweating like a bastard—" (204). He has vague ideas about his life from the monotony, cliché, and "phoniness" of society. But he is certain about shedding his egoistic self one day and regressing into silence. His dream of a future life resembles the kind of life that is demanded of a Hindu monk and Yogi:

> *I thought what I'd do was, I'd pretend I was one of those deaf mutes. That way I wouldn't have to have any goddam stupid useless conversations with anybody. If anybody wanted to tell me something they'd have to write it on a piece of paper and shove it over to me. They'd get bored as hell doing that after a while, and then I'd be through with having conversation for the rest of my life. Everybody'd think I was just a poor deaf mute bastard and they'd leave me alone. (205)*

This idealization of being "left alone" and regression into "silence" is there in Salinger's consciousness right from the beginning. Holden's final inability to wrest himself from the social life which he so utterly detests may be one of the reasons for his mental imbalance. He has discovered the superficiality of life in the metropolis; he has already heard the calling of an inner, more profound life, but he has to stick around and conform to society with the help of psychoanalysis.

Most of Salinger's characters are convinced of their unique, personal destiny beyond the ordinary social life that twentieth century America offers. Their show of disgust cannot be dismissed simply as a protest of a "well-fed youngster against a wrong set of toys" as some critics tend to do. The critics are probably baffled that the precocious youngsters in Salinger do not articulate any identifiable social problem or offer an alternative ideology. On the other hand his fiction's concern is gradually withdrawn from contemporary social problems.

Salinger, it seems, is not content with merely depicting social realism in his novels. He is probably trying through his fiction to communicate epiphanies, the inner reality of characters, enlightening experiences that occur to an expanded consciousness. He is incorporating innovations in the craft by attempting to utilize "transcendental mysticism in satiric fiction" (Gwyner and Blotner 33).

There is however another reason why Salinger turns away from social satire in his fiction to a delineation of inner psychic and spiritual reality. He is becoming increasingly aware that in attacking the evils of the social system the fiction cannot problematize the ideas of the "right living," for, human voice (has a tendency to conspire) "to desecrate everything on earth" (Salinger 78). Ironically, most art reinforces the evil they set out to attack.

In "The Last Day of the Last Furlough", Babe Gallagher comes up with a similar insight. He sees the importance of silence in matters objectionable:

*Babe clenched his left hand under the table. "But if we come back, if British men come back, and Japs, and French, and all the other men, all of us talking, writing, painting, making movies of heroism and cock-roaches and foxholes and blood then future generations will always be doomed to future Hitlers. It's never occurred to boys to have contempt for wars, to point to soldiers' pictures in history books, laughing at them. If German boys had learned to be contemptuous of violence, Hitler would have had to take up knitting to keep his ego warm. (Salinger 62)*

Most of the characters in Salinger inhabit the fringe of the dominant society. They more or less adopt Holden's new theory of action—a compassionate waiting without any motive of profit or success—reminding us of an ideal Hindu monk who devotes all his efforts for self-realization and the greater benefit of the world. Thus the conventional quest theme of Catcher gradually gives way to stories which deal more and more with mysticism. From the busiest places in the world Salinger moves in his later stories to narcissistic autonomous families and cocooned individuals. Like the shift of themes there is predictable shrinking of language. From Holden's slang, signifying a language of mass consumption, there is movement towards a solipsistic voice—a voice that is often a monologue (Buddy's), confiding secrets (Seymour's letter), offering advice (Zooey's advice to Franny), or speaking to and about itself (Buddy as an artist talking about the intricacies of writing a fiction)—almost a voice of the monastery.

From the spiritual perspective enunciated above, the maladjustment of a Holden, Franny, Buddy, or Seymour is in fact the sign of spiritual health. The insistence on social success, and therefore on competition inside a social jungle has resulted in a deep seated confusion of the modern man. The confusion has made it mandatory for us to search for our true identity and authenticity. But since our vision of identity is largely social, we seek to get back our identity through social action motivated by greed and ambition, "to become something" as Franny says. This process alienates the individual further not only from the community but from himself. Salinger's characters refuse to partake of such action. "I am just sick of ego, ego," says Franny to Lane Coutell (*Franny and Zooey* 16). The sane way out for Franny is to withdraw from the play which is an ego-directed action resulting in success that whips up pride.

In such a context Salinger's own act of publishing becomes a paradoxical stance in the sense that it conforms to the very marketing, profit oriented society against which some of his characters rebel so often. Silence—the refusal to publish—then, may be interpreted as a resolution of that paradox. For a significant trait which Salinger has obtained from his multicultural legacy is bridging the gap between art and life practice and profession. By refusing to publish, Salinger voluntarily denies himself success in the marketplace.

The conflict of the writer as a sell-out which is central to Salinger's consciousness appears for the first time in his story "The Varioni Brothers." Joe starts selling his talent by writing popular songs under the influence of Sonny and later is sold out and destroyed by money. The gamblers with whom they are associated kill Joe. Salinger will often make use of this kind of destruction and death of the spirit through ambition, greed and success of which Joe's death is a physical sign.

The very act of appending one's name to the created work of fiction, is in a certain sense an act of ego, a defeat for the cause Salinger wants to stand for. Moreover, the success of such a work makes the author a mercenary, willy-nilly, the kind which come under severe reprimand by the author himself. Being an author is also fulfilling an ambition, maybe of a previous birth. In a similar vein, Zooey suggests that by being an actress, Franny is only fulfilling her own "hankering" to be a good actress in a previous incarnation. Ian Hamilton's biography records how Salinger himself, during his early years, was also hankering after the success and publicity of being an author. This fulfilling of an ambition of a lifetime is the egocentric enterprise which he is trying to overcome through his silence.

Salinger's characters subtly deny success. Joe writes his novel in "bits" of rough paper, Teddy embraces his death in spite of his blazing glory, Franny withdraws from the play because she cannot tolerate the adulation. These are certainly the signs of austerity and voluntary denial of worldly pursuits—the kind of spiritual discipline expected of a sadhaka, the seeker in the quest for perfection. We have also seen the way Salinger reprimands Lane Coutell's lustful designs, in his story "Franny". Sexual abstinence (Brahmacharya) denial of material benefits (aparigraha) and elimination of individual identity (apaurusheya) are the different moral disciplines the seeker has to undertake in the course of his spiritual elevation. Significantly the rishis who composed the verses of the Upanisads never appended their names to their creation. Since their writings were contemplating truth whose nature is eternal, how could they be created by any particular human being conditioned by time and space? Can we see in Salinger's silence and denial of publicity and success such an act of humility? Is the gesture a reminder of the limits to our cultural moorings and the possibility of transcendence?

With the publication of "Teddy" and "A Perfect Day for Bananafish" Salinger moved away from the confines of realistic prose fiction. Salinger seems to be using the insights of Vedanta to analyze the ills of the present predicament. For the explanation of the present he uses the Vedantic Karma Theory in which there is no space-time division. The Jatismara (the person who can remember the details of his previous births) Teddy, remembers that in his previous birth he was an Indian Yogi who fell from the grace of God because of his susceptibility to lust. According to the Karmic law, not only sexual impurity, but any kind of action or contemplation of an action done with a selfish motive or for any social advancement acts as a fetter to the soul in its course for liberation and union with God. Teddy dismisses all such action and contemplation as disgusting apple-eating:

> "The trouble is" Teddy said, "most people don't want to see things the way they are. They don't even want to stop getting born and dying all the

*time. They just want new bodies all the time, instead of stopping and
staying with God, where it's really nice," he reflected. "'I never saw such
a bunch of apple-eaters," he said. (208)*

This is the reason why Teddy advised Bob Peet to stop teaching:

*Only because he's quite spiritual, and he's teaching a lot of stuff right
now that isn't very good for him if he wants to make any real spiritual
advancement. It stimulates him too much. It's time for him to take
everything out of his head, instead of putting stuff in. He could get rid
of a lot of the apple in just this one life if he wanted to. He's very good
at meditating. (212)*

Through the educational system which resembles the Vedantic model
of education, Teddy wants to make people realise the ultimate char-
acter-ideal which the Gita calls Sthitaprajna—the being without any
kind of sentimental indulgence and whose passions are subsumed by
the love of God. One can have better control of the immediate, para-
doxically, by transcending it. "If you opened up wide enough" said
Teddy. "Zooey" develops the idea further:

*Detachment, Buddy, and only detachment. Desirelessness. "Cessation
from all hankerings." It's the business of desiring, if you want to know
the goddam truth, that makes an actor in the first place. (154)*

Unlike many of his contemporaries, Salinger is not merely content at
just exposing the wrong ways of existing world order, he sets out to find
solutions to stem the rot. He was aware that the culture he belonged to
created a lot of aspirations without the means to satisfy them. His
search for an alternative model of living took him to the realms of several cultures which share a holistic vision. For example, in the non-
dualism of Advaita Vedanta, the realms of social and spiritual converge
and coalesce. Teddy's epiphany declares everything to be God. "I mean

all she was doing was pouring God into God." To master the finite, one has perforce to transcend to it.

But the real problem of Salinger would be how to make the medium of fiction, primarily a realistic social document, to communicate metareality. How can fiction really become a spiritual tool in social engineering? How can the language of fiction, so much dependent on logic and a certain historical sense, communicate epiphanies such as Teddy's or the all-knowledge of Seymour? Being muktas—highly developed liberated souls—they are beyond the fetters of time and space which engulf ordinary mortals. How can Salinger articulate to an American audience so very obsessed with the largely mimetic fiction of literature a belief in and understanding of an inner spiritual realization that defies the communicative powers of rational language? The Glass stories dramatise these conflicts and seek a resolution.

Though the narcissistic concerns for the craft of fiction runs through the entire body of Salinger's works, it comes under sharper focus in "Inverted Forest" and "Seymour: An Introduction." Language, as Holden Caulfield has demonstrated, can be a form of reality. James Lundquist suggests how Salinger, by using Holden's preference for certain colloquials and slangs and aversion towards others, shows two sets of realities. We are, in fact, prisoners of our words. In several of Salinger's stories a character's phoniness or sincerity can be discerned from the kind of vocabulary he chooses to use. Lane Coutell's vocabulary for example, reveals his phoniness. Lundquist also compares the art of Salinger with the linguistic philosophy of Wittgenstein. Wittgenstein concludes that there is no discoverable reality outside language and that the world of facts will eternally be beyond human cognition for language cannot reach the world of facts.

The approximation of metareality through both life and art is the ambitious project of Salinger's later fiction. Ihab Hassan (1963) suggests that Salinger has not fully grasped the reality that he wants to depict and that the Glass saga is merely an inchoate voice bordering on silence. Hassan might well have added that what Salinger wants to grasp is really beyond the scope of fictional language. It is a perfection beyond the human realm and language which could only be effectively communicated through silence, the way the Zen and Lama teachers communicate knowledge to their disciples.

Salinger's "Poet" in "The Inverted Forest" plumbs the depth of the world in the pursuit of perfection. The true "beauty" of the world is in the underground foliage. However, Raymond Ford nearly loses his sight in the course of finding that beauteous world of perfect art and imagination. The intimate relationship between art and religion and the possibility of perfection in art is further explored in the two stories, "Raise High the Roofbeam, Carpenters" and "Seymour: An Introduction." Seymour's diary records the ideal Gettysburg speech as a gesture of silence. It is as if the perfection of art leads to the annihilation of the medium itself:

> *I'll champion indiscrimination till doomsday, on the ground that it leads to health and a kind of real enviable happiness. Followed purely, it is the way to the Tao, and undoubtedly the highest way. But for a discriminating man to achieve this, it would mean that he would have to dispossess himself of poetry, go beyond poetry. That is, he couldn't possibly learn or drive himself to like bad poetry in the abstract, let alone equate it with good poetry. He would have to drop poetry altogether. I said it would be no easy thing to do. Dr. Sims said I was putting it too stringently, putting it, he said, as only a perfectionist would. Can I deny that? (74)*

That quest for perfection or the ultimate poetry of silence is basically a spiritual quest. The Sanskrit aesthetician Mammata speaks of the joy of poetry as "Brahmaswadamibanubhabayan"—the thrill of the ultimate divine experience. However, while art experience is finite, and ceases when the stimulus is withdrawn, the joy of "Brahma" realization is infinite. While art experience does not require moral elevation, moral discipline is a precondition for the attainment of blissful spiritual experience. The insistence on moral life, the revulsion against lust and squalor and pleasure of the senses in Salinger is precisely for this reason. Through his art Salinger is subtly persuading his audience towards a higher mode of conduct and character which will be helpful in the ultimate spiritual life. In Sanskrit poetics, the role of art has been recognized as a valid spiritual stimulus (Aurobindo 220). If we accept Salinger's fiction as such a stimulus, his silence can be treated as the flight beyond:

> *I say that the true artist-seer, the heavenly fool who can and does produce beauty, is mainly dazzled to death by his own scruples, the blinding shapes and colors of his own sacred human conscience. (105)*

The Dhvani school of ancient Sanskrit poetics does not accord any great importance to the words, their semantic connotation and the figures of speech. The theoreticians emphasise an inner implicit meaning, the emotional atmosphere that underlies the best poetry. This view corresponds to the Vedantic theory that the objects of experience are not the ultimate reality, but only manifestations of reality. Words, therefore, are merely external appearances of poetry. Seymour, as a practicing poet, not only tries to go in search of the true reality beneath the appearance, he leads a kind of non-dichotomous life. An interesting poem of his is about a boy who becomes the fish he catches and feels all the pain, the way Sri Ramakrishna developed welts on his body when he saw the beating of a cow. Seymour too contracts wounds, pain and colors of others. Through a universal sympathy the pinda or the microcosmic existence of the individual becomes the brahmanda, the macrocosm. For this kind of quest Seymour has started writing poetry which is beyond what Sri Aurobindo calls the "crude actualities of life" making them quite unwestern. This is one of the reasons why he shies away from publishing them:

> *. . . but he felt at times that the poems read as though they had been written by an ingrate, of sorts, someone who was turning his back—in effect, at least—on his own environment and the people in it who were close to him. (124–25)*

At the pinnacle of Salinger's social and spiritual ideal is Seymour, who is more or less a Hindu Seer albeit in the transitional phase of his spiritual transformation. Being a mukta, he is conscious of the spiritual evolution that is taking place and actively contributes to it. This active participation in the divine purpose of evolution is what is known as Sadhana in yoga. However, the ideal to be realized can only be apprehended intuitively, not explained through a rational language. The logical, rational autopsy of an intuitive experience is what Salinger is critical about (he dedicated "Raise High the Roofbeam, Carpenters" to the "Pure reader"). For Seymour, seeing more, is speaking less. His action of not publishing his mantric poems is also an ideal act. His "right living" is complemented by his ideal act, the unpublished poems and silence. As human beings tend to approximate the condition of Seymour in Salinger, all art strives towards the condition of his brilliant, yet unpublished poems. Though they remain unpublished, they continue to inspire future seekers like Buddy, the way the mantras of a Hindu guru passed into a true disciple in total secret brings about his spiritual transformation. In the evolutionary hierarchy of Salinger, man is a transitional being as his art is an intermediate gesture. The moment of the perfect art has been described by Buddy Glass as a kind of "seizure." He is in such a state of happiness in "Seymour: An Introduction," when writing becomes an automatic act. "Of course," he says, "The poets in this state are by far the most 'difficult,' but even a prose writer similarly seized hasn't: any real choice of behavior in decent company divine or not, a seizure is a seizure" (98).

Later, in his on-going meditation on Seymour Buddy feels a panic which prevents him from continuing his action. The actions and efforts of Buddy Glass, Salinger's literary prototype, are clearly to emulate his chosen ideal—Ishtam in Bhakti Yoga—Seymour. In the manner of a true disciple Buddy gradually expands his consciousness of Seymour ("He'd grown too much while I was away" [151]) and merges his self-awareness, the shrinking of ego; there is a corresponding interior-ization of the art. The craft of story writing moves away from the external world and into intense interior meditation on the process of writing itself. This narcissistic interiorization is also the method recommended by Yoga for spiritual aspirants, which culminates in total silent vibrations like the poems of Seymour. In the Samkhya Yoga of Bhagbad Gita there is the description of the tortoise who draws his limbs into itself:

*Yada Samharate Chayam Kurmonganiba sarbasah Indriyani Indri-yarthevyasthasya Prajna Pratisthiti. (Sloka-58)*

[When an individual withdraws his senses comprehensively from the world of objects, the way a tortoise withdraws all his limbs into itself, then only, his intellect becomes established, in the wisdom.]

As we see, the characters in Salinger are in different stages of perfection in their quest for a right living which is largely modeled upon the ideals of Vedanta to which Salinger was exposed initially through the teachings of Sri Ramakrishna and Swami Vivekananda. The process of the quest which begins with a general disaffection with the existing order of sensual and vital pursuits, goes through different stages of intensification like the intellectual awareness of alternative modes, interiorization and meditation upon that true knowledge and simultaneous withdrawal from the mundane trappings of outward other directed life, and culminates in the realization of the ultimate silent blissful state of samadhi where all kinds of duality produced by avidya (false knowledge) of maya (illusion) vanish and the seeker and the sought become one. The life of J. D. Salinger bears out his own disgust with the existing order and subsequent quest for a spiritual alternative. His works are ample proof of his intimate knowledge of his chosen way of life, so much so, that the last stories almost become silent meditation upon those ideals. One could conclude in the fitness of things that Salinger is trying to enact the next phase of the life of the seeker, through his silence—an act of extreme renunciation of action. It would be a kind of luxury to nurture such conjectures; yet, keeping in mind the limited scope and inability of literary criticism to ascertain a writer's inner life, we can decode Salinger's silence as loud protest against the current aggressive, competitive action-ethic of the West, its largely materialistic pursuits with great emphasis on social success which whips up vainglory and pride, its acquisitive spirit and penchant for sensual pleasures that money and hypocrisy can buy. The true Vedanton first seeks to perfect the self before using it as the primary instrument of changing outward society. Salinger's regression into silence may be a reminder of the primacy of self-realization in this clamorous age of ideologies, revolutions, and upheavals whose effect is as temporary as their promises lofty. Silence as a gesture acts as a perfect foil for Salinger's art which retreats in order to recover the silence of the repressed "other" of our modern civilization.

ACKNOWLEDGEMENTS

I gratefully acknowledge the help of Professor Dr. B. K. Tripathy, Head, Department of English, Utkal University, Bhubaneswar, Orissa and Dr. B. K. Nanda, Department of English, Ravenshaw College, Cuttack, Orissa, India while revising the essay.

Works Cited

Aurobindo. *Sri Aurobindo Birth Centenary Library Popular Edition*, Vol. 23. Pondicherry: Sri Aurobindo Ashram Press, 1970.

—. *Letters on Poetry Literature and Art*. Pondicherry: Sri Aurobindo Ashram Press, 1971.

French, Warren. *J. D. Salinger*. New York: Twayne, 1963.

Gwyner and Blotner. *The Fiction of J. D. Salinger*. Pittsburgh: University of Pittsburgh, 1958.

Hamilton, Ian. *In Search of J. D. Salinger*. London: Heinemann, 1989.

Hassan, Ihab. *The Dismemberment of Orpheus*. New York: Oxford UP, 1971.

Kunihiro, Masao. "Indigenous Barriers to Communication." *The Wheel Extended.*

Spring 1974. Cited in Thomas Hoove, *Zen Culture* (London, Routledge, 1978, 225).

Lundquist, James. *J. D. Salinger*. New York: Lungar, 1979.

M. *The Teachings of Sri Ramakrishna*. Calcutta: Advaita Ashram, 1985.

Merton, Thomas. *Contemplation in a World of Action*. London: Unwin, 1980.

Salinger, Jerome David. *Catcher in the Rye*. London: Penguin, 1958.

—. *Franny and Zooey*. London: Penguin, 1964.

—. "For Esme with Love and Squalor." London: Penguin, 1986.

—. *Raise High The Roof Beam, Carpenters and Seymour: an Introduction*. New York: Bantam, 1981.

—. Selections from *The Complete Works of Swami Vivekananda*. Calcutta: Advaita Ashrama, 1989.

—. *The Complete Works of Swami Vivekananda*. Vol. II. Calcutta: Advaita Ashrama, 1989.

# The Sentimental Misanthrope;
# Why J. D. Salinger Can't Write

DAVID SKINNER

J. D. Salinger's cultural significance seems beyond dispute. *The Catcher in the Rye* is a book read even by those who don't read much. When Mark David Chapman assassinated John Lennon in 1980, he said the reason could be found in the novel's pages. When John "Goumba" Sialiano spoke in 1999 of his role in the "Scores" nightclub case against John Gotti Jr., he explained, "I'm the Holden Caulfield of Scores. I'm Goumba in the Rye." In such books as Don DeLillo's *Mao II*, such movies as *Field of Dreams* and *Jerry Maguire*, Salinger has become a stand-in—our living metaphor, holed up in the New Hampshire woods—for the innocence that needs protection from the outside world. A bestselling author from *Catcher in the Rye* in 1951 to *Franny and Zooey* in 1961, Salinger hasn't published since 1965, but he remains as famous as ever—more famous than ever as each year of silence goes by.

Joyce Maynard's *At Home in the World*, published last year, is only the most recent episode in the search for America's best-known hermit. It describes in detail a nine-month affair she had in 1972 with the sometimes sentimental and sometimes misanthropic writer. Salinger was then fifty-three, while Maynard was eighteen; he was a famous author, while she was a precocious and ambitious girl with a *New York Times Magazine* cover story to her credit. Their affair started with a fan letter from Salinger, peaked with Maynard's quitting school to move in with him, and ended in the middle of a trip to Florida—when Salinger told her to pack up and go home.

A few of Maynard's reviewers celebrated her revelations about the reclusive author: She "surpasses [Salinger] in depth of feeling," according to the *San Francisco Chronicle*; a "literary pioneer," agreed the *Washington Post*. But most reviewers recognized that disliking Salinger's behavior didn't necessitate liking the now-forty-five-year-old Maynard, while others seemed to want to believe in the essential goodness of the man whose *Catcher in the Rye* is every adolescent's favorite novel. "To read *At Home in the World* doesn't require a suspension of disbelief," Katherine Wolff snarled in Salon, "but it does require the suspension of literary standards." In *The New Yorker*—the first publisher of much of Salinger's fiction—Daphne Merkin added, "There is something of the stalker in Maynard, the oxygen-eater."

Whatever its faults, Maynard's book contained the first glimpse into Salinger's life in ten years. Since the troubled publication of Ian Hamilton's *In Search of J. D. Salinger* in 1988, no one has added to the few facts available. Hamilton had found in library collections some letters the novelist had written over the years, but Salinger promptly sued to stop their quotation. (The lawsuit did force Hamilton to rewrite his biography, but, ironically, it also put the letters into the court record—where they could be quoted in hundreds of newspaper accounts of the trial.) During depositions, it became clear that Salinger couldn't remember what was in the letters, didn't know which ones were being quoted, and hadn't checked Hamilton's last-minute paraphrasings. He just objected—to all of it: the biography, the letters, the interest Hamilton was generating, the whole idea of exposure.

Salinger's obsession has continued. In 1997, his agent threatened to sue a young fan whose website provided quotations from *Catcher in the*

*Rye* whenever a visitor clicked a red-hunting-cap icon. In November 1998, Salinger stopped Lincoln Center from showing *Pari*, and Iranian film loosely based on *Franny and Zooey*. In a world where recycling Salinger's work is outlawed, only outlaws do it. An "anarchist publishing collective," for instance, has recently printed *Twenty-Two Stories*, a collection of early fiction. Copies are few and distributed only "on a personal level."

Joyce Maynard explains, in her introduction to *At Home in the World*, why she decided to violate Salinger's desire for privacy—and the passage is a fair measure of her silliness, her conventionality, and her prose: "I pray what my children take away from this story is freedom from the kind of shame I experienced as a young person, and the lesson that every child, woman, and man should possess license to speak or sing in his or her true voice." Over the years, Maynard has made herself into a sort of low-rent anti-Salinger. She is public in every way and publishes as often as she can. In newspaper articles, her Web site, and her newsletter, she writes about her children, divorce, baking tips, alcoholic father, troubled relations with her sister. Hers is a life without curtains, and everybody is supposed to want to peek in.

It's enough to make one wonder what Salinger ever saw in her. This is, after all, the man who, by Maynard's account, thinks the vast majority of human beings are phonies and fools. In one poignant scene, Salinger tells her to change her miniskirt: She looks ridiculous, he says—but "don't take it personally, . . . it's a common failing of mankind."

How such a misanthrope could stand someone who later prays for the "true voice" of "every child, woman, and man" is a mystery—until one sees the darling, pixilated, *New York Times Magazine* photograph of the anorexic young Joyce Maynard, the girl whose eyes are too old for her years. She is Phoebe, the sister Holden Caulfield wants to protect in *Catcher in the Rye*. She is the girl in the red tam playing with her dog who makes Zooey Glass realize that there is good in the world in *Franny and Zooey*. She is the child on the beach whose foot Seymour Glass kisses before he walks off to kill himself. She is the Wise Child.

How such a girl could turn into the author of *At Home in the World* is also a mystery—until one sees the dust-jacket photograph of Maynard today. She has a stretched sort of quality, the half-mad appearance of having desperately held on to something for too many years. The French philosopher Paul Ricoeur once distinguished children from saints, the first innocence we are born with from the second innocence we must strive for. Once upon a time, Joyce Maynard was a J. D. Salinger character—and, like all his characters, there was nowhere for her to go as an adult. Shining through the photograph of the grown-up Maynard is the look of first innocence self-consciously cultivated for so long it has grown into something very much like guilt.

Salinger's desire for solitude is perhaps the most famous of its kind. It has inspired half-baked theories about his identity, pilgrimages to his home in Cornish, New Hampshire, and even trickery to make him come outside and greet his cultist visitors. In a 1997 story in *Esquire*, Ron Rosenbaum wrote of a group of boys who dumped one of their party, soaked in ketchup and screaming as though in pain, onto the street in front of Salinger's house. It didn't work. Salinger's seclusion inspired Rosenbaum to argue that silence is the only eloquence in a media-saturated age.

But, in fact, Rosenbaum and Maynard and the ketchup-boy and Hamilton and all the rest of those in search of J. D. Salinger have it wrong. The reason for his silence is not found in his life, but in his fiction—the work that captured perfectly the adolescent who has discovered the world is corrupt. Salinger's compounding of misanthropy and sentimentality was always smart. He knew that the problem is not children but adults, just as he knew that the solution involves God somehow. That's why his late stories filled up with saints and seers and sages and holy fools. But he never quite figured out how it worked, and his stabs at second innocence kept falling back into first innocence. In raising his children too high—in making childhood not just innocent but wise—Salinger damned his adults forever and ever.

The one who came closest to catching this is Mary McCarthy. In

1961, *Time* magazine published a fawning cover-story canonizing Salinger, and McCarthy responded in a scathing essay in *Harper's*. The charm of Salinger's characters, she argued, derives from the intimacy of a small inside group closed to outsiders. Exclusivity is the pre-condition of a sentimental self-love that sensationalizes the insiders' prosaic life. But to perform this, McCarthy claimed, the author must reject the rest of mankind—which is why Salinger, the biggest phony of all, must put in each of his books an extended attack on phonies.

McCarthy, however, underestimated her argument. The sentimentalizing of life and the attack on phonies aren't just explanations of why Salinger did fail; they point to why he had to fail—why he has been unable to publish since his last short story, "Hapworth 16, 1924," appeared in *The New Yorker* in June 1965. Salinger's world has a built-in doomsday, a point beyond which it can no longer be a part of the world of other people.

The first part of Salinger's brief career consists of the 1951 *Catcher in the Rye*, five of the 1953 *Nine Stories*, and various magazine stories from the 1940s, some available only in bootleg editions. The second part of his career tells the saga of the Glass family. It begins with four tales in *Nine Stories*, runs through the 1961 *Franny and Zooey* and the 1963 pair of stories, *Raise High the Roof Beam, Carpenters and Seymour:An Introduction*, and ends with "Hapworth 16, 1924," unavailable except in pirated collections.

As cynical as it is sentimental, *Catcher in the Rye* is easily Salinger's best work. In the novel, only children escape being phonies, but that doesn't save them. To describe the actual dying of a child—as, say, the fearless Charles Dickens would have done—is impossible in the cynical, naive, confused, and knowing voice Salinger developed for his hero. But the reader eventually discovers that not one but two young sensitives have died before the story opens.

The younger brother of the narrator Holden Caulfield "was terrifically intelligent," but he died of leukemia. Just before the expelled Holden leaves school for the wanderings around New York that form the bulk of the book, he writes a descriptive essay for his roommate, using as the subject his dead brother's left-handed outfielder's glove—on which the boy had copied poems in green ink so he would have something to read while waiting for pop flies.

Later, when the hungover Holden is drifting aimlessly through Grand Central Station, he can't stop thinking about a classmate, "old James Castle," a "skinny, weak-looking guy with wrists about as big as pencils." Physical weakness turns out to be proof of goodness: After telling a conceited boy that he is, in fact, conceited, Castle jumped from a dorm window rather than take it back.

About an adult pianist he admires, Holden says, "If you do something too good, then, after a while, if you don't watch it, you start showing off." But children in *Catcher in the Rye* are never conscious of their own goodness. That's exactly what makes them vulnerable to cruelty. At his sister's school, Holden notices an obscenity scrawled on the wall. He can't help picturing his sister and the other innocents, and how they probably don't know the word. But soon enough some jerk will explain it. And then the children will start worrying. Holden imagines smashing the head of whoever wrote it.

The perfection under siege in *Catcher in the Rye* belongs only to children, and it inspires Holden to imagine a playground in a ryefield perilously close to a cliff: He would stand by the cliff, basking in the innocence of the children at play and make sure they didn't fall off—the catcher in the rye.

The thing that allows Holden to recognize the innocence of children—his knowledge of the existence of phonies—is also what sets him against adults. In the end, though, he pays for passing judgment on others, even when they deserve it. Salinger is at his best in *Catcher in the Rye* because the narrator lives out the consequences of being a sensitive, unstable teenager. What few graces the world has for Holden—time spent with his sister Phoebe, his brother's baseball mitt—do not protect him from having to face the reality of other people. The adult world may be filled with horrible people, but Holden Caulfield is no angel either. And in the novel's beautifully ironic ending, the people who burdened him most become, when they are no longer around, the objects of his affection.

Of the five tales in *Nine Stories* from the time of *Catcher in the Rye*, three are mild, anecdotal studies of young, upper-class Manhattanites. In them, however, the victims of life's misfortune are, like Holden Caulfield, also perpetrators of misfortune. Holden is partly to blame for ending up in a psychiatric ward. So the naive husband in "Pretty Mouth and Green My Eyes" is partly to blame for his wife's cheating. So the hero of "De Daumier-Smith's Blue Period" discovers that the art school he has joined as a teacher is a fraud, after he had lied his way into the faculty.

The other tales in *Nine Stories* concern the Glass family—who go on to fill the rest of Salinger's fiction. The Glasses consist of seven precocious geniuses and their parents, two retired vaudevillians. All the children appeared at various points on "It's A Wise Child," a national radio quiz show for pre-teens. The two eldest, Seymour and Buddy (who narrates most of the stories) oversaw the education of the others and taught them the important lessons of life. Interestingly, the story of Seymour's suicide at age thirty-one is the earliest of the stories, while the last, "Hapworth 16, 1924," shows Seymour at his youngest, age seven. This arch from an unbearable adulthood back to an exhilarated childhood represents a journey into perfection, from the world of other people into the utopia of Salinger's Glassland.

Simpletons and phonies surround the Glasses, but in the case of Seymour's bride, Muriel, simplicity is proof of goodness. In a diary entry in "Raise High the Roof Beam, Carpenters," Seymour describes the thrill he receives from Muriel's lack of self-consciousness: "She has a primal urge to play house permanently. She's not a genius and may not even be particularly bright, but how I worship her simplicity, her terrible honesty. How I rely on it. . . . A person deprived, for life, of any understanding or taste for the main current of poetry. . . . She may as well be dead. . . . I find her unimaginably brave."

Muriel's stupid opinions, including her undying respect for her annoying mother's even more stupid opinions, the middlebrow novels she reads nightly, the analyst she sees regularly, her wish to say and do exactly what other married couples do—it's all proof of the innocence that Seymour, like his siblings, needs to find in the world.

Usually, they don't find it. When the Glasses take their chances in the subpar world of other people, the characteristics they most prize within the family—endless curiosity, a poetic appreciation for the funny details of life, the innocence of children—are measured by more fickle standards. The pretentious boyfriend of Franny Glass in *Franny and Zooey*, Lane Coutell, for example, is a bright, Ivy League, literature student who worships false gods like the poets who teach at Columbia where Franny is a student. She tries to correct him: "They're just people that write poems that get published and anthologized all over the place, but they're not poets." Anyway, college, Franny says, is "the most incredible farce."

Franny is headed toward a nervous breakdown—precipitated in part by an attempt to pray without ceasing, as described in a book she found on the dead Seymour's bookshelf, *The Way of a Pilgrim*, written in the nineteenth century by a Russian peasant with a withered arm. Just as her quest is beginning, however, Franny goes on a date with Lane, who explains to her over frog legs his discovery that the novelist Flaubert lacked "testicularity." The contrast between Lane's pretentiousness and the Russian peasant's simplicity is Salinger's standard divide between other people and Glassland, but Lane was doomed from the start. As Franny's train arrives at the beginning of *Franny and Zooey*, Lane "emptied his face of all expression that might quite simply, perhaps even beautifully, reveal how he felt about the arriving person." Such fakers hide the innocence and love Franny needs in abundance to go on with life, and Salinger puts the burden on the world to prove it can live up to the standards raised by the Glasses.

In "Raise High the Roof Beams, Carpenters," the foil is Muriel's matron of honor, Edie Burwick. Her false god is Muriel's mother, who pronounces her son-in-law a "latent homosexual" and a "schizoid personality." Says Edie, "I honestly think she's one of the few really brilliant people I've ever met in my entire life." She doesn't think, she honestly thinks; it's not just ever or in her life, but ever in her entire life. Poor, pretentious Edie can't even begin to see that in meeting Seymour she has met a true genius, "a true poet," as Buddy describes him.

After "Raise High the Roof Beam, Carpenters," Salinger never published a story with a non-Glass character. The second segment of *Franny and Zooey* doesn't even leave the Glass home, a rambling Manhattan apartment described in endless detail. Even the living room is evidence of the simple-hearted geniuses who lived there: *Nancy Drew and the Hidden Staircase* atop *Fear and Trembling* on the bookcase. The Glasses' cozy clutter is detailed in Salinger's listing of fifty items in the bathroom medicine cabinet. As Mary McCarthy put it, "Every single object possessed by the Glass communal ego is bent on lovably expressing the Glass personality—eccentric, homey, good-hearted."

The climax of *Franny and Zooey* comes in the sweetly theatrical spiritual counsel Zooey offers his sister. "I remember about the fifth time I ever went on [the radio program 'It's A Wise Child'], . . . Seymour'd told me to shine my shoes just as I was going out the door. . . . He said to shine them for the Fat Lady. . . . He never did tell me who the Fat Lady was." After many entertaining pages of the bitter sibling squabbling, it comes to this: The Fat Lady, Zooey tells his sister, is everywhere and everyone. In the world of other people, every annoying, everyday person is the Fat Lady. And the Fat Lady, he tells her, is Christ: "Christ himself, buddy." It is a terrific speech, earnest and funny, but also very thin. The enormous intellectual power stacked to the ceiling in the Glass apartment turns cute on a dime.

That speech at the end of *Franny and Zooey*, however, is as close as Salinger gets to escaping the corner into which he painted himself. The Glasses' religious instincts often seem drawn from a freshman survey course in world religions. Zooey does accuse Franny, with her "bide-a-wee-home heart," of thinking that Jesus has to be somebody really nice like St. Francis of Assisi or Heidi's grandfather. But throughout the novel, the Bhagavad Gita, the Islamic mystics, Plato, and the Victorian clergyman Kilvert are all rolled into one uniform collection of sage sayings from indistinguishable seers and holy men.

Throughout the novel, that is, until the end, when Zooey speaks the word "Christ." Every previous mention (Salinger's special interjection "Chrissakes" aside) had only been of "Jesus"—another edifying world-religion character, another seer, holy man, and honorary family member: Franny, for instance, recounts the story that Jesus visited the Glass kitchen one night to ask the very young Zooey for a small glass of ginger ale. Then, suddenly, for a brief moment at the novel's conclusion, Jesus is Christ, the Anointed One, God Himself in Whose image were formed even fat ladies listening all day to the radio, even phonies like Lane Coutell, even precocious little brats like *Franny and Zooey*.

If there was a chance for Salinger to break free from first innocence, to climb out of the well of sentimental misanthropy into which he had fallen, it surely involved something like this. But he couldn't maintain it, or he wouldn't seize it, and his remaining two stories narrow even his Glass world down to an unbearable point.

"Seymour—An Introduction" gives few details that can't be discovered in the earlier stories. What it adds is merely praise, a sweeping of Seymour up into high, holy company. "He was all real things to us," Buddy writes, speaking for the whole family, "our blue-striped unicorn, our double-lensed burning glass, our consultant genius, our portable conscience, our superego, and our one full poet." *Catcher in the Rye* is written as though Holden were sharing confidential information with the reader; "Seymour: An Introduction" as though such sharing is impossible. One digressive sentence contains a hundred and eighty-three words and says nothing except that Seymour was half-Jewish and had unusually intimate relations with his hands.

Last year, a small press in Virginia announced an authorized book publication of "Hapworth 16, 1924," the final Glass story. But Salinger pulled back again, and the publisher now says the book is "indefinitely delayed." "Hapworth" consists entirely of a letter from the seven-year-old Seymour, describing his impressions of summer camp and requesting books for Buddy and himself: Conversational Italian, the complete works of Leo Tolstoy, the Gayatri Prayer, Don Quixote, Raja-Yoga, and Bhakti-Yoga, "George Eliot, not in her entirety," "Charles Dickens, either in blessed entirety or in any touching shape or form. My God, I salute you, Charles Dickens!"—and so on and on through dozens of authors, subjects, and titles.

There's deliberate comedy in this erudite list, but there's another point as well, for it places Seymour firmly among the poets and other holy men, and far beyond our ken. Other characters are simply dismissed: "Few of these magnificent, healthy, sometimes remarkably handsome boys will mature. The majority, I give you my heartbreaking opinion, will merely senesce." And so, at last, are we dismissed: Even Salinger's readers are exiled finally to the unnecessary, unpleasant, phony, non-Glass world of other people.

From this deep, solipsistic well, there truly is no escape for Salinger. To write a new story would require leaving the Glass family, and to publish it would require joining again the world of Edie Burwick and Lane Coutell—and Joyce Maynard and Ian Hamilton and the ketchup-boy and the Fat Lady. It would mean forgetting the wise child's sentimental misanthropy and the precocious adolescent's division of humanity into the wonderful and the horrible. It would mean joining the painful search that actual adults must all undertake for the second, and real, innocence.

# J. D. Salinger, Failed Recluse

ALEX BEAM

J. D. Salinger is inevitably described as the most private man in America (*Esquire*) or the most private of literary figures (*The New York Times*). In the introduction to his just-published Salinger biography, Paul Alexander calls the Bard of Cornish the one figure in the twentieth century who didn't want his biography written. Yet Salinger has already been the subject of two biographies.

If Salinger really wants to be left alone, he is going about it in a very strange way. He doesn't live in a gated community. He summons perfect strangers into his hideaway. He sues people, and then phones the media to spread the story.

Maybe Salinger should take a page from Thomas Pynchon, American letters' other famous recluse, who really wants to be left alone. Two years ago, a *London Sunday Times* hireling bearded Pynchon on the streets of Manhattan and nearly got his head bitten off: Get your fucking hand out of my face! Pynchon bellowed.

Here's the Tale of the Tape in the Battle of the Hermit Divas:

## 1. Location

Salinger: Salinger has lived on the same Cornish, New Hampshire, property for over 30 years. Other than a No Trespassing sign, there is no particular barrier to entry, from the fictional Ray Kinsella of *Shoeless Joe* to the notorious stalkerazzi photographer Paul Adao of the *New York Post*, no one has ever had much trouble finding the place. Up until recently, Salinger used to chat casually with his doorsteppers—unless they were journalists. The next generation of visitors won't even have to interrogate the locals, as Alexander provides directions in his new book.

On the one hand, it's churlish to suggest that Salinger should move just to protect himself from his public. On the other hand, people have moved for less.

Pynchon: Until recently, no one was really sure where Pynchon lived. Seattle? Mexico? Northern California? Probably all of the above. Much ink has been shed in proving that Pynchon spent several years in California's Mendocino County researching his novel *Vineland* and writing letters to the local newspaper under the name Wanda Tinasky. But that may have been a hoax.

## 2. Litigation

Salinger: In 1974, Salinger sued the editor of an unauthorized collection of his stories and 17 bookstores that stocked the book. Lest his filing go unnoticed, he phoned *New York Times* reporter Lacey Fosburgh to alert her to the case. He made Page One.

In 1986, he sued to block publication of Ian Hamilton's biography, *In Search of J. D. Salinger*, and forced the biographer to remove many quotations from the published work. This kept his name in the papers for months, and forced him to give a six-hour long deposition to Hamilton's lawyer, a portion of which appears for the first time in Alexander's book. In 1996, Salinger's agent forbade a nonprofit *Catcher in the Rye* Web site from using quotations from the novel, garnering the usual rash of publicity.

### 3. Lady Friends

Salinger: In 1972, the 53-year-old Salinger wrote the notorious fan letter to the 18-year-old Joyce Maynard, who had just written a *New York Times Magazine* cover story about herself. The rest is herstory. Salinger wrote similar letters to other young female writers. He also had a fascination with actresses. At age 62, he wrote a fan letter to the 36-year old actress Elaine Joyce, whom he had seen in the TV show *Mr. Merlin.* That resulted in a long-running affair. A few years later, he developed a fascination with the comely Catherine Oxenberg, then starring in the TV show *Dynasty.* Salinger traveled to California and had shown up on the set, according to biographer Hamilton. He had to be escorted off.

Pynchon: As befits a man guarding, as opposed to flaunting, his privacy, Pynchon has kept his private life private. Past girlfriends have spoken with journalists, mainly to report that Pynchon was charming and a tad eccentric. In the early '70s, Jules Siegel, a college friend, wrote an article for *Playboy* titled: "Who Is Thomas Pynchon and Why Did He Take Off With My Wife?" The story praised Pynchon as a wonderful lover, sensitive, and quick with the ability to project a mood that turned the most ordinary surroundings into a scene out of a masterful film. . . .

For almost a decade now, Pynchon has been married to his literary agent and kept to himself. Cunningly, Pynchon is hiding in plain view. He lives in Manhattan and escorts his son to and from school many days of the week. A friend of mine says he's active in children's activities and has even been written up in the school newspaper. The mothers love him, he says. Local literati know where he lives and they leave him alone.

Why? Why is Pynchon left alone and Salinger harassed? Theories abound. Some people feel that Pynchon is a cerebral writer, and his fans are mature in age and temperament. Salinger's great classic *The Catcher in the Rye* is about an adolescent and has visceral appeal to adolescents of all ages. John Lennon's assassin, Mark David Chapman, and Ronald Reagan's would-be killer, John Hinckley, were both major *Catcher* fans.

Another major difference is that Pynchon has continued to publish. Unlike Salinger, people have been able to access Pynchon, and his evolution as a writer, explains Ron Rosenbaum, who has followed both writers' careers closely. In 1997, Rosenbaum published an *Esquire* cover story lauding Salinger's self-imposed Wall of Silence as his most powerful, his most eloquent, perhaps his most lasting work of art.

But I wonder: Is the wall really art, or is it an act? And has the act now supplanted the art?

Two years ago, Salinger announced plans to publish a 32-year-old story, "Hapworth 16, 1924," as a book. After some negative publicity, he changed his plans. The way Salinger handled the publicity he said he did not want was a bit too contrived to get attention itself, Paul Alexander concludes at the end of his new biography. He continues: Salinger became the Greta Garbo of literature, and then periodically, when it may have seemed he was about to be forgotten, he resurfaced briefly, just to remind the public that he wanted to be left alone. The whole act could have been cute or whimsical; only, it felt as if it were being put on by a master showman, a genius spin doctor, a public-relations wizard hawking a story the public couldn't get enough of.

# Holden at Fifty

*The Catcher in the Rye* and What it Spawned

LOUIS MENAND

*T*he Catcher in the Rye *was turned down by* The New Yorker. *The magazine had published six of J. D. Salinger's short stories, including two of the most popular, "A Perfect Day for Bananafish," in 1948, and "For Esme—with Love and Squalor," in 1950. But when the editors were shown the novel they declined to run an excerpt. They told Salinger that the precocity of the four Caulfield children was not believable, and that the writing was showoffy—that it seemed designed to display the author's cleverness rather than to present the story. The Catcher in the Rye *had already been turned down by the publishing house that solicited it, Harcourt Brace, when an executive there named Eugene Reynal achieved immortality the bad way by complaining that he couldn't figure out whether or not Holden Caulfield was supposed to be crazy. Salinger's agent took the book to Little, Brown, where the editor, John Woodburn, was evidently prudent enough not to ask such questions. It was published in July 1951, and has so far sold more than sixty million copies.

The world is sad, Oscar Wilde said, because a puppet was once melancholy. He was referring to Hamlet, a character he thought had taught the world a new kind of unhappiness—the unhappiness of eternal disappointment in life as it is, Weltschmerz. Whether Shakespeare invented it or not, it has proved to be one of the most addictive of literary emotions. Readers consume volumes of it, and then ask to meet the author. It has also proved to be one of the most enduring of literary emotions, since life manages to come up short pretty reliably. Each generation feels disappointed in its own way, though, and seems to require its own literature of disaffection. For many Americans who grew up in the nineteen-fifties, *The Catcher in the Rye* is the purest extract of that mood. Holden Caulfield is their sorrow king. Americans who grew up in later decades still read Salinger's novel, but they have their own versions of his story, with different flavors of Weltschmerz— *Catcher in the Rye* rewrites, a literary genre all its own.

In art, as in life, the rich get richer. People generally read *The Catcher in the Rye* when they are around fourteen years old, usually because the book was given or assigned to them by people—parents or teachers—who read it when they were fourteen years old, because somebody gave or assigned it to them. The book keeps acquiring readers, in other words, not because kids keep discovering it but because grownups who read it when they were kids keep getting kids to read it. This seems crucial to making sense of its popularity. *The Catcher in the Rye* is a sympathetic portrait of a boy who refuses to be socialized which has become (among certain readers, anyway, for it is still occasionally banned in conservative school districts) a standard instrument of socialization. I was introduced to the book by my parents, people who, if they had ever imagined that I might, after finishing the thing, run away from school, smoke like a chimney, lie about my age in bars, solicit a prostitute, or use the word "goddam" in every third sentence, would (in the words of the story) have had about two hemorrhages apiece. Somehow, they knew this wouldn't be the effect.

Supposedly, kids respond to *The Catcher in the Rye* because they recognize themselves in the character of Holden Caulfield. Salinger is imagined to have given voice to what every adolescent, or, at least, every sensitive, intelligent, middle-class adolescent, thinks but is too inhibited to say, which is that success is a sham, and that successful people are mostly phonies. Reading Holden's story is supposed to be the literary equivalent of looking in a mirror for the first time. This seems to underestimate the originality of the book. Fourteen-year-olds, even sensitive, intelligent, middle-class fourteen-year-olds, generally do not think that success is a sham, and if they sometimes feel unhappy, or angry, or out of it, it's not because they think most other people are phonies. The whole emotional burden of adolescence is that you don't *know* why you feel unhappy, or angry, or out of it. The appeal of *The Catcher in the Rye*, what makes it addictive, is that it provides you with a reason. It gives a content to chemistry.

Holden talks like a teen-ager, and this makes it natural to assume that he thinks like a teen-ager as well. But like all the wise boys and girls in Salinger's fiction—like Esme and Teddy and the many brilliant Glasses—Holden thinks like an adult. No teen-ager (and very few grownups, for that matter) sees through other human beings as quickly, as clearly, or as unforgivingly as he does. Holden is a demon of verbal incision. He sums people up like a novelist:

> *He was always asking you to do him a big favor. You take a very hand-some guy, or a guy that thinks he's a real hot-shot, and they're always asking you to do them a big favor. Just because they're crazy about them-selves, they think you're crazy about them, too, and that you're just dying to do them a favor. It's sort of funny, in a way.*

> *She was blocking up the whole goddam traffic in the aisle. You could tell she liked to block up a lot of traffic. This waiter was waiting for her to move out of the way, but she didn't even notice him. It was funny. You could tell the waiter didn't like her much, you could tell even the Navy guy didn't like her much, even though he was dating her. And I didn't like her much. Nobody did. You had to feel sort of sorry for her, in a way.*

*His name was George or something—I don't even remember—and he
went to Andover. Big, big deal. You should've seen him when old Sally
asked him how he liked the play. He was the kind of a phony that have
to give themselves room when they answer somebody's question. He
stepped back, and stepped right on the lady's foot behind him. He probably broke every toe in her body. He said the play itself was no masterpiece, but that the Lunts, of course, were absolute angels. Angels. For
Chrissake. Angels. That killed me.*

"*You had to feel sort of sorry for her, in a way.*" The secret to Holden's
authority as a narrator is that he never lets anything stand by itself. He
always tells you what to think. He has everyone pegged. That's why he's
so funny. But *The New Yorker's* editors were right: Holden isn't an ordinary teen-ager—he's a prodigy. He seems (and this is why his character
can be so addictive) to have something that few people ever consistently attain: an attitude toward life.

The moral of the book can seem to be that Holden will outgrow his
attitude, and this is probably the lesson that most of the ninth-grade
teachers who assign *The Catcher in the Rye* hope to impart to their students—that alienation is just a phase. But people don't outgrow
Holden's attitude, or not completely, and they don't want to outgrow it,
either, because it's a fairly useful attitude to have. One goal of education
is to teach people to want the rewards life has to offer, but another goal
is to teach them a modest degree of contempt for those rewards, too. In
American life, where—especially if you are a sensitive and intelligent
member of the middle class—the rewards are constantly being adver-
tised as yours for the taking, the feeling of disappointment is a lot more
common than the feeling of success, and if we didn't learn how not to
care our failures would destroy us. Giving *The Catcher in the Rye* to your
children is like giving them a layer of psychic insulation.

That it might end up on the syllabus for ninth-grade English was
probably close to the last thing Salinger had in mind when he wrote the
book. He wasn't trying to expose the spiritual poverty of a conformist

culture; he was writing a story about a boy whose little brother has died. Holden, after all, isn't unhappy because he sees that people are phonies; he sees that people are phonies because he is unhappy. What makes his view of other people so cutting and his disappointment so unappeasable is the same thing that makes Hamlet's feelings so cutting and unappeasable: his grief. Holden is meant, it's true, to be a kind of intuitive moral genius. (So, presumably, is Hamlet.) But his sense that everything is worthless is just the normal feeling people have when someone they love dies. Life starts to seem a pathetically transparent attempt to trick them into forgetting about death; they lose their taste for it.

What drew Salinger to this plot? Holden Caulfield first shows up in Salinger's work in 1941, in a story entitled "Slight Rebellion off Madison," which features a character called Holden (he is not the narrator) and his girlfriend, Sally Hayes. (The story was bought by *The New Yorker* but not published until 1946.) And there are characters named Holden Caulfield in other stories that Salinger produced in the mid-forties. But most of *The Catcher in the Rye* was written after the war, and although it seems odd to call Salinger a war writer, both his biographers, Ian Hamilton and Paul Alexander, think that the war was what made Salinger Salinger, the experience that darkened his satire and put the sadness into his humor.

Salinger spent most of the war with the 4th Infantry Division, where he was in a counter-intelligence unit. He landed at Utah Beach in the fifth hour of the D-Day invasion, and ended up in the middle of some of the bloodiest fighting of the liberation—in Hurtgen Forest and then in the Battle of the Bulge, in the winter of 1944. The 4th Division suffered terrible casualties in those engagements, and Salinger, by his own account, in letters he wrote at the time, was traumatized. He fought for eleven months during the advance on Berlin, and by the summer of 1945, after the German surrender, he seems to have had a nervous breakdown. He checked himself into an Army hospital in Nuremberg. Shortly after he was released, and while he was still in Europe, he wrote the first story narrated by Holden Caulfield himself, the real beginning of *The Catcher in the Rye*. It was called "I'm Crazy." (It was published in *Collier's* in December, 1945.)

"A Perfect Day for Bananafish," published a little more than two years later, is, of course, the story that both introduced Seymour Glass, the oldest and most improbably gifted of the improbably gifted Glass children, and finished him off, since Salinger has Seymour kill himself on the last page. If we know Seymour only from the later stories in the Glass saga, in which he appears as a kind of saint—"Franny" and "Raise High the Roof Beam, Carpenters" (both published in *The New Yorker* in 1955), "Zooey" (1957), "Seymour: An Introduction" (1959), and "Hapworth 16, 1924" (1965), Salinger's last published work—we are likely to assume that he killed himself because the world's stupidity had made him crazy. But in "A Perfect Day for Bananafish" it is clear that Seymour kills himself because the war has made him crazy. He has just been discharged from an Army hospital, and his behavior in the story isn't saintly or visionary or engagingly eccentric; it's nutty and, in the end, psychotic. Seymour is a war casualty. So, much more obviously, is the unnamed protagonist of "For Esme—with Love and Squalor," an American soldier who is befriended by a thirteen-year-old English girl just before he goes off to take part in the D-Day invasion. *The Catcher in the Rye* was a best-seller when it came out, in 1951, but its reception as some sort of important cultural statement didn't happen until the mid-fifties, when people started talking about "alienation" and "conformity" and "the youth culture"—the time of *Howl* and *Rebel Without a Cause* and Elvis Presley's first records. It is as a hero of that culture that Holden Caulfield has survived. But *The Catcher in the Rye* is not a novel of the nineteen-fifties; it's a novel of the nineteen-forties. And it is not a celebration of youth. It is a book about loss and a world gone wrong.

By the mid-nineteen-fifties, Salinger had disappeared down his New Hampshire rabbit hole. *The New Yorker's* rejection of *The Catcher in the Rye* plainly had no effect on him as a writer. Criticized for creating a family with four precocious children and for writing in a style that

# Smile Makers®

In the US:     call 888-800-SMILE
www.SmileMakers.com

In Canada:    call 888-456-SMILE
www.SmileMakersCanada.com

SPS53-#209620

OPTIMUS

TRANS FORMERS

DARK OF THE MOON

© Hasbro. All Rights Reserved.

drew attention to itself, he proceeded to create a family with *seven* precocious children, and to produce, in "Zooey" and "Seymour," works of supreme literary exhibitionism.

"Zooey" and "Seymour" are exhibitionistic because the emotional current driving the characters has become unmoored from anything that has actually happened to them. They are not thrown into a state of higher intensity by trauma or by grief. They are just in a state of higher intensity. In "Franny," Franny Glass's spiritual crisis is a kind of screen shielding the rather mundane circumstance that she has been made pregnant by a man who she realizes will remain, all his life, a pompous English major. But in "Zooey," published two years later, Franny's spiritual crisis is genuine, because, apparently, having spiritual crises is the price one pays for being a Glass in this lousy world. There is no suggestion of pregnancy. We get Seymour's Fat Lady instead. After 1955, Salinger stopped writing stories, in the conventional sense. He seemed to lose interest in fiction as an art form—perhaps he thought there was something manipulative or inauthentic about literary device and authorial control. His presence began to dissolve into the world of his creation. He let the puppets take over the theatre.

*The New Yorker* had no trouble publishing "Zooey" (which remains the longest piece of fiction it has ever run) and "Seymour." The magazine seems to have got over its anxiety about credibility and transparency. Salinger changed *The New Yorker's* aesthetic, at a time when *The New Yorker's* aesthetic was the gold standard for short fiction, and that is one testament to the impact he has had on American writing. There are many more. Philip Roth's early stories, collected in "Goodbye, Columbus," have something of Salinger's voice and comic timing, and it is hard to read Roth's later funny, kvetchy, mournful monologuists without imagining Holden Caulfield and Zooey Glass as ancestral presences.

Still, Roth was not trying to rewrite *The Catcher in the Rye*; Salinger's complete lack of irony could hardly have appealed to him. But other writers have tried, at least one in every decade since it appeared. Sylvia Plath made a version of it for girls, in *The Bell Jar* (1963); Hunter Thompson produced one for people who couldn't believe that Nixon was President and Jim Morrison was dead, in *Fear and Loathing in Las Vegas* (1971). Jay McInerney's *Bright Lights, Big City* (1984) was the downtown edition; Dave Eggers' *A Heartbreaking Work of Staggering Genius* (2000) is the MTV one. Many books featuring interestingly unhappy young people have been published since *The Catcher in the Rye*, of course, and some of them were written by people who no doubt regarded Salinger as a model and an influence. But that doesn't make those books *Catcher in the Rye* rewrites. The bar is set a good deal higher than that, and the reason has to do with the Salinger mystique.

Why Salinger chose to drop out of sight and then out of print is his own business, and it probably ought to have nothing to do with the way people read the work that he did publish. But it does. Readers can't help it. Salinger's withdrawal is one of the things behind, for example, Holden Caulfield's transformation from a fictional character into a culture hero: it helped to confirm the belief that Holden's unhappiness was less personal than it appears—that it was really some sort of protest against modern life. It also helped to confirm the sense, encouraged by Salinger's own later manner, that there was no distinction between Salinger and his characters—that if you ran into Salinger at the Cornish, New Hampshire, post office (which is where his stalkers generally seem to have run into him) it would be exactly like running into Holden Caulfield or Seymour Glass. By dropping out, Salinger glamorized his misfits, for to be a misfit who can also write like J. D. Salinger—a Holden Caulfield who publishes in *The New Yorker*—must be very glamorous indeed.

This is why the narrator in a *Catcher in the Rye* rewrite is always a magazine writer. So, of course, is the author of the *Catcher in the Rye* rewrite, and the author and the narrator are separated by barely a hair. The model for the narrator is no longer Holden Caulfield. And it is not J. D. Salinger imagined as Holden Caulfield. It is the author imagined as J. D. Salinger imagined as Holden Caulfield. You can't, in other words, rewrite *The Catcher in the Rye* simply by telling the story of an unhappy teen-ager and updating the cultural references, or transposing the events to a different city, or changing the sex of the protagonist. You have to reproduce the Salinger mystique, because the mystique has become part of what *The Catcher in the Rye* is. The end product of the ideal Salinger rewrite isn't a Salinger story. It's Salinger. To rewrite the story of Holden Caulfield you have to become a melancholy genius, too. You have to be your own sorrow king.

The book that seems, in some ways, closest to Salinger's is Plath's. Plath belonged to the first generation of *Catcher in the Rye* readers. She read it sometime before 1953, when she spent part of a summer in New York City as a twenty-year-old intern at *Mademoiselle*. (When she arrived at the magazine, she asked to be assigned to interview Salinger, whose *Nine Stories* had just been published. She got Elizabeth Bowen instead.) That internship and her subsequent breakdown and hospitalization became the basis, ten years later, for *The Bell Jar*.

Reviewers noticed the similarity to *The Catcher in the Rye* immediately, and there are echoes of Holden's voice and story in the voice and story of Plath's heroine, Esther Greenwood. But Plath was not merely borrowing. She must have felt that an aspiring magazine writer in New York City in 1953, when Salinger was in his prime, would naturally see life in a Salingeresque way. When Esther says, for example, "I'm stupid about executions" (1953 is the year the Rosenbergs were executed), she is adopting a Caulfield attitude. Esther's vague loathing of sex is a loathing learned partly from *The Catcher in the Rye*; her obsession with madness and suicide is partly the obsession of an admirer of "Teddy" and "A Perfect Day for Bananafish." In other ways, though, *The Bell Jar* and *The Catcher in the Rye* are very different books, and the difference can be summed up by saying that no reader has ever wanted to be Esther Greenwood. Holden (despite the confusion of the Harcourt Brace executive) is not crazy; he tells his story from a sanatorium (where he has gone because of a fear that he has t.b.), not a mental hospital. The brutality of the world makes him sick. It makes Esther insane.

*The Bell Jar*, too, has become a staple of ninth-grade English, an officially approved text for adolescents, a book about the culture of youth. The later *Catcher in the Rye* rewrites—Thompson's and McInerney's and Eggers'—are not yet canonical in this way. People don't read them because their parents recommended them. They read them for the same reason they listen to alternative rock or go to see *Pulp Fiction* six times—because these are things that teach them an attitude. They are sensibility manuals; they show what sort of unhappiness is in style this decade.

*Catcher in the Rye* rewrites are all constructed on roughly the same pattern: a trauma triggered by a death (in Thompson's book, it's the death of the sixties), followed by an episode of emotional regression and a kind of shadow war, mostly in the head, with the rest of the world. They share with *The Catcher in the Rye* and *The Bell Jar* a fuzzy Christian thematics about salvation, redemption, and rebirth, and they draw heavily on the Salinger and Plath catalogue: mummies, fetuses, comas, sensational headlines, perversions, botched sex, suicide attempts, suicides, death fantasies, deaths. The narrators have a mordant contempt for everyone and everything, including themselves. The books are funny, but they are about loss and frustration and defeat. And each one seemed to hit a generational nerve, as though no one had ever told that story, or sounded those notes, before. What makes their melancholy so irresistible?

We think of nostalgia as an emotion that grows with age, but, like most emotions, it is keenest when we are young. Is there any nostalgia more powerful than the feelings of a third grader revisiting his or her kindergarten classroom? Those tiny chairs, the old paste jars, the cubbies where we stuffed our extra sweaters—we want to climb back into that world, but we're third graders now, much too large. We've fallen off the carrousel. Although "youth" is supposed to mean an enthusiasm for change, young people don't want change any more than anyone else does, and possibly less. What they secretly want is what Holden wants: they want the world to be like the Museum of Natural History, with everything frozen exactly the way it was the first day they encountered it.

A great deal of "youth culture"—that is, the stuff that younger people actually consume, as opposed to the stuff that older people consume (like *Lord of the Flies*) in order to learn about "youth"—plays to this feeling of loss. You go to a dance where a new pop song is playing, and for the rest of your life hearing that song triggers the same emotion. It comes on the radio, and you think, *That's when things were truly fine*. You want to hear it again and again. You have become addicted. Youth culture acquires its poignancy through time, and so thoroughly that you can barely see what it is in itself. It's just, permanently, "your song," your story. When people who grew up in the nineteen-fifties give *The Catcher in the Rye* to their kids, it's like showing them an old photo album: *That's me*.

It isn't, of course. Maybe, in fact, the nostalgia of youth culture is completely spurious. Maybe it invites you to indulge in bittersweet memories of a childhood you never had, an idyll of Beach Boys songs and cheeseburgers and convertibles and teen-age crushes which has been constructed by pop songs and television shows and movies, and bears very little relation to any experience of your own. But, whether or not the emotion is spurious, people have it. It is the romantic certainty, which all these books seduce you with, that somehow, somewhere, something was taken away from you, and you cannot get it back. Once, you did ride a carrousel. It seemed as though it would last forever.

PART IV:

FAMILY, FRIENDS, AND FANATICS

*Excerpt from*
# Dream Catcher: A Memoir

MARGARET SALINGER

M y father let me come with him to the Dartmouth College Library, where he browsed the stacks and sometimes borrowed books. It was a sanctuary of cool in the summer and cozy warmth in the winter and smelled wonderfully of dust, lemon oil, and old leather. You entered through a revolving door, exciting to begin with, and found yourself in a vast, quiet space with, I couldn't believe it, a huge black-and-white tile floor like almost endless chessboard. Daddy taught me how to play checkers, which I liked if I won, and chess, which took too long, especially when the only thing I really liked was to move my bishops—tall, oval-headed things with slits for mouths— on the diagonal. While Daddy went about his business in the stacks, I happily played games of patterns on the black-and-white squares.

At the end of the squares, just off the main hall, students sat reading at long tables by lamplight surrounded by a cozy glow. I hopscotched back across the main floor to look at the huge murals on the walls. I think they were of Indians, but I wouldn't show too much interest. It would have been a betrayal of the unwritten Salinger code of good taste. My father had made it stingingly clear that murals, as an art form, were beneath contempt. Ditto anything "primitive," like the African art at my friend Rachel's house. For him, there are those such as his "wondrous Chinese, and novel Hindus with their "fine and subtle minds"* and delicate features; and then there are the primitive, the physically strong, the great unwashed, including Negroes, Hispanics, and the vast majority of Caucasians. He has the taste in physiognomy of an Hasidic Jew; the paler and frailer and more studious looking, the more valued the being. For my father, there is something most definitely suspect—not kosher—about physical robustness. When I brought home an A in Spanish one year, he said, "Oh, terrific, now you're studying the language of the ignorant!"

It's not that in his day these were atypical cultural prejudices, but they are strange attitudes, it seems to me, for someone who considers himself to be well read, to think Spanish-speaking writers and poets and painters, for example, are ignorant. Though my father considers himself to be widely read, I discovered as I grew older that what he is, in fact, is deeply and passionately read in very selected areas. He becomes an expert in whatever he falls in love with, whatever he is passionate about, and leaves the rest untouched.

His worldview is, essentially, a product of the movies of his day. To my father, all Spanish speakers are Puerto Rican washerwomen, or the toothless, grinning gypsy types in a Marx Brothers movie. Once, when he was criticizing me about my black friends in high school—"coarse" was what he called my friends and me—he said that blacks had no subtlety of humor at all. "Wasn't it all that crap?" he said as he put on a big stupid grin and rolled his eyes and waved his hands. I said, "Dad, that's in the movies, they don't do that in real life amongst themselves. That's for the camera, because that is what white people want to see." His expression changed and he said thoughtfully, "No . . . of course you're right. That makes sense." He is by no means a heartfelt bigot who will hold to an idea in the face of evidence to the contrary. But his frame of

---

* "Hapworth."

reference is Hollywood in the twenties, thirties, and forties. When I was a teenager and announced my engagement to my karate teacher, who was black, my father was terribly concerned, but for fictional rather than real-life reasons, of which there were plenty; e.g., you've only known the guy for a few months, you aren't out of school, he doesn't have a job except teaching karate and the occasional guitar gig, and so on. Instead, he cautioned me, saying he saw a movie once called *The Jazz Man* or something where a white woman married a black singer and "it worked out terribly."

He used to borrow movies from the Dartmouth film library, and we often stopped there after a trip to the regular library. But someone at the film library apparently let it be known which movies J. D. Salinger borrowed, and he's never since darkened their door. It's not that he had cause whatsoever to be embarrassed about his choice of movies; it was the violation of his privacy that so infuriated him.

After Daddy finished his business at the libraries, he'd take me to Lou's or the Village Green for a tuna fish sandwich and french fries. Then we'd either go next door to the Dartmouth Bookstore or we'd go to do his marketing at the Hanover Co-op. He loved the fresh food but hated to go there because he stood a good chance of running into someone he knew and, to be polite, would have to stop and talk. The dreaded human encounter. I liked the Co-op better than the local stores because it didn't smell like ammonia and old sour-milk sponges or death at the meat counter, the way the others did, like the old wooden-floored IGA or the Grand Union with its S & H green stamps booklets we filled but never redeemed. When, years later, Purity Supreme, which he referred to as Puberty Supreme, built a megastore in Lebanon, he gave up the Co-op, even though he liked the Co-op's food better. He preferred the impersonal atmosphere.

On the way home from a trip to Hanover, I mostly just looked out the window because if you engaged my father in conversation while driving, he'd turn and look right at you, forgetting he was at the wheel. He'd swerve back onto the road or into his lane at the last instant. It was even worse if you were in the backseat. He'd turn his head all the way around to listen to you. If my brother made a peep, I shot him my most murderous look that said, "Shut up, will you. Do you want to get us all killed?" In an era of two lane highways—your lane and the traffic coming toward you—he was an absolutely terrifying passer. When someone ahead of us was going too slowly, being a "road hog" (one of his favorite movies is one where W. C. Fields inherits a million dollars and spends it all smashing, one by one, into the cars of offensive drivers), he would pull up to the offending car's bumper, lurk there at forty-five miles an hour or so until he reached what was technically a passing zone, and then pull out to pass. We'd careen down the wrong side of the road heading straight for an oncoming car. He'd duck back in just in time. In the Jeep it was always dicey whether it would have enough pickup to pass the car in front before hitting the oncoming one. Terrifying. My hands, he noticed, were never unclenched as we drove. He thought it was just a habit of mine.

Right by the beaver pond, before the Plainfield town line, a solitary road sign said NO PASSING. "Will you look at that," he's say, "tsking" his teeth. "What would Miss Chapman say? 'No Pissing!' Can you imagine?" I fell out in giggles every time he said it.

# *Margaret Salinger, Daughter of J. D. Salinger, Discusses Her New Book,* Dream Catcher

Interview with Susan Stamberg on NPR's *Morning Edition*

**BOB EDWARDS,** host: J. D. Salinger, who wrote *The Catcher in the Rye*, is one of America's most read authors, despite the fact that his last work was published in 1965 and he's lived in seclusion for the past half century. Two biographies have come out in recent years, plus a memoir from an ex-lover. Now Salinger's daughter offers further testimony on life in that isolating house in Cornish, New Hampshire. Special correspondent Susan Stamberg reports.

**SUSAN STAMBERG** reporting: J. D. Salinger makes beautiful soups, perfect eggs, too, according to his daughter and he's a superb dog whistler. Margaret Salinger's earliest memories are warm.

**MS. MARGARET SALINGER:** When he would come back from his trips or come back from a long spell of writing or even come back at the end of the day, it was, 'Daddy's home.' He was a really wonderfully, huggy dad. You know, his tweed jacket smelled wonderful. You could hide your head in when he told a scary story. It's somewhat like being in love. You loved the way somebody's shirt smells.

**Stamberg:** And his bulk and Subrani(ph) pipe tobacco and the apple wood smoke from his firewood. But Peggy Salinger's memoir, *Dream Catcher*, begins with this sentence: 'I grew up in a world nearly devoid of living people.' And in those isolated New Hampshire woods, J. D. Salinger ran his family with increasingly strict rules and harsh judgments.

**Ms. Salinger:** Laughing at something in the movies that he doesn't think is funny, that's the end of a relationship.

**Stamberg:** Peggy Salinger, who is 44 with huge eyes and lovely smile, says her father had broken off many relationships. She hasn't been in touch with him for two years. Salinger's agent says he will have no comment on her memoir. His life, Peggy says, has grown narrower and narrower. The daughter sees that in his writing. In 1951, *Catcher in the Rye* embraced readers, took us into the struggling world of young Holden Caulfield. After that, Salinger made us honorary members of the Glass family, the intense, loving, brilliant inhabitants of a series of short stories. Over time, Peggy Salinger says the stories become more and more insular, tough to follow. The last one published, "Hapwood 16, 1924," it came out 35 years ago, is an interminable letter home from a seven-year-old camper genius who memorizes 25 new, difficult words a day and then keeps on using them. Peggy Salinger finds "Hapwood" hard to read in many ways.

**Ms. Salinger:** It is a sermon and it's one I have heard over and over growing up, I mean, about what you should read, what are good books, what are bad books, how to breathe, how to eat. There's not one recommended practice that didn't send me back to being sort of 13 and slouching and rolling my eyes and saying, 'OK. OK. OK,' you know?

**Stamberg:** Difficult doesn't begin to describe the childhood Peggy Salinger unfolds in her memoir, complete with notes she passed in seventh grade. 'My mom came at me like a jackhammer,' she writes, 'my father like a guillotine.' She says her mother was unstable, broke down, beat her brutally. The father either off alone writing—to interrupt was sacrilege—or if around, gave Peggy and her brother Matthew his interminable sermons and judgments. Peggy left home for boarding school at 12, had terrible emotional and health problems, a suicide attempt, wonderful friends who pulled her through and something else.

**MS. SALINGER:** Years of therapy.

(SOUNDBITE OF LAUGHTER)

**MS. SALINGER:** Years of therapy.

**STAMBERG:** Married now with a son in elementary school near Boston, Peggy Salinger has produced a memoir that reveals the private world of a man who has made privacy a career. Why?

**MS. SALINGER:** My real motivation was understanding, not, 'Oh, you're bad,' the blame's here. You can't spend that many hours—I mean, maybe you can. I don't . . .

**STAMBERG:** You mean if it's only out of revenge.

**MS. SALINGER:** Yeah.

**STAMBERG:** See to me, if somebody said to me, 'Is it a "Daddy Dearest," I don't think so,' I think it's a, 'Daddy, why?'

**MS. SALINGER:** Yes. Yes.

**STAMBERG:** She said she wrote to support her family financially. Her advance reportedly was $250,000 and emotionally to examine her past so she doesn't repeat it raising her own child. Now Peggy Salinger reads her father's best-known work in a new way.

**Ms. Salinger:** Holden said, 'I keep picturing all these little kids playing some game in this big field of rye and all, thousands of little kids, and nobody's around—nobody big. I mean, except me. And I'm standing on the edge of some crazy cliff. What I have to do I have to catch everybody if they start to go over the cliff. I mean, if they're running and they don't know where they're going, I have to come out from somewhere and catch them. That's all I do all day. I'd just be the catcher in the rye and all. I know it's crazy, but that's the only thing I'd really like to be.'

When I read this passage as an adult with a child of my own, my first reaction was outrage, not at Holden. It's a nice dream for a boy to have, but outrage at the fact that I was once one of those kids. Where are the grownups? Why are those kids allowed to play so close to the edge of a cliff? And where are the responsible adults who should build a secure place for those kids to play, or a fence at least so that some young boy like Holden or some young girl like me doesn't have to engage in perpetual rescue.

**Stamberg:** Peggy Salinger graduated with honors from Brandeis, went on to Oxford, worked five years as a car mechanic, is getting a degree from Harvard Divinity School where she trained as a hospital chaplain.

**Ms. Salinger:** I give people permission to be crabby, to complain, to kvetch, you know, to talk about the Red Sox. People are so phenomenally alone in hospitals these days. It's amazing the people who have no family.

**STAMBERG:** So Peggy Salinger goes, volunteers, to help someone through a psych evaluation or a sexually abused woman who must have intrusive examinations.

**MS. SALINGER:** If there's the trust there, I can say, 'Look, I will watch. I will make sure nothing happens.' And I don't know. It's lovely to feel that some of the lousy breaks you've gotten turn into something that can help somebody else. It wipes the slate clean.

**STAMBERG:** It seems that Margaret A. Salinger has herself become a kind of catcher in the rye. Her memoir is called *Dream Catcher*. I'm Susan Stamberg, NPR News, Washington.

**EDWARDS:** This is Morning Edition from NPR News. I'm Bob Edwards.

1998, revised 2006

# Excerpt from
# At Home in the World

JOYCE MAYNARD

**Author's Note:**

*The excerpt that follows, from my memoir,* At Home in the World, *tells a part of the story of my relationship with J. D. Salinger, embarked upon in 1972, when I was eighteen, and severed almost exactly a year later.*

*For twenty-five years, I did not write or speak of what happened then. The memoir I published in 1998—telling the story of this experience, and the way in which it shaped the years that followed— was met with contemptuous critical response on the part of a vast majority of the literary establishment, charging me with having violated the privacy of a man whose place in the firmament of writers appeared close to that of a god. The attacks, not only on my book but on my character, were brutal, intensely personal, and relentless, and even now—several years later— hardly a week goes by in which someone or other, usually an individual who has not read my memoir, remarks to me, "Oh, you're the one who wrote the book about Salinger."*

*In fact, I wrote a book about my life, not his. The book I wrote—an excerpt of which appears here—tells a story of shame and secret-keeping, and perhaps of exploitation, but it is a curious phenomenon to me that a*

259

*reader, hearing the story of a fifty-three year-old man, sending letters to an eighteen-year-old, would conclude that it was the woman she became who ultimately exploited him, by revealing her story.*

*Evidently it appeared to many of my critics that the sole significance of my life had been sleeping with a great man. This was disheartening, not only personally, but for what that portrayal of me and my story indicated about those writers' perceptions of women. One day I hope some feminist scholar will examine the way in which a woman's recounting of her history is so often ridiculed as self-absorbed and fundamentally unimportant. I believe it is a measure of the hostility toward women still deeply woven into the texture of our culture that when a female writer gives voice to the struggles that are the stuff of women's lives, she is so often dismissed as emotional, self-indulgent, and trivial. One need not look far for examples of male writers who have written freely and with no small measure of self-absorption about the territory of personal experience, who are praised for their courage and searing honesty.*

*I did, however, receive affirmation of the work I'd written. I received letters from women and men well-acquainted with shame and secret-keeping in their own lives, thanking me for my willingness to speak openly of experiences they had supposed were theirs alone, or simply too painful to speak of. I heard from women and young girls who had given themselves over to relationships with more powerful older men, and known the damage of their rejection or—equally harmful—the cost of transforming themselves into someone they were not, for the sake of that man's love. My story might have involved any man of vastly greater power to myself, any child who ever took upon herself responsibility for an alcoholic parent's sobriety, or a family's happiness. It might have been their story, and often they told me it was.*

*Not wholly surprising to me were letters I received from three other women telling me they had engaged in correspondences with J. D. Salinger eerily like my own—one, within weeks of his dismissal of me. I have no doubt these women's stories were true. They quoted lines from Salinger's letters to them nearly identical to ones in his letters to me, whose contents had never been made public. Like me, these women had been approached by Salinger when they were eighteen years old. Like me, they once believed him to be the wisest man, their soul mate, their destiny. Like me, they had eventually experienced his complete and devastating rejection. Also like me, they had maintained, for years, the belief that they were obligated to keep the secret—out of fear of the very form of condemnation I was now receiving for having refused to do so.*

*Based on what was so often said about me for breaking my own silence, the fears of these women to speak of their experiences appear justified. Even now, it seems, there are many who would say it remains a woman's obligation to protect the secrets of a man for the simple reason that he demands it. More than that, it appears to be a matter of some dispute whether a woman has the right to tell the truth about her life— and if she does, whether the story of a woman's life is viewed as significant or valuable.*

*The pursuit of privacy has been portrayed by many as evidence of purity of character, just as the refusal to bow to the genteel notion of secret-keeping has been depicted as inappropriate and invasive—a profound betrayal of trust. I have come to believe that sometimes what is truly inappropriate and invasive are certain activities on the part of the very individuals who will later invoke their sacred privacy as a cloak for the concealment of their behavior. To suggest that an individual enjoys immunity from scrutiny or accountability for his actions because he holds some position of power (whether as a priest, a professor, a politician or a man of great wealth and accomplishment) is to clear the way for the exploitation of the very people most vulnerable to influence and manipulation—generally, the young. There lies the true betrayal of trust. It is yet another instance of indignity that the victims of these individuals are so often blamed and humiliated themselves when they give voice to their experience.*

*So long as we question a woman's right to her own story, we allow the perpetuation of the same dangerous and damaging patterns generations before us experienced. The most powerful tool most of us possess is our own voice. Take that away, and what do we have?*

When I was 18, I wrote a magazine article that changed my life. The piece was called "An 18-Year-Old Looks Back on Life." It was published in *The New York Times Magazine* on April 23, 1972, with a photograph of me on the cover. In it I described growing up in the 60s, expressing a profound sense of world-weariness and alienation. I spoke of wanting to move to the country and get away from the world.

This was only part of my story. I had grown up in the household of brilliant and ferociously ambitious parents, both sidelined in their own creative careers, who coached me from the earliest childhood to achieve great things in the world. Before I knew how to form alphabet letters, I gave dictation. I spoke: my mother wrote down what I said and told me how to make it better. Soon enough she gave me a typewriter. By the time I was 12, I was entering writing contests. By the time I was 14, I'd sold my first piece to *Seventeen* magazine. It was my work for *Seventeen*, sent by me to the editor in chief of *The New York Times*, in the spring of my freshman year at Yale, that led to the cover story in the magazine.

In that article, I talk about the national events that shaped my generation's worldview—the Cuban missile crisis, the Kennedy assassination. "Like overanxious patients in analysis, we treasure the traumas of our childhood," I write. But I never mention the real traumas of my childhood: my father's drinking, our family's inability to discuss it. I do not mention my obsession with dieting and being thin, though this is another issue that has haunted me for at least a year, probably longer. When I talk about sex, I revert to the third person, speaking of "the embarrassment of virginity" I observe on campus—unable to admit that the embarrassed virgin is myself.

Within 24 hours of the publication of my piece in the *Times*, I'm getting phone calls from magazine editors inviting me to come into the city to have lunch. Under normal circumstances, I would pick up my mail at the Yale Station post office, where I have a box. But on the Tuesday morning following that weekend I open the door of my dormitory room to find a couple of mail sacks filled with letters from all over the country. Hundreds. A movie director invites me to the Palm Court at the Plaza hotel. Several editors write to ask if I have a book contract. Senator Hubert Humphrey writes to tell me I'm a credit to my generation.

Most of the letters are from young men around my age who tell me they are my soul mate. They listen to the same music, feel the same feelings I did growing up, the same alienation, the same longing for love.

There is this other letter. I could easily have missed it. After I read this one, none of the others matters. The return address says Cornish, New Hampshire, a small town 60 or 70 miles northwest of the one where I grew up. The salutation reads, "Dear Miss Maynard." The author of this letter explains that the nature of what he says must be kept totally private. Like me, he says, he is half-Jewish, right-handed, and lives in New Hampshire. The writer says he figures I'll be getting a lot of intriguing mail in response to my article in the *Times*. He urges me to be careful before signing up for the stuff they offer me. My talent should be allowed to develop quietly and without haste, he says, rather than being plastered over the pages of a bunch of magazines.

The author of the letter concludes with apologies for taking such a dark view of things, but the fact is, he likes my writing quite a bit, and he has experienced the dangers as well as the appeal of youthful success. He signs his letter "Sincerely." The signature reads J. D. Salinger.

I am probably one of the very few people on the entire Yale campus—or any campus in 1972—who have not read *The Catcher in the Rye*. Or *Nine Stories*. In fact, I haven't read any book by Salinger. I have a general sense of his avoidance of publicity, but I know nothing of his legendary solitude. Still, the fact that a famous man has conferred approval on me thrills me. I spend a long time composing my response on my yellow legal pad. When I'm done I type it carefully.

"I will remember your advice every day of my life." I write back. "I read your letter over and over, and carried it in my pocket all day. I no longer need to read it. I know it by heart. Not just the words, but the sentiments expressed . . ."

I tell J. D. Salinger that I like to ride my bicycle into the country-side outside New Haven. I don't have many friends here. I tell him. I make dollhouse furniture. I listen to a lot of music and I draw. I don't like writing all that much. I love acting in plays. I am also working hard in my letter to maintain J. D. Salinger's high opinion of me as a writer and observer of the world. So I entertain him with stories of my world—my Yale dormitory, my English class, the dining hall, the play I'm acting in. I don't fit in very well in this place, I tell him. I do not need to pretend with this man, as I would with boys my age, that I am cool or knowledgeable about things that make me enormously uncom-fortable. Where, all year, I have tried to act like other girls, with this person about whom I know virtually nothing I feel I can speak in something approaching my real voice.

J. D. Salinger's first letter was dated April 25. His next letter is dated May 2. He writes to me from a plane headed for New York City, rather than waiting till his return to answer my letter to him. He thanks me for writing and calls my letter nice—twice. He offers a kind of regretful apology about his compulsion for privacy. He cautions that a glimpse of fame can distract a writer, so it might be just as well if I like acting better. His guess, though, is that what I will always be is a writer. He tells me never to stop writing whatever it is I feel I must write about, the things I love writing about, and to pay no attention to any voices from within myself, or from the outside world, that might cause me to ques-tion what I'm doing.

He signs off with a weather report and the news that he and his 12-year-old son, Matthew, recently attended a baseball game at Dartmouth. Reading this, I get a comforting picture of J. D. Salinger as a man who takes his boy to a ball game: an all-American dad.

I write back immediately. I tell him about my sense of panic that I will never again be able to produce another piece of good writing. He also writes the day he gets my letter to say he doesn't see how this thing I have could ever be extinguished, no matter what the future holds for me. I am a girl, he says, who will make a wonderful life for herself. A life like nobody else's. I'm a girl with the world on a string.

"Dear Mr. Salinger," I write (in a letter that has crossed paths with the one in which he instructed me to call him Jerry). "What is a day in your life like? I don't mean to intrude. I am not a scoop-seeking fan, just—I hope you'll believe me—a friend who has slightly but trustingly opened the door herself, and feels the one on the other side should do the same."

His answer comes swiftly, as they always do. A big part of his days, he says, is spent in the practice of homeopathic medicine, which he applies on his children and himself. He talks with a certain ruefulness about the way his study of homeopathy, like the studies of religion and mysticism, has taken him away from his writing for long periods. But he takes comfort from the understanding that eventually the things that interest him are likely to show up in his fiction.

He offers me a list of the things he loves and cares about that fill his day: Jane Austen, vaudeville, his daughter's basketball playing, Hui Neng, the neighbors on *I Love Lucy*, samadhi, Bert Parks. Among the items named on his list is myself.

I continue to attend my classes that spring. I write papers and study for exams. But I am not engaged in any of it anymore. I act in another play—a jazzed-up production of *Measure for Measure*. I ride the train to New York City more than once on the invitation of the various magazine and book editors who have called, suggesting that we meet at some expensive restaurant and discuss some project that would have thrilled me only weeks earlier. I am invited to read for the role in *The Exorcist*. But the part goes to Linda Blair.

I have lunch with an editor at *Mademoiselle*, and the editor of *McCall's* and an editor at Random House. Within a couple of weeks, I have signed a contract with Doubleday for more money than my father ever earned in a year of teaching at the University of New Hampshire. I am going to write my memoir.

My days now revolve around my trips to the post office to pick up my letters from J. D. Salinger.

He wonders if I am familiar with the word "landsman"—and I am. It's a word my mother used interchangeably with our family phrase "one of ours." Literally, a landsman is a person who comes from the same place, back in the Old Country. A landsman is someone with whom you find a connection of the heart and soul. Jerry tells me we are landsmen, he and I.

I write back, as always, the day his letter arrives. "Oh yes, I know the word landsmen well, the people to whom it refers very little—well, landsmen are, to me, a rare and valuable group of just a few. Finding one makes me happier than I can say."

On the surface of things we could hardly seem more different. That he's 35 years older is just the first of a very long list of differences between us. He grew up in a family of increasing privilege in New York City in the 20s and 30s. I'm a small-town girl. He fought in World War II, landing on Utah Beach on D-day. I organized a Kids for L. B. J. headquarters on our tree-lined street in Durham, New Hampshire, and later handed out daisy stickers for McCarthy. He has been married before—twice. I have kissed one boy my whole life.

Then there's the huge matter of our attitudes toward worldly success. He was the toast of New York in his early 30s and chose to leave all that. He wants quiet and solitude. I want to go to parties full of famous people. I want to go to Hollywood. I see myself performing on Broadway, dining at Elaine's, posing for *Vogue*.

There is probably no square mile in the nation, the spring of 1972, with a higher density of bright, ambitious young people than the mile or two that constitutes the epicenter of the Yale campus. I don't know this at the time, but at the law-school dining hall, where I clear dishes for my scholarship job, one of the students whose dishes I am clearing is Bill Clinton, and another is Hillary Rodham.

With the publication of my *New York Times* article, I seem at last assured of getting all the things I've wanted for myself. Just as that's happening, along comes Jerry Salinger.

As I become familiar with his voice in the pages of his letters, I recognize a certain irony in the way that J. D. Salinger is worshiped by so many of my contemporaries. The actual man behind the beloved character of Holden Caulfield, and the characters of the Glass family, possesses contempt for much of what young people embrace on campuses like mine. Jerry despises what he perceives as the watered-down variety of Eastern mysticism popularized by the Beatles' visit to see the Maharishi in India. He barely mentions politics or world affairs—even in this election year, with the Vietnam War still going on.

All through his letters are the comings and goings of his children. His 16-year-old daughter, Peggy, goes to boarding school but comes home a lot of weekends to see her boyfriend at Dartmouth. Matthew splits his time between his mother's house up the road and his father's.

In almost every letter there is some reference to a day spent treating one or the other of his children homeopathically. I mention that on a bike ride into the countryside I've picked up a case of poison ivy. Two days later a little package arrives: a remedy he's fixed for me—spotted jewelweed saturated in high-proof vodka. I use it and the poison ivy's gone. No surprise. Jerry Salinger has secret powers, greater than those of any person I've ever known.

I read and reread his letters daily. He tells me we're cut from the same cloth, he and I, and that, more than anything, fills me with comfort and joy. The bond he has with me, he suggests, is something he has never experienced before.

On paper, all the other differences that separate us fall away, and we are simply two people with a shared vocabulary. In one of my letters, I used the word "good-sense-ish" to describe myself. Jerry tells me how he loves it that I chose that word over "sensible." I hadn't given any thought to the word when I wrote it. Now I consider every line I send him. Knowing what he likes, I tailor my language to suit him.

His letters never carry the slightest hint of sexual feeling. Although my letters to him are full of stories, I do not recount for him my experience of lying on the top bunk, listening to my roommate making love on the bed below, or my own agonized sense of unworthiness at my lack of a boyfriend. He never mentions any woman in his life, past or present, including the mother of his children.

I have now studied Jerry's photograph in the pages of an article I found in an old issue of *Life* magazine at the Yale library. I know by this time that he and I are bound to meet. But for a highly inexperienced and fearful girl, uncomfortable in her own skin, I find a certain safety in the fact that Jerry is not a physical presence in my life. What our physical separation offers him—why a man of his age would want to carry on what is now a correspondence of considerable intensity with a girl he's never met—is something I don't ask myself.

The correspondence begins in late April. For the remainder of the semester, letters go back and forth between us almost daily. By May he has given me his telephone number and suggests that I call collect.

He has a wonderfully deep, rich voice—no discernable trace of New York, although Jewishness is there in it, and intelligence, and humor, and a sense that the person speaking is doing so with a kind of self-assurance and authority few others possess.

"Is this Jerry?" I begin. "This is Joyce Maynard calling."

"What do you know? That's terrific," he says. He's a little out of breath. "I was just down at the garden, putting in the last of my tomato plants. Blackflies are murder this year. What have I been telling you? Everybody's after your blood."

I tell him what's going on in my life—the people in my classes, my teachers, my parents, exciting developments in my publishing career, meaning assignments from *McCall's* and *Newsweek* and *Mademoiselle*. "I know you didn't think it was a good idea, my taking so many jobs," I say.

"You'll weary of it before too long," he says. "I wrote for *The Saturday Evening Post* myself, in my day. The moment will come when you'll want to put a lid on all that. The kick of the thing will wear off soon enough."

I describe for Jerry the details of the junior prom I attended in Cheshire, Connecticut, the other night, which I'm writing about for *The New York Times*. I am only a year or two older than most of the participants in this prom, but my description of the event, and the one I will ultimately publish in the *Times*, suggests the perspective of a much older person, somebody for whom things like proms and boyfriends with corsages and dancing to rock 'n' roll bands and making out in cars afterward would be strictly *material*.

"The whole thing sounds altogether too poignant for this kid," he says.

In the conversations we have almost nightly now, Jerry is interested in everything I have to say. He wants to know what my room looks like. What I had for dinner. (A broccoli spear and a container of yogurt.) One thing I do not share with him is the story of my endless anxiety about my body. Lately, in fact, I have begun feeling insatiably hungry, and put on five pounds. This is making me terribly nervous.

Although we're talking regularly on the phone, the letters continue. He writes about the movies he loves best, and how, some years back, he got himself a 16-mm projector so that he could watch prints of old movies: *The Lady Vanishes*, *Lost Horizon*. With the exception of a handful of movies—*From Here to Eternity*, *The Pink Panther*—his favorites were made long before I was born.

In my dormitory, as we speak, the music playing is likely to be Led Zeppelin, James Taylor, Carole King, or the Rolling Stones. When I ask Jerry what music he listens to, he mentions somebody named Blossom Dearie, Glenn Miller, the Andrews Sisters, Benny Goodman.

The frame of reference we share is television—the one current medium where his otherwise withering critical sense seems suspended. "We're both *watchers*, you and I," he tells me—though I have already known this about myself for years, and recognized it to him too. We are not just talking about television, either.

"The worse the television—the more *American*—the more I love it," he says. We reminisce about particular episodes of *The Andy Griffith Show*: the time Andy catches Barney serenading his girlfriend over the phone at the diner, the wonderful performance of Ron Howard as Andy's son Opie. Mostly, though, Jerry hates the idea of putting children in front of a camera, and regards child actors as the worst kind of frauds, because they manage to *affect* this look of innocence without possessing anything close.

He works on his fiction daily, though he hasn't published a story since 1965. Another night, sitting on my bed eating the container of yogurt that is my dinner, I ask him why he doesn't publish his work.

"Publication is a messy business," he tells me. "You'll see what I mean one day. All those loutish, cocktail-party-going opinion givers, so ready to pass judgment. Bad enough when they do that to a writer. But when they start in on your characters—and they do—it's murder. It's just more of a damned interruption than I can tolerate anymore."

He often says how much he loves my writing. "I haven't had a pal like you before, you know, kiddo," he tells me one night. "Don't quite know what to make of it, and I don't much want to worry the thing to death. God knows what's to be done about it. I'm just happy knowing you exist on the planet of aliens. Or maybe you and I are the aliens. Either way, it would be a lonely world for me without you."

Somewhere over the course of our correspondence, Jerry starts signing his letters "love."

Early in June, classes at Yale end. Sometime in those last days I get on my bike with a copy of the classified in hand and ride around New Haven in search of an off-campus apartment to rent when I come back to school in the fall. I find one and, with money from my book advance, put down the deposit.

My editor at *The New York Times*, invites me to come talk with him. I take the train to New York again and make my way to West 43rd

Street. A pleasant, gray-haired man, he tells me that one of the members of the editorial board, Fred Hechinger, will be on leave this summer. He invites me to come and use Hechinger's office in the position of apprentice editorial writer.

I have never read the editorial page of *The New York Times*. I had been thinking I'd stay at my parents' house in Durham this summer, to be closer to Jerry, and to work on my book. But now I say yes, I'd like that job.

A totally unrelated invitation comes my way around the same time—also brought about by my recent *Times* story. A psychotherapist and his wife, who own a brownstone just off Central Park West, will be vacating their place for the summer. They send me a letter asking if I might like to stay there, rent-free, and take care of their dogs.

So now I have a job as an editorial writer and a dog-and-house-sitting position, complete with daily maid service. Before embarking on my summer plans, though, I want to spend a few days in New Hampshire. I have to meet Jerry Salinger.

My mother is very proud that I have attracted the attention of such a famous and brilliant man. Up in my bedroom, she and I lay out the pattern pieces for a dress we will make together for my trip to Cornish. It's a sleeveless A-line shift, made of stiff white broadcloth, printed with the ABC's in bright primary colors. It fastens at the shoulders with oversize mother-of-pearl buttons. I am so thin and flat-chested the dress requires no darts. I wear it with purple Mary Jane–style flats.

I am gong to ride a bus, but then we find out that my English teacher from Exeter, our good friend Mark, who has business that weekend at Dartmouth, can deliver me to Hanover, where Jerry will meet me.

I spot Jerry right away, standing on the front porch of the Hanover Inn as Mark's car pulls up. He's very tall—six feet two or three—and his height is more startling because he is so lean. He wears blue jeans and a crewneck sweater. His arm rests on a pillar on the porch of the inn with the debonair grace of a performer in a musical or a soft-shoe artist. He still has the thick hair of a young man, but where, in the pictures I've seen, it was black, he's all gray now. There is something gangly and boyish about him—long legs, long arms, and long fingers on his hands, one of which he runs through his hair as he catches sight of me, the other raised high over his head in a wave.

I jump out of the car. Jerry steps over the railing at the Hanover Inn to meet me. I run as if I were meeting an old friend I hadn't seen in years. He doesn't quite run, but there is a look of pure joy in his face.

We talk all the way to his house—a 20 minute drive over a two-lane highway, followed by winding uphill roads that go from tar to dirt.

He drives fast, and skillfully, but now and then he looks over at me sitting on the passenger side and smiles. Finally I'm here. It's hard to know where to begin. On the other hand, there seems no need to say anything. For the first time in as long as I can remember, I feel no need for speech.

"We are *landsmen*, all right," he says. My heart lifts.

We're in Cornish now. We pass the elegant Augustus Saint-Gaudens house, now a museum, and, a few miles farther up the road, he points out the house that belongs to his ex-wife, Claire, the mother of his two children. His own place lies just beyond her, at the top of a long driveway, off a winding dirt road. There's no name on his mailbox. A sign posted at the end of the driveway says PRIVATE, NO TRESSPASSING. The house is a single-story, ranch-style place with a deck that looks out to the north, a horizon dominated by an unobstructed view of Mount Ascutney. Except for Jerry's vegetable garden, the land around the house is wild, with acres of open fields below. Jerry's dachshund, Joey, lies in the sun on the deck as we pull up. "We're home," he says.

I have spent less than an hour in the company of Jerry Salinger, but I am feeling something I have never experienced before.

"I've waited a long time for you," he says. "If I didn't know better, I'd say you belong here."

"Some people could call this an awkward situation," I say. "Actually, it's the first unawkward situation I've been in for a while."

He looks at me hard. I don't look away.

We enter Jerry's house through the basement, where he keeps a giant chest freezer filled with nuts and fiddlehead ferns and vegetables from his garden. We go upstairs from there, into the living room. Inside are a couple of worn velvet couches and comfortable chairs, tables piled with books and homeopathic journals, catalogues, film reels, and newspapers. A couple of Oriental rugs cover the floor. It's a small house—a kitchen, a living room, and a bedroom each for Jerry and his two children, plus a small, cluttered room filled with books and papers where Jerry keeps his typewriter. Beyond that, though he doesn't show me this (and never will), there is a safe—as large as another room—where he keeps his unpublished manuscripts.

He has prepared lunch: whole-grain bread, a little cheddar cheese, some nuts mixed with honey. He sets two folding TV tray tables on the deck.

"I hope this is all right," he says. "I don't entertain much. Not exactly the Junior League here."

"That's a relief," I say.

After lunch, we take a walk up the hill behind Jerry's house.

I tell him about my family—my mother's frustrating career as a ghostwriter for a famous psychologist, my father's paintings, which nobody ever buys or even sees, the distance my sister has chosen to put between herself and the rest of us, and the feeling I am left with, that responsibility for my parents' happiness lies with me. Jerry listens soberly to everything I say, though he offers little personal information of his own.

"I keep catching myself talking to you as though we're veterans of all the same sorry pieces of history," he says. "I want to ask you some dopey question like where you were on V-E Day. Then I have to slap my forehead and remind myself you're a kid."

"I never really fit with my age group," I tell him.

"That makes two of us, my friend," he says. "I can take society well enough, so long as I keep my rubber gloves on. Although lately I keep feeling the irrepressible urge to cut off my ear and catch the next train to Antarctica."

"Same reason I ended up in my psychological single at Yale," I say. Then I tell him about the roommates and the bunk bed and the noises in the night.

"I'd call that a hell of an imposition," he says.

"Maybe I'm just not cut out for collegiate life."

"Try the army," he tells me.

Somewhere along the path, climbing the hill behind his house with the dog following, he takes my hand.

For dinner that night, there is more bread, a plate of steamed fiddle-head ferns, and slices of apple. Afterward, Jerry pops a bowl of popcorn for us and tosses it with tamari sauce rather than butter. He clears a spot for me on a couch and wraps a blanket around my feet. I have been coughing slightly, which worries him.

The first movie he screens for me is one of his favorites, an early Hitchcock, *The Thirty-Nine Steps*. After that one's over, he puts another reel on the projector—*The Thin Man*. I fall asleep somewhere in the middle of the second half.

Earlier that day, Jerry set my suitcase on the spare bed in Peggy's bedroom. I haven't met her yet. Now he makes sure I have everything I need. Towels. Water. A pillow. He stands next to the bed, smoothing the sheets. I have taken out my contact lenses, so I'm wearing my glasses now. I remove them and set them on the nightstand.

"Now I can't even recognize you," I say. "You could be anybody."

"I'm actually Clark Gable," he says. "Make that Gomer Pyle."

Sometime in the night Peggy comes in and lies down on the single bed beside mine. When I wake up, she's still asleep. I put on my jeans and T-shirt and go out into the kitchen.

Jerry is already up. He serves us a breakfast of Birds Eye Tender Tiny Peas and whole-grain bread on the deck.

"I want to teach you about this diet of mine," he says. "Cooking food robs it of all the natural nutrients, he explains. Not only that: refined foods like sugar and white flour—even whole-wheat flour, honey and maple syrup—take a very heavy toll on the body. Although he has served me cheese, dairy products are also a bad idea, especially if they're made from pasteurized milk, which has, after all, been heated above 150 degrees, the temperature at which crucial nutrients are destroyed, he says.

Jerry has developed a particular technique for preparing meat. First he takes the special, organic ground lamb he buys at the health-food store and forms it into patties, which he freezes. He believes this will kill whatever bacteria might be there. Then he cooks them, but only at a temperature of 150.

It's close to noon when Peggy emerges from the bedroom.

"I want you to meet Joyce," Jerry says.

"She's the one I told you about. She wrote that magazine article."

"Hi," she says. Then she picks up a magazine and flips through it.

"What do you say we drive into town for the paper?" Jerry asks me. It's a 10-minute drive, back over the dirt roads and onto a covered bridge that spans the Connecticut River, leading into the town of Windsor, Vermont. When we pull up in front of the newsstand on Main Street, both of us hop out of Jerry's car and walk into the store together. Jerry says hello to the man behind the counter. He picks up a yo-yo for Matthew.

"That was pretty unusual for me," he says as we drive away.

"Getting a yo-yo?"

"Bringing somebody into the store like that," he says. "A guest. Except that you don't feel like a guest."

Just when we turn into his driveway, Jerry shifts the car into neutral and pauses a moment. He leans over, puts his hands on my shoulders and kisses me. I kiss him back.

Two days after I leave Cornish a letter arrives from Jerry. He's missed me all day, he writes. I'm on the move again now, this time to my job in New York City and the Central Park West brownstone of the people I'll call the Mendelsons, who have invited me to use their house and watch their dogs while they're away. The Mendelsons' house on West 73rd Street, a block from the famous Dakota apartment building, is huge, and filled with original art and very modern furnishings. I reach my bedroom on the top floor via private elevator.

At *The New York Times*, too, my circumstances are impressive. I am installed behind a huge desk, facing a wall full of books about world history and current affairs. I am supposed to sit and compose editorials.

Still, I feel oddly depressed. Jerry Salinger has moved into my head. We talk together on the phone every night, and sometimes during the day.

"All these years you haven't been around, and it hasn't seemed like a problem," he tells me on the phone. "But now that I've met you, and you're gone, things seem out of balance. This morning I found myself looking over at the chair where you sat, and it seemed unbearably sad that you weren't in it."

He sends me a flyer for an antiques auction taking place near White River Junction the next week, and suggests that we go. He calls to say he picked the first peas from his garden. He calls to say he just finished reading the editorial page of the *Times*. "When are they going to run something you have to say?" That page is crying out for the voice of a girl like you, if you ask me."

Ten days after I began my job with *The New York Times*, Jerry drives five hours to New York to pick me up—me and the Mendelsons' two dogs. This time, when he pulls up in front of the brownstone on West 73rd Street, I go running into his arms. He strokes my hair. "God, I've been waiting forever for this," he says.

We buy a big bag of bagels and lox on the Upper West Side. Then he turns right around and drives, very fast, the full five hours straight back to New Hampshire. This time, when I walk into his house, I know where I'm headed.

After five days in Cornish, Jerry drives the Mendelsons' dogs and me back to New York. I rest my head in his lap most of the way. In the front hall of the brownstone, he sets my bags down.

"Exciting place, New York," he says. "A girl like you could go far in a city like this."

"It's not that great," I say.

"This bachelor business doesn't seem to be as hot an idea as it used to," he says. "You've got me impossibly distracted. I keep wanting to hear what's on your mind."

"Maybe we could get one of those wire-service machines, like the ones at *The New York Times*, and I could send you hourly bulletins. Matthew could run out to the garden with the latest updates." But I'm not in the mood for joking and I'm trying not to cry.

"I couldn't have made up a character of a girl I love better than you," he says.

In July, two of the editorials I've written run in *The New York Times*—"Not bad for a girl who grew up on the wrong side of the tracks in Kalamazoo," Jerry says when he calls. "I'd hardly even know your first tongue was Lithuanian."

I start work on my memoir, with a deadline for delivery of the book set for October, shortly before my 19th birthday. My publisher, Doubleday, is eager to have the book come out while I'm still in my teens so that it can make the claim that I am the youngest girl since Franáoise Sagan and Anne Frank to publish a book.

For someone who would once have described a book contract with a major New York publisher as one of the better things that could happen in her life, I am not really thinking about my book much anymore. All I really care about by now is being with Jerry Salinger.

His letters to me are full of longing for me, missing me, and plans for how we might be together. Maybe he'll call up his old friend Bill

Shawn and take an office at *The New Yorker*, he suggests. Maybe next fall, when I'm back in New Haven, he'll rent a little house in Westport, to be closer to me.

Knowing how I love to perform in plays, he speaks often of the two of us acting scenes from Shakespeare together in his living room. *Antony and Cleopatra*, maybe, for starters. In one letter, he suggests that he and I write a two-character play together and take it to London to perform ourselves, in the West End.

I believe him. Yes, I say. Why not?

"Why don't you find someone else to take care of those goofy dogs and move in here for the rest of the summer?" Jerry says. "A girl like you shouldn't have to put up with the Upper West Side in August, when she could be eating fresh-picked corn and swimming in New Hampshire ponds. You've had a nice big taste of *The New York Times*. What you really should be doing now is working on that book of yours. I'll help you."

At the beginning of August I tell my editor I'm leaving *The New York Times*, offering no explanation. I find a house-sitting and dog-walking replacement for the Central Park West brownstone, and Jerry drives to New York again to pick me up.

Every day, in the late afternoon, we take the same walk to the top of Jerry's hill. On this particular day, I am telling Jerry the story of my visit the previous fall to the Miss Teenage America pageant in Fort Worth for *Seventeen* magazine. Along the path, I perform imitations of the talent presentations of the various contestants: a girl who twirled her baton to "Stars and Stripes Forever," a medley of songs from *The Sound of Music*, including one number in which the contestant, dressed in a nun's habit, whipped off her long black robe to reveal a sparkly leotard and then broke into a tap dance.

He looks at me hard, " I have no doubt you could go to town on a story like that, Joyce," he says. "Not a lot gets by you. You'd get all kinds of hugely gratifying pats on the back while you were at it, too, as some kind of goddamn female Truman Capote, hopping from one hollow scene to the next.

"But one day, kiddo, you're going to ask yourself what the point is. Does anybody actually need to open up *Esquire* magazine and take in one more hysterically amusing little exercise in assassination by typewriter? Sooner or later you need to soberly consider whether what you write is serving any purpose but to fan your own ego."

For several minutes we walk up the hill with no sound but the one our shoes make along the path. Now and then we stop to throw a stick for Joey. I put my hand in Jerry's pocket.

"Most writers aren't in the position you are, Jerry," I point out. "A person has to write things somebody will be willing to pay for and publish."

"That article you wrote for *McCall's* about your wonderful, perfect relationship with your parents," he says quietly. "Skillful. Clever. Eminently publishable. And there wasn't one honest sentence in the whole damn thing. Your father's an alcoholic, for God's sake."

We have reached the top of the hill, where we always turn around and head back to the house. I study the dirt and draw breath as a terrible wave of sadness comes over me. " I could never write about my father's drinking," I whisper. "I can't even talk about it with my mother. She'd be so upset."

He shakes his head. "Someday, Joyce," he says, "there will be a story you want to tell for no better reason than because it matters to you more than any other. That's when you'll finally produce the work you're capable of."

In September, Jerry drives me to New Haven. He and I carry my trunk up the stairs to my apartment, along with a bag of vegetables from his garden.

The next morning I'm supposed to register for classes. Jerry is driving home to New Hampshire. "I'll call you tonight," I say.

"Who knows?" he tells me. "Maybe you'll meet up with some irresistible Joe College type and I'll never hear from you again."

The next day I buy a schefflera plant and an African violet. I go over to the Hadassah Thrift Shop and buy a hooked rug and an overstuffed armchair and a bunch of mismatched dishes and cooking utensils. By nightfall everything is in place. I call Jerry, collect as usual.

"You wouldn't recognize it here, my place looks so homey," I tell him.

"Wish I could say the same about this one," he says. "Things aren't the same around here."

The next day I buy books and notebooks. But I don't attend the art class I've signed up for. I ride my bike for hours through the Yale campus.

That night I call Jerry. "Come get me," I say.

"God I missed you," he says. "It's about time."


It's lonely in Cornish. Even the telephone is largely off-limits, but I write a few letters. "I've hung my clothes in the closet here," I write to my sister. "I've decided that this is really the only place I can live. I can no longer imagine being apart from Jerry."

It's not that simple. Jerry can be moody and cranky, and even his humor is often tinged with a sharp, practically sneering bitterness that scares me. His assessments of most people around him are withering, even brutal. I hear him on the phone with some acquaintance, someone from his New York days. He sounds patient and concerned. Then he puts down the receiver and groans. "God, the world is full of dreary fools," he says.

Even though I never question that he loves me, he now voices criticisms of me of a sort I never used to hear from him. It's bad enough that I bake a banana bread. But I leave the bowl in the sink. There are banana peels on the counter, and drips of batter.

I scatter clothes on the floor. My red-and-white-checked sneakers, which he had noted in the photograph on the cover of *The New York Times Magazine*, are less charming to him in the middle of the bedroom floor.

The division between us goes deeper. What Jerry wants is freedom from wanting. The self-denial that he practices is his diet— "abstemiousness," he calls it—is what he believes in for all other areas of his life, too. His goal, in meditation, is letting go of desire, obliterating the ego. His goal is nothing less than to empty his brain of thought.

Jerry meditates daily, but not the way certain college students do, for 10 or 15 minutes on the mat, or like a follower of the form of transcendental meditation popularized by Maharishi Mahesh Yogi. "Not a pleasant thought, knowing I can take credit for getting the whole, rotten, faddish thing going," he tells me.

There is a certain kind of heavy cotton broadcloth jumpsuit, of a sort generally worn by car mechanics, that Jerry favors. Every morning after breakfast, he puts on his, which is navy blue, with a zipper down the front, and disappears into his study to write and meditate. I may not see him again until the middle of the afternoon. He wants me to meditate, too. But every time I assume my yoga position and begin my breathing, worldly thoughts seep in.

Except for the hours in the day when he retreats to his study, I stay very close to Jerry—sitting on his lap, resting my head on his shoulder when we watch movies, holding his hand when we walk down the street. But even in our affection there's a kind of mad, clutching desperation.

His irritation with me becomes more pronounced. I left wet laundry in the washer. My editor has raised the question: Would Jerry consider making some kind of statement about my book that could be used to promote it, and though I should have known what he'd say, I mention her request to him. It isn't what he says that shames me. What he says is simply "I think I'll pass." But the look on his face is one of just barely concealed horror.

I put one of my old miniskirts on a day when Peggy's over. "Don't you have something else you can wear?" he says.

"I like this skirt," I say.

"You look ridiculous," he says. I start to cry. "Don't take it personally," he says. "It's a common failing of mankind."

My birthday in November passes as just an ordinary day. Three days later Nixon is re-elected.

Jerry writes for hours every day. In the years since he last published his work, he has completed at least two books. He doesn't show me his writing. One thing he does show me is his archives of the Glass family, who seem as real to him as the family into which he was born, and for whom he feels far greater affection. He has compiled stacks of notes and notebooks concerning the habits and backgrounds of the Glasses—music they like, places they go, episodes in their history.

About his own family he says nothing, except for the one time he tells me his sister works at Bloomingdale's. Over the months, we will make numerous stops at Bloomingdale's, on our trips into Manhattan. But he never introduces me to her.

I spend a good portion of that fall writing my book, which is called *Looking Back: A Chronicle of Growing Up Old in the Sixties*. I approach the project with weariness and something close to dread.

I may not have a highly realistic view of my relationship with Jerry and our prospects for a future together. But I recognize that the completion of the book and its publication the following spring are bound to bring about a crisis between the two of us. Writing *Looking Back* represents everything Jerry has told me not to do and everything he hates: Early publication. Exploitation of my youth, my face, my name; pandering to the fickle tastes of what he calls "newsstandland," cashing in on the precocious facility with language my parents fostered from such an early age at the expense of true thoughtfulness. Delivering more of what the marketplace demands.

My book has undergone its final editing now, and is heading toward the galley stage. Almost every day I receive a letter from my editor or agent, discussing some aspect of the book's promotion. Sale of the paperback rights. Foreign translations. Radio interviews. I tell my agent I'll have to pass on those.

"Nobody sells books anymore purely on the strength of what she writes," she tells me. "You have to go out and sell yourself too. Why do you think they put your photograph on the book jacket?"

Jerry and I argue daily about this. "A writer's face should never be known," he says.

"If you hadn't seen my face, would you have written to me?" I ask him. He doesn't answer.

I write a 160-page book that fall, ostensibly about my life, in which I never once mention that I grew up with an alcoholic father. Or with a mother who never felt able to talk with me about my father's drinking.

I talk about Joan Baez and Jackie Kennedy, about hearing the Beatles on *The Ed Sullivan Show*, the prevalence of pot smoking among my friends, the women's liberation movement. I talk about college without mentioning that I've dropped out. I do not say that I spent one whole summer, once, living on a diet consisting of little besides a single apple and Baskin-Robbins ice cream. I do not talk about how I get rid of the ice cream I eat, now, by going into the bathroom and sticking my finger down my throat.

*Looking Back* ends with a scene that finds me sitting by the fire in New Hampshire, preparing to make myself a dinner of steamed squash. It's New Year's Day, 1973, I say. I do not say, in my book, that January 1, 1973, is also the 54th birthday of the man I intend to live with forever, J. D. Salinger.

One day that January the phone rings. When Jerry answers it, his voice turns icy. "Yes. No. No. No. I have nothing more to say to you. Don't call me again. Good-bye."

He hangs up. "That was a reporter from *Time* magazine," he says.

"Asking about you. He said he heard from some friends of yours that you were living here with me."

"All these years I've done everything I could to maintain my privacy," he says to me. "Now *Time* has my phone number."

We were in the bathroom when the call came. He paces the floor. He looks out at the mountain, his back to me.

"I'm sorry," I say, weeping. "Forgive me. I'll do better."

He seems barely to hear me. He has sunk onto the edge of the bed, staring at the floor, talking to himself more than to me.

"How could you have done this? How did I let this happen? What have I brought on myself?"

I climb onto the bed behind him. I put my arms around him. He still won't look at me.

"Maybe it's hopeless," he says. "This book of yours could be the end of us."

In March, Peggy and Matthew are on a week's vacation from school and the four of us travel to Daytona Beach, Florida.

The first night we eat in the hotel dining room. The kids order spaghetti and garlic bread. Jerry and I get a salad, no dressing. Other patrons of the hotel, surveying our table, would suppose what they are seeing is a single father vacationing with his three children. But my behavior is very different from that of his children. I am careful and anxious, fearful always of displeasing him.

The next day we put on our bathing suits and take our towels and books down to the beach. Peggy has to lie under a beach umbrella. Matthew sprints toward the water, calling for his dad. Jerry has bought him a kite and he wants Jerry to fly it.

Jerry and I sit on our folding beach chairs alone together for a moment. He stares out at the water, the children, the hungover college students on spring break, the cars racing up and down across the sand. He looks very old. His shoulders are hunched. He rests his forehead in his hands.

"You know," he says. "I can never have any more children. I'm finished with all this."

Then he turns to me and speaks, with a coldness I have never known before from him. Here is the chill wind I have always feared.

"You'd better go home now," he says. "You need to clear your things out of my house. If you go now, you can have everything gone before the children and I get back. I don't want them upset having to witness all this."

I get up from the sand. I must be breathing, but it feels as though the air has left my lungs. My vision blurs. I walk back to the hotel.

Back in the room, I dial the number of the airline. "When is the next flight to Boston?" I ask. There's a blizzard going on up north. No planes are expected to fly into Boston until the next day at the earliest.

Sometime late that afternoon Jerry and the children return to our two adjoining rooms. "I got a flight back tomorrow," I tell Jerry.

"Joyce's father is sick," Jerry tells Matthew and Peggy.

Matthew looks momentarily concerned.

"But he'll be O.K., right?" he says. I say sure.

Later we prepare for bed—I in my room with Peggy, he is his with Matthew. He says good night, barely looking at me. I say good night.

Lying there in the darkness, all I want is to be able to cry freely. But I know I mustn't wake Peggy. So I go into the bathroom. The sound of my crying wakes Jerry. He stands in the doorway in his pajamas. "You've got to be more quiet," he whispers. I let my knees give way. He catches me. Then he sighs very deeply.

He sits down on the closed toilet set. I sit on his lap. His pajama top is wet with my tears.

"I don't think I can live without you anymore," I say. "Don't send me away."

"You know the story, Joyce," he says. "We've been through all this before. Let's not make it harder."

In the morning he gets a taxi for me. "Don't forget to turn the heat down and lock the door after you, once you leave the house," he says. "I'll give you a call." He pats my shoulder, kisses my cheek, and hands me a couple of 50-dollar bills. I watch out the window as the taxi pulls away. He looks at his watch and runs his hand through his hair. He turns and walks back to the hotel.

*Twenty-five years pass. The author has continued to live and work as a writer, having published numerous novels and articles in the intervening years, but having maintained her silence concerning Salinger. Maynard is now forty-four years old, divorced, and the mother of three nearly-grown children, the oldest of whom—her daughter—has recently turned the age she was when Salinger first wrote to her. She has decided to re-examine what happened when she was young, and so she has traveled back to New Hampshire to pay him a visit. She has not seen him since she was nineteen years old.)*

By the time I get to Jerry Salinger's house, it's four o'clock. The last light of the day is closing in. Dark clouds fill the sky. Dry leaves swirl around in the wheels of my truck.

I recognize the spot, though the only marker is the NO TRESSPASSING sign still posted at the foot of the driveway leading up the steep hill to his house.

When people made their pilgrimages to see him in the days when I lived here, they would park their car on the side of the dirt road and walk up the hill. Usually these visitors would be young people. I know, when I reach this spot, that I am not going to park. I'm driving up the hill.

As I come over the crest, the house comes into view. A few years ago I read that there was a bad fire here, but he must have taken great care to rebuild the place. It looks exactly as I remember. The deck looks out to the mountain and the garage is underneath, though there is a second garage now, too, with bays for three more cars. The satellite dish is also new.

I turn off the ignition and get out of the truck. I look out at Mt. Ascutney, watching the clouds building and the way the shadows fall over the field. His garden has been cleaned for winter.

I walk up the last stretch of hill to the house. I go around the back, to the door by the kitchen. My heartbeat is surprisingly steady. I'm standing at the door now, next to the bird feeder. Through the window, over-looking the doorstep, a young woman stands at the sink washing dishes.

I ring the bell.

The young woman moves back and forth in and out of view for a moment or two, then calls out through the window, not unpleasantly, "What do you want?"

"I've come to see Jerry," I say. "Could you tell him Joyce Maynard's here?" The steadiness of my voice surprises me. A flicker of a smile crosses her face.

She goes into one of the back rooms. "Someday, you may find your-self in a situation where it may help you to say this word," he told me once. Om.

There are certain moments in your life when all the senses seem to enter a state of intensified acuity, and you notice every single thing. Your eyes take in more, and what they take in, they take in with a sharpness they didn't possess ten minutes earlier, and will not possess ten minutes later—a cloud formation, a stick on the ground that looks chewed by a dog. You hear the sound your boot heel makes touching the rubber mat on the doorstep, and the pecking of a bird picking up a single grain of birdseed. You can feel your own blood moving through your veins.

Childbirth was one of those times for me. Holding a baby for a few hours at a time, watching her nurse. So was sitting beside my mother while she lay dying, and all I had to do was watch the breath come out of her.

It's hard to say how long I stand on this doorstep. Five minutes maybe. More likely ten. There is no reason in the world why he would come out of that room. Only I know he will, and he does.

All these years I have thought of him as such a tall man. Now, as Jerry emerges slowly from the bedroom and stands in front of me in the doorway, he seems shrunken. He is a little bent over.

He's wearing a very fine bathrobe and slippers. He is thinner than ever. At seventy-eight, he still has all his hair. It is pure white now. He is clean-shaven, and his face is deeply lined.

He does not invite me in. I remain standing on the step. I have never looked a man in the eye before who looked back at me with an expression of greater bitterness or rage.

"What are you doing here?" he says. The words come at me. *Spitting.* "Why didn't you write me a letter?"

"I wrote you many letters, Jerry," I say. "You never answered them."

"What are you doing here?" he says. His voice comes from that place deep in the diaphragm the orgonomist taught him to use. It's a voice that doesn't have to be loud to make itself heard.

"I came to ask you a question, Jerry," I say. "What was my purpose in your life?"

I would not have believed that a person could ever look more angry than he did the moment he first laid eyes on me. But now his mouth, which doesn't speak yet, curls as if he has bitten into a piece of fruit, and found it to be filled with maggots.

"What was my purpose in your life?" I say again. The image that comes to me is of Rumpelstilskin, as I always imagined him, and even acted him out, there on my bed all those years ago with my sons and daughter snuggled up beside me—that moment when the miller's daughter has one chance left to guess his name, or her baby will be lost to her forever. And she guesses right. That is how Jerry Salinger looks now, when I put my question to him.

"That question—" he says, almost too angry to speak. "That question—that question—that question is *too profound.* You don't deserve an answer to the question."

"Oh yes I do," I say.

I am still calm. I can feel warm water washing over me. I am swimming my crawl stroke, and my breathing is steady. I am skating on black ice over Loon Pond on a moonlit night with Steve's arm around my waist. I am cutting up apples for pie, with a baby propped in an infant seat on the counter next to me. I am hitting a tennis ball with my son, under the lights at the Keene State courts, at midnight. I am riding with my daughter on the chair lift, and I know just when to lift the bar and lower the tips of my skis.

"You're writing something, aren't you?" he says.

"I'm always writing," I say. "I'm a *writer*." I have never called myself that, before. I have always left it that I write.

"You're writing a *book*, aren't you?" he says. He says it as if it were a pornographic act. "I've heard you're writing some kind of . . . *reminiscence*."

"Yes," I say. "I am writing a book."

"You have spent your career writing gossip," he says. "You write empty, meaningless, offensive, putrid gossip. You live your life as a pathetic, parasitic gossip."

I am looking at his hands, his fingers wrapped around the belt of his bathrobe. The same long, elegant fingers that I loved—fingers that touched my naked skin before any other man had, before so many other things happened.

"I'm not ashamed of the work I've done," I say. "I've worked hard to be an honest writer."

He throws back his head as if to laugh, only no laughter comes out of him—only the stifled sound of the syllable "Ha." "You always did have an inflated notion of yourself and your so-called talents," he says.

"You know," I tell him, "I've never took myself seriously as a writer until you told me I was one."

He stands there for a moment. Then, taking a step backward, he raises his long thin finger so it's pointing directly at my heart.

"You, Joyce—" he says, finger still pointing. "You. You. You." His whole body is quaking, and his eyes stare out at me as if he were beholding a sight of unspeakable horror.

"The problem with you, Joyce, is . . . *you—love—the—world.*"

"*Yes,*" I say, smiling. "Yes, I *do* love the world. And I've raised three children who love the world, too."

"I knew you would amount to this," he says. "*Nothing.*" He, the man who told me that if there was anything he knew at all, it was that I would be a true writer no matter what. Nobody, ever, could take that away from me, he told me once. Never forget that, he said. Let no one ever tell you what to say. *Trust nothing but your own strong voice.*

"I want to say good-bye to you, Jerry," I say.

"I don't hear well," he says. His voice seems less powerful than it was a few minutes ago. I can no longer smile. I feel nothing but a wave of sorrow. This was a wonderful man one time. I loved him more than anything on earth. I danced with him in the living room to the magic accordion of Myron Florin, Lawrence Welk's finest. I have no desire to hurt him. Only to let him go at last.

"You mean to exploit your relationship with me, I suppose?" he says.

"It may be true that someone standing in this doorway has exploited someone else who's standing in this doorway. I will leave it to you to meditate on which one of us is which."

As I walk away he calls out one more thing: the last words I am ever likely to hear from the first man I loved.

"I didn't exploit you!" he calls out. "*I don't even know you.*"

# On First Looking into Chapman's Holden

## Speculations on a Murder

DANIEL M. STASHOWER

Mark David Chapman, the young assassin, was carrying two things with him when he shot and killed John Lennon on the steps of the Dakota apartments in Manhattan: a pistol and a paperback copy of *The Catcher in the Rye*. The function of the pistol was obvious. Less obvious was the function of J. D. Salinger's novel. Yet the book, it seems fair to say, must have had some special significance to Mark Chapman. Any attempt to uncover its significance is, in the nature of the case, highly speculative. Yet some aspects of *The Catcher in the Rye*, set beside Mark Chapman's murder of John Lennon, seem so suggestive that not to speculate upon the connections between the two seems a temptation impossible to forgo.

J. D. Salinger's *Catcher in the Rye* was published in 1951. Like the Beatles, whose rise to fame came about roughly thirteen years later, the novel's adolescent hero, Holden Caulfield, became a spokesman for a generation of rebellious, supposedly much-misunderstood youth. An oversimplified yet functional reading of the Salinger novel might conclude that all that the book advocates would fall under the heading of "innocence" and all that it condemns falls under that of "phoniness."

Holden Caulfield, during his somewhat aimless ramble through New York, feels overwhelmed by the phoniness he finds all around him. He struggles to preserve his own tenuous hold on youthful innocence—or, as he sometimes puts it, "niceness"—and despairs when he finds that innocence lost or threatened in the young people around him. At his trial, Mark Chapman read what is perhaps *The Catcher in the Rye's* most famous passage:

> *I keep picturing all these little kids playing some game in this big field of rye and all. Thousands of little kids, and nobody's around—nobody big, I mean—except me. And I'm standing on the edge of some crazy cliff. What I have to do, I have to catch everybody if they start to go over the cliff—I mean if they're running and they don't look where they're going I have to come out from somewhere and catch them. That's all I'd do all day. I'd just be the catcher in the rye and all. I know it's crazy, but that's the only thing I'd really like to be. I know it's crazy.*

While scarcely as succinct as John Wilkes Booth's "Sic semper tyrannis," or as compelling as Brutus's "Romans, countrymen, and lovers," the above passage was Chapman's sole attempt to justify the murder of John Lennon. It ought to be examined for anything in it that might have led Chapman from Salinger's rye fields to the Dakota apartments.

Probably no one will object too strenuously to the notion that Mark Chapman identified himself rather heavily with Holden Caulfield. Chapman would, after all, be only one of millions who felt that Salinger's book was written especially for him, that it addressed itself to his problems and, in the way that certain books do, eased his pain. If Chapman identified with Holden, what sort of view of the world would accompany the identification? *The Catcher in the Rye* is a book almost wholly concerned with the preservation of innocence. When Holden speaks of "coming out from somewhere" to catch the children, he hopes to save them from becoming the adult "phonies" of the kind he has been encountering in New York. He doesn't want children to grow up into people who will "talk about how many miles their goddamn cars get to the gallon." If Chapman also saw himself as a protector of innocence, why was he inspired to shoot Lennon? Here is a question of the kind Holden himself might have called "a real bastard."

Two possibilities come to mind: either Mark Chapman saw John Lennon as a corruptor of innocence, or he saw him as an innocent about to be corrupted. If Chapman imagined that Lennon was a threat to the innocence of youth, he certainly took his time in doing anything about it. After all, the man who in his music sang the joys of "Lucy in the Sky with Diamonds," and later posed nude on album covers while exhorting listeners to "open their thighs," was not exactly what one would call a samaritan. But Lennon's last album, *Double Fantasy*, was, by contrast, a Girl Scout manual. This album, which came after a silence of six years, dealt largely with the joys of home life and fatherhood. There was little in the album's songs that could be considered threatening; and the interviews that Lennon gave to promote it showed that he had settled into a comfortable, somewhat embourgeoisified life of baking bread and clipping coupons. Surely, this John Lennon was not the sort of person likely to threaten the innocence of children or of anyone else.

It is more likely, then, that Chapman saw Lennon as an innocent who was himself about to be corrupted. Some problems arise here, but the idea becomes at least plausible if considered in tandem with *The Catcher in the Rye*. Holden Caulfield provides some useful standards by which to judge innocence. His older brother, D. B., is the novel's clearest example of innocence gone bad. D. B., it will be recalled, was apparently a writer of great promise who "sold out" and began to "prostitute himself" in Hollywood by writing cheap movie scripts. Commercial success at the expense of artistic integrity is, in *The Catcher in the Rye*, the worst expression of phoniness. Throughout the novel Holden despairs that his once-noble brother has fallen.

This model of the fallen artist is easily applicable to the world of

Mark Chapman. As a teenager, he idolized the Beatles, and a large part of the charm of the Beatles lay in their absolute unwillingness to compromise their integrity for the sake of commercial gain, as Holden's brother, D. B. had. As it happens, the Beatles made fabulous sums of money anyway, but they often risked both their fortune and their popularity in unorthodox creative ventures. Sometimes, as with the album *Sgt. Pepper's Lonely Hearts Club Band*, they succeeded in spite of their heterodoxy. Other times, as with their disastrous merchandising firm Apple Corps., they failed. But they always preserved their dedication to their fans and their art, which made them easily the world's most exciting rock band, while other bands clung to tested, profitable, and second-hand formulas. When the Beatles disbanded in 1970, their fans—including, one imagines, Mark Chapman—watched with interest to see what the individual members would do. Could any of the four men who had formed the Beatles achieve anything like a similar success on his own? Ringo Starr and George Harrison pursued fairly steady and largely uninteresting solo careers. Paul McCartney and John Lennon, divided by the stresses that had disrupted the Beatles, took off in two wildly divergent directions. Salinger himself couldn't have wished for two characters whose careers more clearly defined the two sides of *The Catcher in the Rye* dilemma.

James Paul McCartney, as almost everyone who once cared for the Beatles is aware, became the most successful male pop artist the world has ever known, but in the process he completely alienated his former fans. The man who had written such songs as "Hey Jude," "Let It Be," and "Yesterday" now churned out material that was designed, almost scientifically, to sell. From a purely commercial standpoint, McCartney was several times more successful than the Beatles ever were, but he had, like Holden's older brother, clearly sold out in producing obviously commercial music. If Chapman held to the definitions of "phoney" and "nice" as outlined by J. D. Salinger, Paul McCartney had become a phoney.

Turn now to John Lennon. Lennon's solo career was easily the most erratic of the four Beatles. He released a series of albums that were alternately brilliant and peculiar, sometimes both, and they he dropped out of sight. "Dropped out of sight" actually means that he stopped recording and dedicated six years to raising his son, Sean, while his wife, Yoko, managed their business affairs and sold holstein cows for enormous sums. While McCartney was so much in the news that even his toes were once photographed for *Time*, John Lennon—and all his various parts—were hidden from sight. No one has ever made much sense out of Lennon's post-Beatle years, but one thing is certain: in the code of rock music, he preserved his Beatle integrity. He was not a phoney. Even his artistic failures were dignified, and his self-imposed exile did nothing to damage but rather strengthened the claim of some music critics that Lennon was, after Elvis Presley, the "king of rock."

Lennon's exile suggests an interesting and possibly illuminating parallel to *The Catcher in the Rye* as it might have been interpreted by Mark Chapman. Possibly America's most famous recluse is J. D. Salinger. For more than twenty years Salinger has isolated himself in his bunker-like retreat in New Hampshire. Like Lennon, Salinger has preserved the mystique that surrounds his early work, and he has accomplished this simply by removing himself from society. This isolation has done nothing to damage but rather has strengthened the claim of some literary critics that Salinger is one of the more important American writers in the postwar era.

Salinger's retreat from society is anticipated in *The Catcher in the Rye*. On a date with the pretty but vapid Sally Hayes, Holden suddenly asks:

> *How would you like to get the hell out of here? Here's my idea. I know this guy . . . we can borrow his car for a couple of weeks. What we could do is, tomorrow morning we could drive up to Massachusetts and Vermont, and all around there, see. It's beautiful as hell up there . . . I have about a hundred and eighty bucks . . . we'll stay in these cabin camps and stuff . . .*

Holden's plan is, obviously, unrealistic, a fact that, in the novel, Sally Hayes belabors at somewhat tedious length. But the desire to "get the hell out of here," which Holden expresses several times, is entirely consistent with the uncompromising line Holden draws between "nice" and "phoney," and his fantastical if winning desire to become a "catcher in the rye." "There were goddam phonies coming in the windows," Holden complains at one point. Thus overwhelmed, the logical recourse is escape. Salinger's own decision "to get the hell out of here" must mark one of the rare cases in literature in which an author has taken his character's advice.

Though one can hardly call holing up in the Dakota "getting the hell out of here," John Lennon did follow a course roughly like the one outlined by Holden. He, too, "got the hell out." If Chapman shared the views of Holden Caulfield, then the chances are fairly good that he very much admired Lennon's withdrawal from public life. When Lennon resurfaced in 1980, suddenly granting interviews and appearing in public, Chapman may have perceived a threat to the Salinger credo and a crack in the wall that protected Lennon's splendid innocence.

The self-promotion accompanying Lennon's re-entry into the world of high publicity was unlike anything he had ever done before, and it seems likely that Chapman found him listing dangerously toward commercialism. After six years of seclusion, news of John Lennon's doings was everywhere. The hermit of rock had become all too accessible, in a *People* magazine, vulgar way. In many respects he resembled Paul McCartney promoting his albums, which led John Lennon's fans to wonder, with some trepidation, what Lennon's long-awaited album would sound like.

Since his death, Lennon's last album, *Double Fantasy*, has been hailed as a rock classic. At the time of its release, however, when Lennon was still alive, the album received a very lukewarm reception. In England, his home country, *The National Music Express* suggested that "the old man" ought to have stayed in retirement and pointed out striking similarities between this album and the work of Paul McCartney, which Lennon was known to have found distasteful. Fans who hoped for, or expected, another album of the quality of *Imagine* were disappointed.

We can only speculate, of course, upon what effect Lennon's re-emergence might have had on Mark Chapman. Perhaps Chapman had been perfectly content as long as Lennon remained in Salinger-like isolation. Now, however, Lennon thrust himself into the open with a McCartney-like publicity blitz and released what was generally acknowledged to be a mediocre piece of work. Lennon was in trouble; he was in danger of falling off the cliff, à la D. B. Caulfield and Paul McCartney. What could Mark Chapman do about it? If we examine the question with *The Catcher in the Rye* in mind, a most distressing, twisted solution arises. Simply put, it appears Chapman misread *The Catcher in the Rye*. He took the "catcher" passage to be the novel's solution, when in fact it is the crisis.

No one who has read *The Catcher in the Rye* will argue that Holden Caulfield was a seriously disturbed sixteen-year-old. He wanders through New York with a genuine desire, to quote an old Beatles tune, to "take a sad song and make it better," but he doesn't know how to begin. As a result he develops and all-purpose, self-protective cynicism. When challenged by his younger sister Phoebe to justify this cynicism, he offers the famous "catcher" speech. But the book doesn't end there. What Holden has outlined in his "some crazy cliff" plan, and in his earlier "get the hell out" plan, is impossible. Holden Caulfield wants to stop reality. He wants to keep the children in the rye field from growing up. But growing up is the natural order of things. It cannot be stopped. Yet Holden longs to do the impossible. This is what brings about his crisis in *The Catcher in the Rye*.

Can it be that Mark Chapman, devoted J. D. Salinger reader, had his own difficulty in dealing with reality and responsibility in a world of grown-ups? In addition to *The Catcher in the Rye*, Chapman was known to favor a song of Lennon's called "Strawberry Fields Forever." Like

Salinger's rye fields, Lennon's strawberry fields offered a frozen, unrealistic approach to life; it promised an eternity in a land where, to quote from the song, "nothing is real." If Chapman was madly drawn to both Holden Caulfield's "catcher" and John Lennon's "Strawberry Fields," it is not inconceivable that he would have wanted Lennon himself to remain "caught" in his protective retreat, where "nothing is real." Especially now, with the release of the mediocre album *Double Fantasy*, Mark Chapman could have viewed John Lennon poised on the edge of the crazy cliff, and it was up to him, Chapman, to play catcher in the rye.

So Chapman flew to New York and began a sojourn very much like the one that takes place in *The Catcher in the Rye*. Although it is difficult to know for certain how Chapman filled his time, he was in the city for two full days before the shooting. He is said to have switched hotels (as Holden did); walked out of a movie theater ("I hate the movies," Holden says, "don't even mention them to me"); and regaled a cab driver with tales of a forthcoming Lennon/McCartney album, which he claimed to be producing ("I'm a terrific liar," Holden admits, "I have to watch myself sometimes").

Now comes the large question: Why did Chapman shoot Lennon? Given his Holden Caulfield state of mind, wouldn't it have made more sense to invite Lennon out for a nightcap somewhere or to go skating at Radio City, there to caution him against selling out? But Chapman was a confused, disturbed man. There are no easy explanations for why he did what he did. One answer is suggested in the pages of *The Catcher in the Rye*. Chapman may have believed that the highest possible attainment, at least as viewed through Salinger's novel, would be to achieve that permanent state of innocence suggested in the "catcher" passage. Only one character in *The Catcher in the Rye* manages that unimpeachable innocence—Holden's younger brother Allie. Allie is the only character in the novel, including Holden, who never shows any hint of phoniness, and who never will. How is this possible? It is possible only because Allie is dead.

Immediately preceding Caulfield's "catcher" speech, which Chapman found so significant and which he recited at his trial, there is a section in the novel in which Holden's sister Phoebe asks if her depressed brother can "name one thing" that he likes. Holden has a lot of trouble responding. He recalls a boy at school, James Castle, who, rather than taking back something he had said about a bully, jumped out of a fifth-floor window. Then he reveals what at first seems to be an unrelated piece of information: that he likes his brother Allie. "Allie's *dead!*" Phoebe cries, "You always say that! If somebody's dead and everything, and in *Heaven*, then it isn't really—"

"I know he's dead!" Holden returns. "Don't you think I know that? I can still like him though, can't I? Just because someone's dead, you don't just stop liking them for God's sake—especially if they were about a thousand times nicer than the people you know that're *alive* and all."

In the traditional interpretation of the novel, Holden's reference to his brother is simply another indication of his unrealistic desire to freeze innocence and thwart phoniness. But Chapman, who wrote "this is my statement" in the flyleaf of his copy of the Salinger novel, was not a typical reader. To him, the "catcher" speech was the book's final and transcendent message, which would make Allie the real hero of *The Catcher in the Rye*. Allie, in this reading, is the only character to come out unscathed. Death, then, would have presented itself to Chapman as the only safeguard against loss of innocence.

Holden Caulfield and Mark Chapman were faced with the same crisis: an assault on innocence. Holden Caulfield could not find a way to preserve innocence forever and was forced to entertain the notion of growing up. If I am correct in my speculation, Chapman found a way. Taking as a model the only character in *The Catcher in the Rye* who achieved perpetual innocence, Chapman found his course clear. For John Lennon's innocence—which was essential to Chapman's own spiritual well-being—to remain intact, Lennon himself would have to die. Only then could his innocence, like Allie's, be preserved forever.

Unfortunately, this idea, as I have set it out here, is not as absurd or outrageous as it sounds. If Chapman's intention was to secure and even improve, the legend of John Lennon, the artist of perfect integrity, he succeeded. Gone now is the John Lennon who once smeared excrement on the walls of his dressing room; who claimed that the Beatles were a bigger item than Christ; and who appeared in a Los Angeles nightclub with a Kotex on his head. In his place is a sort of rock-and-roll Gandhi. Because of his violent death, anything about him that is base or even unkind has been erased. In the most extraordinary way, John Lennon today is viewed as a man of pristine innocence—"a genius of the spirit," Norman mailer has called him. And all because Mark Chapman, standing outside the Dakota apartments, caught him in the rye.

# Selections from
# Letters to J. D. Salinger

Dear Mr. Salinger,

Some years ago, actually in the summer issue of the *Paris Review,* 1981, we published an account of a curious interview with you conducted by one Betty Eppes, a young part-time tennis professional, who was a Special Assignments Editor for the "Fun" section of both the Baton Rouge *Advocate* and *State Times*. In the spring of the previous year she had persuaded her managing editor (much against his better judgment) to let her spend her summer vacation trying to interview you. She flew to Boston, rented a sky-blue Pinto, and drove into the Green Mountains to Windsor, which is the nearest place to Cornish which has lodgings. She wrote you a letter which she left with the Windsor post office, knowing you would get it. In it she said she was a budding novelist, needed some advice, a great admirer, of course, that she was tall with green eyes and red-gold hair, and that at 9:30 the next morning she would wait by the covered bridge in her sky-blue Pinto for thirty minutes before heading back to Louisiana.

You may remember that something in her letter touched you in some way—the effort she'd gone through, the green eyes and red-gold

hair or whatever—and that you'd gone down over the river to see her.
You leaned in the car window and she had time for seven or eight questions ("Did you consciously opt for a writing career, or did you just
drift into it?") before you realized she was actually a reporter on the
prowl and abruptly you turned back for the covered bridge.

In the process of preparing our lengthy account of her trip (including
your increasingly peremptory answers) Ms. Eppes told us that eleven
days after her story was published, you sent her care of the *Advocate*
photostats of an order blank you had sent away to New York. In it you
asked for two over-sized schoolbags, gift-wrapped from Denmark (at
$16.50 each) that had been advertised in the then current *New Yorker*.

Ms. Eppes told us that she had been driven "just about crazy" trying
to figure out why you would send her such a thing. We too are
intrigued. Is there some hidden meaning here? Why a "Danish"
schoolbag? Why is the letter dated five years earlier? Is there some significance to "over-sized"? Does the Chocolate Soup address (there is no
such place today) suggest that Zimbabwe is somehow involved in the
Glass family history? Is the number 100003 a clue of some kind?

In sum, Mr. Salinger, much to be considered, and I hope you will
take the time to do so.

Sincerely yours,
George Plimpton

Dear Mr. Salinger,

In 1970, a bookmobile traveled up my dirt road twice a month. By
age eleven I'd read every book on its shelves. I was then allowed to
accompany my mother to town once a week, where she shopped for
groceries and I visited the newly-opened library. There was a four-book
limit per library card, but I got around that by getting cards in my siblings' names, two of whom could not read. I read sixteen books a week.
My all-time favorite was *Harriet the Spy* because it was about a little girl
who carried pencil and paper and wrote notes about her friends. I loved

the genre of misfit kids who came out ahead. The best books involved a boy who hit the winning homerun and suddenly everyone liked him. All I really wanted was acceptance and I found it through reading.

The town library was staffed by volunteers and one afternoon an ancient woman would not leave me alone. She insisted on helping me find books, an endeavor I preferred to do alone. Out of politeness, I allowed her to dig around in the card catalog for me under the heading, "Baseball." There were too many books and she asked me to narrow my interest. I told her my favorite player was Johnny Bench, catcher for the closest big league team, the Cincinnati Reds. She continued to flip cards and I continued to wait with growing impatience. Finally she led me to a part of the library I had not yet explored and removed a book from the shelf. I dutifully checked it out along with my other fifteen books. After supper I opened the book. It was *The Catcher in the Rye.*

I stayed up all night reading that book. It literally changed my life. I didn't know a book could be that way—honest, about real life, and with the word "goddamn" on the first page. This was not a book about a made-up misfit kid who suddenly everyone liked; here was a genuine misfit who did the best he could—same as me. I never read another juvenile book again.

Chris Offutt

Dear Mr. Salinger,

During the past three years, we have used your novel, *The Catcher in the Rye*, as the focus for an online discussion between two very different sets of students: a high school class in a suburb of Chicago and a college class in rural Kentucky. The Web forum is held each September, when the high school students are beginning their senior year at Benet Academy and the college students are in the last stage of training as secondary English teachers at Murray State University. When we first thought of bringing our classes together in an electronic discussion, we weren't convinced the project would work since the two groups seemed worlds apart. What is clear now, however, is that Holden Caulfield can unite students of varied ages, interests, and economic resources, if not in agreement, certainly in relevant and sometimes heated debate.

Although we provide the prompts for some of the discussion threads and require our students to complete a set number of postings, we usually step back from the exchange, allowing the students to assume control of the conversation. They soon become intensely engaged in online chat, posing questions, offering interpretations, and even sharing links to relevant Web sites. Invariably, the threads that provoke the most varied and emotional responses are those dealing with Holden as a character and those addressing the value of teaching the book in the secondary classroom.

Even though you created Holden more than fifty years ago, the students today still see a part of themselves in him. One of the high school students, Dave, explained, "Holden is easy to identify with for all teenagers, for he is struggling to come into his own, face the world, and decide if he agrees with everything that is going on in it." Another senior, after admitting, "I am very Holdenish," invited others to explain how they saw themselves mirrored in this protagonist. The response to this prompt was phenomenal! Students spoke of being "not yet an adult and no longer a child," of longing for the simplicity of their younger years, of hating the game-playing they associate with growing up, and of wanting to protect even younger children from the ugliness of the world.

Through your book, students are moved to question themselves. Kelly attested to this fact when she wrote, "Holden made me look at things differently. He made me look at my own life to see if I was playing the game. I didn't want to be a phony." Holden intrigues these young people. The complexity of his character calls forth fairly sophisticated analysis—from diagnoses of attention deficit disorder and chronic fatigue to claims that he is "a self-contradicting, irony-laden hypocrite." Jeff saw him as "both honest and a liar, both mature and immature, both loving and misanthropic." And Wesley labeled him a "human oxymoron." Diana provided even more insight: "There are two dueling parts of Holden's character—one that would like nothing better than to completely change the world but also another part that wishes he could escape from society completely. He's running, not only from all the 'phoniness' in the world, but also from himself."

Thank you, Mr. Salinger, for creating a book that engages adolescents, that prompts them to critique the world around them, and that continues to haunt all of us who have read it. One of the best testaments to the lasting power of your novel came from Shannon, who confessed, "I finished the book more than a week ago, but it is still with me. For example, in the grocery store the other day I wondered what Holden would think of all the brainwashing we receive by packaging and brand names in the store. . . . J. D. Salinger's writing style has also stuck with me throughout the week. I find myself saying certain *Catcher* phrases such as 'it killed me' in conversation and writing."

Those training to be teachers benefit greatly from being exposed to Holden and from seeing the way high school students react to him. Soon, they will be teaching young people who will undoubtedly exhibit the same angst and the same mixture of cynicism and idealism that we see in Holden. To become the kind of teacher that Mr. Antolini represents, they must recognize the complex emotional lives of adolescents. The Web forum is also useful in preparing these future teachers for the level of sophistication that they can expect from classes on the secondary level. The Benet seniors, who are enrolled in Advanced Placement English, are bright and engaging, eager to challenge interpretations made by their fellow students and their teachers. With any luck, by being exposed to the articulate and insightful comments of adolescents early in their training, the college students will be less likely to deserve the censure Holden delivers: "You don't have to think too hard when you talk to a teacher."

Although the posting from the Benet students should make it

obvious that your book is an excellent choice for the high school curriculum, the college students from rural Kentucky, who tend to be from very conservative backgrounds, usually have misgivings about teaching controversial works. When these future teachers voice their concerns online, the high school students become quite vocal in arguing against censorship. We want to share a few of their eloquent responses with you:

Mac: "Saying that *The Catcher in the Rye* is not for adolescents is going against the whole purpose and message of the book. Ignoring the swearing and the sexual content, which is as much part of adolescence as school and drivers' education, the book centers on the struggle of Holden, a teenager, to fit into and make sense of the adult world. How much more appropriate of a topic can there be for high school students?"

Suji: "I'm sorry, but if you think that teenagers don't drink, smoke, or have sex, then you are living in an alternate reality and you need this book to bring you back. On another level, however, *Catcher* is hardly going to influence teenagers to go out and have sex. I disagree with the idea that the reader necessarily sees Holden as a role model. I see him as a charter that I can relate to, nothing more, nothing less. If I can pick out a character in a novel from AP English class and emphathize with his situation, then I wholeheartedly believe that the text is appropriate for school."

Steve: "My Dad loved *The Catcher in the Rye;* who would've thought that more than three decades later, it'd be just as important and relevant to me as it was to him. *The Catcher in the Rye* is banned for the lifestyle it portrays by people who perfectly fit Holden's description of 'phonies'; they are ignorant, judgmental people who ignore the underlying message and ban things for superficial detail. As long as conservative adults do that, kids will read the book; as long as there are kids like Holden who are atypical outcasts and get pushed around by peers who mindlessly play 'the game,' this book will be near and dear to teenagers."

Besides prompting these wonderful defenses, the discussion about whether or not *Catcher* is appropriate as a school text also leads to worthwhile analysis of language, heroes, and the purpose of literature. What more could we as English teachers ask of an online discussion?

If you ever want to see a sample of the conversations your novel still has the power to elicit, please feel free to visit our Web forum at this URL: http://campus.murraystate.edu/academic/faculty/carol.osborne/ forums/eng529/threads.cfm>.

Each September, two new sets of students will be logging on to give their impressions of Holden's "whole crummy story."

Sincerely,

Carol Osborne and Mike Stracco

# My Salinger Year

JOANNA SMITH RAKOFF

I f you really want to hear about it, if you really want to understand how and why I spent a year of my precious life as Jerome David Salinger (Jerry to his friends, J. D. to his fans), you'll need to do some goddamned work. Picture, if you will, a map of the Eastern seaboard. Halfway down the coast, you'll find Winston-Salem, North Carolina, its air eternally tinged with the sweet scent of tobacco. Somewhere within the city limits, on a narrow street in Old Salem, perhaps, sits a four-bedroom Victorian, recently renovated, surrounded by magnolias and azaleas. In this house is a boy—a boy I do not know, have never met, never will meet—and this is the person on whom you must zoom in. Tonight he sits at the dark wood desk in his bedroom, still half-dressed in his rumpled school uniform—blue Oxford, gray flannel pants—attempting to write a story for his English class. Though he looks rather like the other boys at his school, he is most emphatically not like these boys, boys who spend all their time thinking about football and lacrosse and the SATs. He has just finished reading *The Catcher in the Rye* for the third time. He is sixteen years old.

Now, trace your finger up the map and let it rest on New York City, a place our boy from Atlanta has never visited. Much of what he knows about the city he gleaned from *Catcher* and his other favorite novel, *The Great Gatsby*. He imagines smoky rooms, red-lipped Vassar girls drinking tumblers of whiskey in hotel bars, wisecracking taxi drivers. He cannot picture Brooklyn, particularly not a tiny apartment in a dilapidated back house—an apartment without heat, without a sink in the kitchen. The girl that lives in this apartment washes her dishes in the chipped, pink bathtub. She is not much older than the boy, six or seven years. She rouges her lips like a '40s film star, dons kilts and twin-sets and loafers, and imagines herself, like Franny Glass, as "a languid, sophisticated type," even as she stoops over her bathtub, scrubbing pots in a tattered kimono. Each morning, she gets on the subway in her crummy neighborhood and emerges from it under the starry ceiling of Grand Central, a few blocks from the Madison Avenue office in which she works, an office virtually unchanged since the days in which Holden Caulfield roamed the city, trolling for a date.

Finally, I need you to go to New Hampshire, where a tall, dark-eyed man meditates in the back room of his simple, wood-frame house. In his eighties now and mostly deaf, he thrives on routine: Each morning, he rises, eats breakfast, kisses his wife goodbye, and heads to his study, where he meditates and, allegedly, writes. He is a Buddhist, a vegetarian, the son of a man who made his living processing meat. His wife, thirty years his junior, is a nurse at the local hospital. She enjoys weaving tapestries. He enjoys watching television. A satellite dish crowns the top of their farmhouse. Every five years or so, he visits New York, the city in which he was born and raised, the city he made inti-mate—and eccentrically romantic—for several generations of readers. He hates the city now, but he needs to come, needs to meet with his agent, make sure she's handling the business of his books in exactly the way he likes. He visits her office and they head out to lunch. He says hello to the low-voiced girl who assists his agent, the girl who fields his questions about royalties and contracts, repeating her answers three and four times on the days when he doesn't feel like using his special, amplified phone, bought for him by his wife. The girl has dark hair and wears a plaid wool skirt, red lipstick.

The man, you already know, is Jerome David Salinger.
  The boy, we'll get to later.
  The girl, of course, is me.

Some years ago, J. D. Salinger shook my hand with an air of salty kindness, and I experienced an unparalleled surge of excitement—not because I was meeting the notoriously reclusive writer (how many members of the Salinger cult would have killed to be in my place?), but because I was in possession of a secret, a strange and goofy secret that, if disclosed to the surprisingly sweet old man who held my right hand in both of his, would perhaps lead to some kind of angry scene and, I supposed, the loss of my peculiar and beloved job.

During that year—the Salinger Year—I was newly-minted Ph.D.-in-English drop-out, filled with my own sense of myself as a Young Intellectual, imagining my future as a kind of latter-day Susan Sontag or Mary McCarthy. I drank at parties for New Important Books, attended readings at KGB, and read long, labyrinthine novels by Pynchon, Amis, Dos Passos. I devoured Faulkner and Jean Rhys and Joan Didion and Jane Bowles, writers whose bleak, relentless styles stood in stark opposition to the insufferable cuteness of Salinger, a writer whose aggressively quirky view of the world had always slightly irked me. My parents owned his entire oeuvre.

At work, however, it was nothing but Salinger, Salinger, Salinger. A few months after turning in a terse, uninspired Masters' thesis on the landscape poems of—who else?—Sylvia Plath, I unwittingly landed a position at Harold Ober Associates, one of the city's original literary agencies, assisting the firm's president, who also happened to be J. D. Salinger's agent. Salinger had been an Ober client from the start of his career. I took a curious thrill from looking up the submission record for *The Catcher in the Rye*—noted on a colored card preprinted with the names of publishers and inscribed with the dates the manuscript was sent to them—and seeing that the book had not sold immediately, had not been the subject of the fierce bidding wars I read about in *Publishers' Weekly*, editors fighting over nonfiction accounts of Ivy League murders or first novels from Iowa grads. Publishing, I surmised, was different then, a half-century ago. Or, at least, publishing *houses* were different, while Ober hadn't changed at all since its inception in the 1920s. The older agents, like my boss, chain-smoked in their dark, wood-lined offices, dictating letters into boxy tape recorders, which we assistants would then type up on our IBM Selectrics, left foot gently peddling the Dictaphone's start-and-stop button. The year was 1996. Two blocks to the west, my best friend sat in a foam-board cubicle on a high floor of the McGraw-Hill building. Her boss had decided to eliminate paper. All but the most official correspondence would be sent via email. At Ober, my boss had just recently decided that we could use the Xerox machine to copy our correspondence—rather than making carbons as we typed.

Ober, you see, believed resolutely in Ober-ness. From its inception, Ober had been the best. Harold Ober, and later Dorothy Olding, his successor, represented many of his generation's greats: F. Scott Fitzgerald, Dylan Thomas, Nathanael West, Langston Hughes, S. J. Perelman. But while other agencies grew and changed, responding to changes in the publishing industry, hiring new agents who might bring in young and interesting clients, Ober—like a curmudgeonly old man—retreated into the business of *being* Ober. Being Ober meant drinking single malt scotch at 4 o'clock each Friday, clustered around the departed receptionist's desk. It meant saying things like, "We've always done our contracts this way, so this is the way we're going to do them now, no matter what St. Martin's Press says about electronic rights." and "Computers waste time, rather than save it." and "You're an Ober type of person." My boss declared the latter to me on my first day at the office, while lighting a slender cigarette with her pale, nervous hands. I sat in the large wooden chair that faced her large wooden desk.

I wore a kilt, black watch plaid, with a dark green Pendleton sweater and a pair of black loafers, my hair parted deeply on the side and my lips rouged a matte red. It was a scene that could have taken place fifty years prior, Jerry Salinger in the foyer, manuscript in hand.

Each day, as I sat at my own massive wooden desk, I fielded any number of phone calls from rabid Salinger fans, curious reporters, and the occasional clueless scholar ("Would Mr. Salinger be interested in delivering the commencement address at Bergen College?") all asking for access to Salinger. And then, one day, a month or two into the job, one of the agents—the sweet, cardigan-wearing fellow who tended to most of the agency's dead clients—dumped a pile of mail on my ink blotter. These, he explained, were the Salinger letters. He had been holding them for me—letters that had collected over the past few months—until I acclimated to the job. It was my responsibility to answer them, when I wasn't busy with more pressing tasks (like scrutinizing contracts or hounding publishing houses for checks), as they came in.

I looked at the envelopes. Many were addressed by hand or on obviously ancient typewriters, and quite a few came from overseas, from Japan, Denmark, Sri Lanka. The flimsy, pastel airmail stationary struck me as particularly suited to Salinger's fiercely nostalgic world. Opening the letters, I found variations on a theme: Holden Caulfield, the fans wrote, is the only character in literature who is truly like me. And you, Mr. Salinger, are surely the same person as Holden Caulfield. Thus, you and I should be friends. "I'd get one helluva kick outta you if you wrote back and told me I was a bastard!" enthused one North Carolinian. "My mother says you won't write back," wrote a Canadian high school girl, "but I told her you would. I know you will, because you understand what it's like to be surrounded by phonies."

But Salinger, of course, would not write back. Salinger did not want to see or hear about any of his fan mail. He cared not a whit what we did with it—we could burn it, for all it mattered to him. Certain fans have indeed accused Ober of putting a torch to Salinger's fan mail.

These people do not realize the logistical and legal problems faced by those who build bonfires on the sixteenth floors of Madison Avenue office buildings. Rest assured, each and every piece of mail was opened and read. And during the year that it was my job to open and read it—scanning for death threats or other random dangers—it was all answered.

Along with the backlog of letters, I was given a few crumbling, yellowed carbons of sample responses. Composed in the Sixties, these terse little numbers possessed the starched formality of pre-email correspondence: *Dear Miss So-and-So, Many thanks for your recent letter to J. D. Salinger. As you may know, Mr. Salinger does not wish to receive mail from his readers. Thus, we cannot pass your kind note on to him. We thank you for your interest in Mr. Salinger's books.* Etched quite clearly between the lines was a warning: *Do not respond to this letter.*

Over the days that followed, I dutifully responded to the Salinger fans, updating and personalizing the Ober boilerplate (changed the "Miss" to "Ms."; added a few "sorry"s). As the weeks wore on, it became clear that the Salinger fans were of a different breed than devotees of other authors. First, because they really were *fans* (as opposed to mere *readers*)—their love for Salinger resembled a teen's slobbery obsession with her favorite pop star, an adoration I, as a bookish, overly serious teen, had never succumbed to—but, more intriguingly, because they spanned all age groups, nationalities, classes, races, and sexualities. At least half of the fans made it very clear that they *never* write letters to authors and they *knew* Salinger probably wasn't going to get their letters and if by some weird chance he did, he wouldn't respond—but they still hoped, had a *goddam* feeling, that maybe he would, maybe he would see something (some glimmer of talent, some shared sensibility) and grace them with a response. The Salinger fans were smart. They were misfits. And, for all their cynical posturing, what they loved about Holden Caulfield—what they still love about Holden Caulfield, I am certain—was not just his smart-alecky whinging or his refusal to conform to the expectations of adults, but his hopeless, dewy-eyed naiveté, his utter idealism. If Holden Caulfield were to write a letter to Salinger, he too would hope to hell that somehow, some way, in some world that irascible hermit would write a goddam letter back.

Across from my desk stood a built-in bookcase filled with Salinger's books in their unadorned covers—no images, no author photos, as stipulated in his contracts—each text translated into every known language. Each day, as I typed letters for my boss, the straight spines of Salinger's works played background to my tasks, always lurking in my peripheral vision. Whenever I glanced up or daydreamed or stretched, there they were, an unchanging screen. Inadvertently, I memorized their titles, began to see their characteristic fonts and colors (mustard yellow, dead crimson) on the backs of my eyelids as I fell asleep each night, my eyes spinning in their sockets from reading manuscripts for the Ober agents. "Seymour," my mind would shoot out at me, "an Introduction." *Nine Stories.*

Maybe, I thought, I should give Salinger another chance. Or, no, I didn't actually think such a thing, not in any straightforward way. For all my intellectual posturing, I was not a particularly reflective girl, more interested in the inner lives of the characters in the books I read—their epiphanies and losses—than in my own. Rather, I became prone to telling others—the people at the parties I went to each weekend, in badly renovated Financial District lofts and dingy Williamsburg floor-throughs—that they should *really* re-read Salinger, for they would find that the stuff *does indeed hold up*, though I had no idea, hadn't done so myself, and they *wouldn't believe the kinds of letters the guy gets from fans.* What kind of letters? they would ask, tell us more.

And so I would tell them about the Japanese girl and her Hello Kitty stationary—she included two letters, one in Japanese and one in English, thinking perhaps Salinger knew Japanese, because he was so smart, and because she'd read the book in Japanese. I told them about the Swedish man, exactly the same age as Salinger, who read *Catcher* when it first came out and has re-read it every year since, and now, finally, has decided to write to Salinger, who he believes to be a genius, the greatest author of the 20th century. (Salinger, my friends would cry, the greatest writer of the 20th century? Oh my God, that's *so* funny!) I told them about the crazy people who sent scrawled, scary letters on dirty scraps of paper—I called these people Holdens Gone Awry—the people who had never outgrown their adolescent anger. I imitated their strange imitations of Holdenspeak—their liberal use of 1940s adjectives (How *marvelous!*) and pet names (My *crumb-bun*, Steve, also adores *Franny and Zooey*), their insistence of modifying every noun with *helluva* (I bet everybody tells you this, but *The Catcher in the Rye* is one helluva book). And I told them about the teenage girls who professed their love for Holden—and, though they didn't always say it explicitly, Salinger—a boy who, they felt, really *understood* girls.

What I didn't tell them, these acquaintances of mine, was what I wrote back.

One morning, a bright day in late winter, a handwritten letter arrived, bubbly girlish script crowding three sheets of wrinkly pencil-smudged paper. The writer explained that she was a freshman in high school. She hated school, particularly English class, which she was failing (the only book she liked was, of course, *The Catcher in the Rye*). Her mother, she said, would kill her if she failed English, so she asked her teacher if she could do something, anything, to bring her grade up—perhaps a special project on J. D. Salinger, her favorite writer. "There *is* something you can do," the teacher told her. "Write a letter to J. D. Salinger and make it good enough that he'll write back. If he writes back, I'll give you an A." I put the letter aside for an hour, then took it with me while I went to buy lunch. Each day I ate the same thing: A cheap salad from Au Bon Pain. I opposed chain food shops, on principle, but couldn't afford a salad at any of the other restaurants or take-out shops near the Ober office, in a quiet deco building across the street from Saks' Madison Avenue entrance. The surrounding blocks were filled with delis peddling nine-dollar sandwiches and hushed Japanese restaurants, inside which customers ate at small tables separated by rice paper scrims. With the letter in my pocket, I grabbed my salad from a low refrigerated shelf, took my place in line behind a group of secretaries in polyester suits, pulled the letter out of my pocket, and read it again. Watery lettuce sloshed around the plastic container, studded with sour feta and two slim, salty olives. "I really need this A," the girl wrote. "it will bring my GPA up. My mother is mad at me all the time now. I know you understand."

Of course she knew he would understand. This is a man who created a character who boasts of being "the most terrific liar you ever saw in your life." Would Holden miss the opportunity for a work-free A? Actually, he probably would. Since he cared about passing his classes at Pencey about as much as Salinger cares about his fan mail. Or, for that matter, as much as Salinger himself cared about his own academics—like Holden, he failed out of numerous high schools.

Back at the office, I sat down at my Selectric, chewed an olive, and pattered out a response to the girl, suggesting that it was decidedly *not* in the spirit of her hero to be worrying about grades or her mother's fury. If she wanted to be like Holden, she should accept her failing grade—a grade she, by her own admission, deserved—and tell her mother to go to hell. Okay, I didn't really say *hell*, but I did imply that she was behaving like a coward—like a *phony*, even—trying to trick herself into a grade she hadn't earned. Would Salinger help out such a pathetic fool of a girl? No, he most certainly would not. By this point I had read and re-read his books—stayed late at work one night and slipped slim paperback editions into my tote bag—and I *knew* what Salinger would and would not say or do, like or not like, approve or not approve. I'd been surprised by how much I liked the work—it wasn't cutesy at all, I saw. In fact, it was dark, as dark and bleak as Jean Rhys, in certain ways. Franny Glass, pale and fainting in her sheared raccoon coat, beating at the tired trappings of her life—the tennis lessons and French classes and ersatz poets—struck a particular chord with me, of course. Now, as I lay beneath my old paisley comforter, I imagined her lying on the couch at Sickler's, mouthing "soundless words." Salinger, as any reader of his work could see, liked girls who were honest, girls overcome with the world's thorniest questions, girls obsessed with saints and martyrs, genius girls like Franny. Not stupid little girls who couldn't even admit to their own failures "If you desire an A—or, at the very least, a passing grade—there's only way to earn it," I typed, the Selectric humming in its satisfying, cat-like way, "you must study and do the work assigned to you. An 'A' earned by trickery means absolutely nothing."

It should be clear by now that if there was a line to cross—the loosely sewn seam between bemused interest and freaky over-involvement—I had most certainly crossed it. Each morning, when the mail was dumped on my desk, I stopped whatever I was doing and ripped open the latest crop of letters. While I mocked the Salinger fans with my friends, when I was alone with their letters I felt a certain *charge*, a mixture of anger and love, disdain and empathy, admiration and disgust. You see, these people wrote to me—or, to Salinger, care of me—about their lives, their social problems, their marital frustrations, their hatred of the workplace. And if at first I found this weird, after a few months I found it—well, *still* weird, but also many other things: sad, sweet, stupid, hopeful, obsessive.

Mostly I found it impossible *not* to respond in kind. Insert yourself into the situation: Day after day you must bear witness to the confessions of twenty strangers. You are expected to respond in the most formal, impersonal manner imaginable. *Dear Ms. So-and-So, Thank you for your letter.* At a certain point, would you not break down and respond to their questions? Well, maybe you wouldn't. But I did, and it wasn't long before I was firing off consolation to the mother whose daughter, dead of some unmentionable disease at a young age, loved "A Perfect Day for Bananafish" and dreamed of writing a novel in the adult years she would never have. Now, the mother wanted to start a literary magazine in honor of her daughter and call it, yes, "Bananafish." Writing long letters to Salinger fans was, if not explicitly against the Ober rules, certainly frowned upon. Thus, I took to filching the fan letters, nervously stuffing them in my bag at the end of the day. The boring ones I tossed, sometimes right away, casually depositing them in the trash can outside the 51st Street subway station. The more interesting ones I took home and saved, not sure exactly what I would do with them, but certain they shouldn't be trashed, these documents of people's lives.

Salinger, I thought, would have done the same thing. And so would have Franny, Zooey, Seymour, and Holden, certainly they would have. Franny, clutching her little cloth copy of *The Way of the Pilgrim*, would cry over these letters from the ends of the earth, would keep them in her overcrowded purse, folding and unfolding them until they fell apart at the creases.

It embarrassed me, this affinity I felt for weepy, world-weary Franny and the rest of the Glass family. I spoke of it with no one—not my friends, all involved in their own private dramas, nor my parents, who had long abandoned literary fiction for the comforts of spy novels and mysteries, and certainly not my iconoclastic, Mailer-esque boyfriend, who prodded me to tell amusing Salinger stories at gatherings of his friends, all of whom seemed to be writing experimental novels or obtaining graduate degrees in mysterious fields like "liberal studies" or backing low budget arts magazines with the interest from their trust funds. I obliged him, trotted out the goofs who sent Salinger locks of their hair, but thought of Franny, how she would frown on my cavalier irony and, of course, the company I was keeping, these self-satisfied pseudo-intellectuals, who treated me rather as Lane Coutell treats her. Which is to say, like a soft, shiny-haired pet, an audience for their Big Ideas. One of those men—for they all were men, these dreamers of the boho dream, friends of the man I thought was going to show me The Way of the Writer—particularly irked me, bugged me so much that I, at times, shook off my habitual reserve and argued with him, shocking the bunch of them. An uncritical champion of all things that struck him as avant garde or obscure or politically bombastic—you know him, I'm sure—this man constantly attacked the writers I admired, both living and dead, dismissing them as commercial and trite, as "mainstream." He found my line of work—if you can use that term to describe a 23-year-old's first job—an affront to all true writers. Literary agents? Bah! Vampires who suck the life force from writers. (This firmly held opinion did not prevent him from seeking such a ghoul to represent his drawer-full of unsold manuscripts. Unsuccessfully.) His favorite pastime was, in fact, denouncing the entire trade publishing industry. Editors have no taste, he decreed, they pander to the masses. There's no place in this world for literary writers, for genius. All the fiction published today is crap.

And while I knew there was the tiniest grain of truth to this view—editors can sometimes have a difficult time getting books past the marketing department—every cell in my body railed against it. Still, I often sat silently, listening to the men discuss the tragic state of current fiction, nodding my head and asking questions. Yes, yes, if only a time machine could transport us back to the salons of 1920s. Yes, yes, everything is crap. We would be in a bar, always, in the East Village or Williamsburg—for each night I seemed to find myself, at one point or another, in a dark, smoky bar with a generic name like "Joe's" or "The Homestead," and a following among the ironic youths who had done time in San Francisco, Seattle, and Portland, before coming to New York to get serious. I drank whiskey, straight up with a soda back. Being the only girl of the group—always, it was me and this group of talky men—I needed a drink that would somehow even the playing field, prove that beneath my wool skirts beat the heart of a serious intellectual, a person who had read Derrida and liked it. But with each burning sip I would grow more and more tired, tired or angry, or both. I'd hated Derrida, hated all the theory I'd been forced to read in grad school, hated it so much I dropped out. "That's just not true!" I would cry, some nights, after listening to all their talk, citing some of the living writers I then loved, though I knew it would make them laugh. "It's not true," I would say, near-apologizing as I said it, whiskey fumes rising up from my tumbler, but not knowing why, why had I—the most outspoken member of every Oberlin English class, the Young Intellectual in the making, the girl who read a novel each day, the would-be Mary McCarthy, the almost Ph.D.—lost the ability to defend the books I loved and the writers who wrote them. The answer, of course, is that what I loved was changing. The answer, of course, is J. D. Salinger.

You are probably wondering, right about now, if I signed my own name to the letters—or if I actually pretended to be Salinger, signed a loopy "J. D." at the bottom of the page. It would be, perhaps, a better story had I done the latter, but, you see, I believed so utterly in the Salinger myth—in Salinger's right to be left utterly and completely alone—that I *needed* to write the letters as me, puffing with pleasure at my role as gatekeeper, as defender and guardian angel to Salinger, as explainer and channeler of Salinger, as reminder of the Way of Salinger. It was, indeed, my own name that I used. The Salinger fans received responses, on creamy Ober letterhead, from Joanna Rakoff (no title specified). On several occasions, rabid fans wrote back to me, suggesting that I was not a real person, but a character invented to take the heat off the Evil Agent who refused to send on letters to Salinger: *Dear Miss Rakoff, If that's really who you are.* And once an ancient Midwesterner responded to my brief note, asking if I bore any relation to some other Rakoff—a Daniel or Joseph—whom he'd known in the service, the Second World War. This letter, shakily scratched on two sheets of plain white stationary with a leaking blue ballpoint pen that left greasy smudges on the margins of the page, had me near tears. This man had written a letter to an author—an author who never, ever writes back—and instead found a girl, the daughter or granddaughter of his Army buddy, a connection to his past, to his *Catcher in the Rye* days. I wanted, badly, to write back, to say, "Yes, that man is my father"—for it could have been, easily, in some fictional, pre-digital universe of coincidence and kismet, in Salinger's sepia-toned New York, where letters are a conduit to understanding, a key to discovery. In my world, people corresponded in the short blips allowed by e-mail, forwarding jokes or information without regard to punctuation or even capitalization. For days, I kept the letter at my side, pressed flat against the Selectric, until I found a moment to call my dad—a veteran of Korea, not WWII—and ask him if he knew the man mentioned, the other Rakoff. He didn't.

And so I didn't write back, just as I didn't write back to the people who accused me of not being me (what would I say? *Dear Ms. So-and-So, I assure you that I am in fact an actual person. Enclosed is my driver's license and passport, for your perusal.*), just as I didn't write a second time to schoolgirl seeking an easy 'A', who responded to my note with expletives, angry that I wouldn't pass on her note to Salinger, and even angrier that I had taken her to task for her efforts. Who was *I* to judge *her*, she asked in her response to my note. Did I know what it was like to be a teenage girl? No, I most certainly did not. She wondered if I had ever been young, or was simply a dried up old bitch of a person, a spinster with nothing better to do than berate strangers, to meddle in their business, much like her English teacher. I began to wonder the same thing, or something like it. Was my life so wonderful, so flawless—my teen years holed up in a wallpapered bedroom, re-reading a dog-eared copy of *Jane Eyre*; this new adulthood in a coldwater flat, scribbling poems in cafes—that I could offer advice or consolation to this girl and the others like her?

For the Salinger fans—maybe you have seen this already, maybe you are way ahead of me—books were not texts to be taken apart, as I was taught in my Ph.D. program, nor were they springboards for progressive thought, as I was taught at Oberlin, nor big piles of paper from which one can make a nice ten percent commission, as I was told daily at my office, nor attempts rip apart language, to challenge the reader's bourgeois sense of comfort, as my boyfriend and his friends kept saying. No, for the Salinger fans, books were simply worlds to inhabit—sad and electric worlds in which smart, funny, disappointed people discuss ideas and smoke cigarettes and speak their minds. And this, ultimately, is what books were—are—for me, too. But Salinger Land—much like Disneyland or Never Never Land—is a place in which the trappings of adulthood, the deadlines and toothpaste ads and hairstyles and bridesmaids and skill sets, are something to be feared. The only proper response to such terror is to take to one's couch, weeping into a little book, or to have a nervous breakdown, or—I hate to write this—to kill oneself.

Alternatively, one could hide out in a dark office, writing letters to complete strangers.

Or one could publish a number of best-selling, well-received books, then simply refuse to have any further contact with the world.

Or one could obsess over a reclusive author. One could begin to regard the characters created by this author as something akin to real people. One could adopt their speech patterns and mannerisms and trademark red caps.

Or, to look at it another way, one could—like one of my correspondents, the one I call The Boy from Atlanta, the one I've never quite been able to get out of my head—sit in one's room, reading and re-reading *The Catcher in the Rye*, much as the novel's hero sits in his dorm room, reading Isak Dinesen and Thomas Hardy. "What really knocks me out," Holden explains, in his strange and intimate voice, "is a book that, when you're all done reading it, you wish the author that wrote it was a terrific friend of yours and you could call him up on the phone whenever you felt like it." Like the letters from Salinger fans, Holden dares you to engage him in a dialogue. *The Catcher in the Rye*, I began to realize that year, the Salinger Year, is a love letter, a love letter and suicide note.

The Boy from Atlanta, he sees this. Late at night, in his suburban bedroom, he puts down his worn paperback of *Catcher*. The crimson has rubbed away from the cover's edge. He sits down at his new computer and types "Dear Mr. Salinger." He explains that he's just finished *The Catcher in the Rye* for the third time, that the book is a masterpiece and Salinger should be proud of it, that most of what he reads bores him, most writers are utterly insincere.

> *I think about Holden a lot. He just pops into my mind's eye and I get to thinking about him dancing with old Phoebe or horsing around in front of the bathroom mirror at Pencey. When I first think about him I usually get a big stupid grin on my face. You know, thinking about what a funny guy he is and all. But then, I usually get depressed as hell. I guess I get depressed because I only think about Holden when I'm feeling very emotional. I can get quite emotional. Don't worry, though. I've learned that, as phony as it may be, you can't go around revealing your goddamn emotions to the world.*

No, you can't simply bleed all over the world—at least, not after puberty hits. The Boy from Atlanta was right, though I don't think I realized this until a good deal later in life. (Maybe, like Holden, *I act quite young for my age.*) But you *can* write a letter to J. D. Salinger, explaining your thoughts on love and books, you can have the weird confidence to picture Salinger—looking as he does in his most famous photo, black hair and blacker eyes, eager grin—reading your letter and smiling to read your description of it as a masterpiece, thrilling to find you agree with him about Gatsby ("What a determined sonuvabitch! I really liked him.") and girls ("I used to get nervous as hell around them, especially the really good-looking ones."), to find that—what a coincidence!—you express yourself in much the same way as Holden Caulfield.

When the real, actual J. D. Salinger—with his thin grey hair and saucer-sized ears and same kind, self-deprecating smile—visited our office, I shook his hand (or, really, he shook mine), said "nice to meet you," smoothed my skirt and turned back to my typing. In my desk lay the letter from Atlanta, two neatly typed pages, unfurled from a laser printer, and ending:

> *I'll write you again soon. I can hardly wait. Anyway, my line of thought is this: If I was the guy who put myself onto paper and I came out in the form of* The Catcher in the Rye, *I'd get a bang out of the bastard who had the nerve to write me a letter pretending (and wanting) to be able to do the same thing.*

As the door to my boss's smoke-stained office closed, a thought slashed through my brain—What if I gave Salinger the letter? Wouldn't he be, at the very least, amused by it? With my left hand, I slid open the cold metal drawer, fingered the slightly ragged white sheets—I'd read it several times, unsure of how to respond. Should I write back and tell him what a kick the letter had given me, even though I wasn't the bastard to whom the boy had addressed his note? Should I tell him he could certainly do what Salinger did—write a groundbreaking, beloved book—if he simply applied himself?

I slipped the note into the pocket of my white fur thrift shop coat, read it while standing in line to buy my salad. When I returned to the office, Salinger and my boss had left for lunch at the Intercontinental. My boss returned to the office alone. I read the letter again, wondering if Salinger might come back to finish up some business, knowing he wouldn't, knowing he was gone, gone back to New Hampshire. He didn't, of course. And neither did he—or my boss—ever find out about my personal responses to the Salinger letters. Or, to all the Salinger letters except one. I never wrote back to The Boy from Atlanta. Instead, I kept the letter, occasionally re-reading it, wondering if he ever wrote again to Salinger. You see, I didn't really stick around to find out. I left Ober after a year, six months after receiving that letter, left to become a writer myself. Each season I scan the publishers' catalogues, looking to see if that boy ever wrote that novel. This would be a better story, wouldn't it, if he had?

That's all I'm going to tell about. I could probably tell you about what happened to me after I left Ober—that I left that boyfriend, signed over the lease on our dingy apartment; that I've never gone back and visited Ober, never set foot inside those book-lined walls again. I rarely talk about that time, rarely think about it. A lot of people though—especially my old friends who wondered what was going on with me during that year, the Salinger Year, why I was so quiet and thin and strange—still ask me about the Salinger letters, what they mean to me and to the world, and do I think people still write them? Do the people who have held my job in the intervening years—the parade of Bohemian youths willing to work for nearly nothing in order to be around *literature*—answer them the way I did? Holden would say those are stupid questions, for how do you know what anything really means? Or what anyone else might do in any given situation? If you want to know the truth, I don't *know* what I think about it. In certain ways, I'm sorry I've told so many people about the Salinger fans, sorry to have mocked their letters at cocktail parties, sorry not to have kept their love private, between the typewriter and myself, sorry to have ever been so young. About all I know is—and, again, maybe you've guessed this, for I've already told you I'm not a girl who's prone to reflection—about all I know is, I sort of *miss* them.

# Salinger and Me

J. B. MILLER

I had just finished *The Catcher in the Rye* and I really liked it. I wanted to call the author and tell him how much I liked it. But I didn't have his phone number. So I called his publisher.

"Hello, can I have J. D. Salinger's phone number?" I asked them.

"What for?"

"I just want to call him and tell him how much I liked his book."

There was a pause on the line. "You're not some kook, are you?"

"Oh no."

"OK then." The woman gave me the number. It was (603) 947-3309. I dialed the number. A man answered. "Yes?"

"Is this J. D. Salinger?"

"Yes. Who's this?"

"Um . . . You don't know me, but I just finished *The Catcher in the Rye* and I wanted to tell you how much I liked it."

"Yeah? Wow. That's really nice of you."

There was a pause. I wasn't sure what else to say. "Yeah, well, I really liked it."

Another pause. This was getting kind of awkward. I heard Salinger clear his throat. "So . . . um . . . Would you like to come up for a visit?"

"Gee, I don't know, Mr. Salinger. I wouldn't want to intrude."

"No no, come on up. Do you know how to get to Cornish, New Hampshire?"

"I'm sure I can find it."

"OK. I'll pick you up in front of the post office on Thursday at 3 P.M."

"Great. Wait a minute—how will I recognize you?"

"I'm a big guy with a happy face."

"Yeah? Funny, that's just how I pictured you."

On Thursday I went up to Cornish and waited in front of the post office. But there was no Salinger.

Finally, a huge gray Lincoln Navigator pulled up and a tall guy in Levi's and a red plaid shirt got out. "J. B.?" he asked.

"That's me."

"Sorry I'm late. I was on the phone with a bunch of New York editors."

"They're all a goddam bunch of phonies," I said.

"You're telling me."

J. D. had to do some errands in town, so I accompanied him while he bought some magazines (*Vanity Fair, Premiere, Seventeen, YM,* and *Homeopathic Monthly*) and rented some videos from the Cornish Video Shack (*Roman Holiday, Baby Doll,* and *Lolita*).

On the drive up to his house we talked about stuff. As it turned out, we had a lot in common. "My name is made up of initials too," I observed.

"Yeah, it's better that way," said J. D. "It's different."

Two black Labradors, Franny and Zooey, greeted us at the house, a surprisingly unassuming two-story Colonial style filled with piles of books, papers, magazines, burning incense, scented candles and old movie posters tacked to the wall. "Gee, what a mess," I said.

"Yeah, I know," said Salinger. "I keep meaning to clean it up."

That evening Salinger cooked up a bucket of boiled wheat germ, and we ate it while watching the videos. We didn't talk much.

Between a couple of films I tried to make some conversation.

"So, uh . . ."

Salinger was trying to put the video in the VCR the wrong way. I helped him. "I bet a lot of people call you up like I did, huh?"

"No, actually, you're the first. It's been kind of surprising. I think people are just scared to bother me. But I get kind of lonely up here."

After a couple of weeks I started cleaning up the house, sorting out the piles, throwing stuff out. I was making a lot of long-distance phone calls, calling this chick I knew in France who refused to believe I was staying with J. D. Salinger. "You don't believe me? I'll put him on." I shouted to the den where Salinger was working. "Hey, Jerry!" No answer. "JERRY!"

"What is it? I'm working."

"Get on the phone, I want you to talk to my friend."

"I'm kind of busy here, J.B."

"Just get on the phone, this won't take a second." Salinger picked up the phone in the den. He talked with the French chick for a while. "The French are a bunch of phonies," he finally said and hung up.

The next morning at breakfast Salinger seemed a little tight-mouthed. "I think you should leave," he said. Apparently I'd thrown out some papers he'd wanted to hold on to. Also, all the long-distance calls. I decided to cheer him up by feigning some interest in his work.

I went into his den. There were piles of pages everywhere. "These are my manuscripts," he explained, following me into the room nervously. He showed me a 2,000-page novel he'd been writing called "Glass House." "I've been working on it for 35 years."

"Can I take a look?"

"Well, I really don't . . ."

I grabbed the manuscript and started reading it. It was pretty funny. I was laughing. Salinger was trying to look over my shoulder at what I was laughing at. "Which part are you reading?"

"Where Zooey gets his foot caught in the trash compactor."

"Oh yeah." He chuckled. "That really happened." I marveled at all the pages, painstaking typed, with a myriad of hand corrections on each page. I looked around the room. No computer.

"You still use a typewriter?" I asked him.

"I find it's the only way I can think. I compose on the typewriter." He patted the old Underwood affectionately. I noticed the dust between the keys.

I opened the window to air out the place a little. A sudden gust of wind tore through the blinds, blowing the stack of pages around the room. "Oops." I knelt down to pick them up, accidentally knocking a candle onto the floor.

By the time the fire department got to the house, it was a mass of charred ruins. J. D. was sitting on a stump by the frog pond. He was whimpering a bit, staring into his hands.

Just then a car drove up. Out stepped the most beautiful girl I'd ever seen: tall, thin, with alabaster skin, chiseled features and fine, golden hair. She ran over to Salinger. "Hey, Dad!"

Salinger wouldn't look up. "Hi, Phoebe."

"Wow, what happened here?"

But Salinger couldn't answer. He fell on the ground and began coughing, and we called an ambulance.

After we'd made sure Salinger was safely delivered to the hospital, I took Phoebe out for lunch in Cornish and tried to explain what had happened. Salinger had been trying to cook some soy muffins when the oven had caught fire and it quickly spread through the house. I managed to pull him out of the flames, but everything else got lost in the fire. The firemen came soon enough, but it was too late. Phoebe hugged me. "Those firemen are a bunch of goddamn phonies," she mumbled.

We were married in the spring. Salinger was too sick to attend the wedding. He'd become a weird recluse. Rather than have Phoebe change her name to mine, I decided to change mine to hers. J. B. Salinger.

We have eight kids: Phoebe, Zooey, Booboo, Walter, Walker,

Holden, Buddy and Franny. We were going to call the last one Seymour, but we thought that'd be kind of cruel. And anyway, it was a girl.

Last month we moved to Hollywood. We're angling for a family
sitcom, something like *The Brady Bunch*, but "real." I've been talking
to a few producers, trying to put together a deal, but it's tough. The
town's full of goddamn phonies.

# ABOUT THE CONTRIBUTORS

PAUL ALEXANDER holds an M.F.A. from the Writers' Workshop at the University of Iowa. He is the author of biographies of Sylvia Plath, James Dean, and Andy Warhol, as well as J. D. Salinger.

A graduate of Yale College, ALEX BEAM worked for the House Select Committee on Intelligence, and also as an English-Russian interpreter for the U.S. Information Agency in Russia. As a journalist, he's worked for *Newsweek*, *Business Week*, and the *Boston Globe*, where he is now a columnist for the *Globe's* Living/Arts page. Beam is also the author of two novels, *Fellow Travelers* and *The Americans Are Coming!* and a nonfiction book about McLean Hospital, *Gracefully Insane*. Beam lives in Newton, Massachusetts, with his wife and three sons.

As a Vermont high school student in 1953, SHIRLIE BLANEY managed to get a rare interview with J. D. Salinger.

MICHAEL CLARKSON was a newspaper reporter for 38 years and recently has had five books published on fear. His works are now being purchased for television, and he is also a professional speaker (www.michaelclarkson.com). He is the father of two sons and lives with his wife, Jennifer, in Toronto.

JOHN DUGDALE is the author of books on Thomas Pynchon and Sam Shepard. He writes for the *Guardian*, *Sunday Times,* and *Literary Review*, and is deputy media editor of the *Guardian*.

LACEY FOSBURGH was a longtime reporter for the *New York Times* in New York and San Francisco, as well as the author of three books, *Closing Time: the True Story of the Goodbar Murder*, *Old Money,* and *India Gate*.

ERNEST HAVEMANN was a writer for the *St. Louis Post-Dispatch*, *Time* magazine, and *Life* magazine, and also co-wrote a handful of psychology textbooks. He once won $61,908 on a single bet at a Mexican racetrack in 1963.

A literary critic for the *New York Times*, MICHIKO KUKUTANI has also worked as a *Washington Post* reporter and a writer for *Time* magazine. In 1998 she won a Pulitzer Prize for Criticism.

ALFRED KAZIN was an editor at the *New Republic* and an influential critic and cultural historian. His books of essays and criticism include *On Native Grounds*, *A Walker in the City*, *Starting Out in the Thirties*, and *New York Jew*.

JOYCE MAYNARD is the author of five novels, including *The Usual Rules* and *To Die For*, and numerous works of nonfiction. Her latest book is *Internal Combustion: The Story of a Marriage and a Murder in the Motor City*. Her contribution on these pages is excerpted from her best-selling memoir, *At Home in the World*, which was published in 1998 and has been translated into nine languages.

MARY MCCARTHY was a prolific author and critic and was also very active in left-wing politics for much of her life. Her 1963 novel, *The Group*, was a runaway *New York Times* best seller. McCarthy, who contributed to the *Atlantic Monthly*, *The New Yorker* and *Harper's*, was once famously involved in a literary spat with Lillian Hellman. In 1984 she was awarded the MacDowell Medal for Literature and the National Medal for Literature.

LOUIS MENAND is a writer and regular contributor to the *New Yorker* and *The New York Review of Books*. He is a professor of English and American Literature and Language at Harvard University. His book, *The Metaphysical Club*, won the Pulitzer Prize for History in 2002.

J.B. MILLER is a playwright and novelist who lives in New York. His most recent book is *The Satanic Nurses and Other Literary Parodies*. He also wrote the plays *Bobby Supreme*, *The Dorchester*, and *Post-Mortem*, and a novel, *My Life in Action Painting*. He is currently working on a multidiscipline project called *Fear of Jazz*.

ARTHUR MIZENER graduated from Princeton University in 1930, earned a masters at Harvard University, and then returned to Princeton to receive his doctorate in 1934. Mizener taught English at Yale University, Wells College, and Carleton College before becoming Cornell University's Mellon Foundation Professor of English in 1951. He retired from teaching in 1975. Mizener's most popular work was the first biography of F. Scott Fitzgerald, *The Far Side of Paradise* (1951). His other writings include *The Saddest Story: A Biography of Ford Madox Ford* (1971), and *The Sense of Life in the Modern Novel* (1964).

SARAH MORRILL is the proprietress of Morrill Books, an underground bookstore in San Francisco.

CHRIS OFFUTT is the author of two collections of stories, *Kentucky Straight* and *Out of the Woods*, a novel, *The Good Brother*, and a memoir, *The Same River Twice*.

CAROL OSBORNE directs the Humanities Program and teaches contemporary literature and English education at Murray State University.

JOANNA SMITH Rakoff has written for the *New York Times*, the *Los Angeles Times*, the *Washington Post*, *Vogue*, *O: The Oprah Magazine*, and many other publications. Her poetry has appeared in *The Paris Review*, *Western Humanities Review*, and other literary journals. She currently completing a novel set in Brooklyn.

MORDECAI RICHLER was a prolific Canadian author, scriptwriter, and essayist.

RON ROSENBAUM is the author of *Explaining Hitler*, *The Secret Parts of Fortune* and most recently *The Shakespeare Wars* (Random House, October, 2006). He writes a column for *The New York Observer*, and his work has appeared in *The New York Times Magazine*, *The New Yorker*, *Harper's*, *Esquire*, and *The Atlantic*.

MARGARET SALINGER is J. D. Salinger's eldest child.

DAVID SKINNER is an assistant managing editor at *The Weekly Standard*. He has written for *Education Next*, *Slate*, the *Washington Times*, the *Wall Street Journal*, and several other publications. He edits *Doublethink*, a quarterly journal for young writers published by America's Future Foundation, and is on the usage panel for the *American Heritage Dictionary*.

DANIEL M. STASHOWER is the author of two mystery novels and a winner of the Raymond Chandler Fulbright Fellowship in Detective and Crime Fiction Writing.

MIKE STRACCO has been teaching high school for twenty-five years in Illinois. He also teaches an integration of writing and photography at the College of DuPage.

JOHN UPDIKE is an American novelist who has published 21 novels and over a dozen short story collections. He's best known for his *Rabbit* series. His most recent book is a collection of essays on art titled *Still Looking* (Knopf, 2005).

EUDORA WELTY was a major American writer of short stories and novels, whose books include *The Ponder Heart* and *Losing Battles*. She was an American Book Awards recipient and in 1973 won a Pulitzer Prize for her novel, *The Optimist's Daughter*.

JONATHAN YARDLEY is the book critic of and a columnist for the *Washington Post*. He was awarded the Pulitzer Prize for Distinguished Criticism in 1981.

# ACKNOWLEDGMENTS

PAUL ALEXANDER: "Salinger: A Biography," St. Martin's Press, 1999. From Salinger: a Biography by Paul Alexander, Copyright © 1999 by the author and reprinted by permission of St. Martin's Press, LLC.

ALEX BEAM: "J. D. Salinger, Failed Recluse," *Slate.com*, June 29, 1999. Used by permission of the author.

SHIRLIE BLANEY: "Interview with J. D. Salinger," *The Claremont Daily Eagle*, November 13, 1953. Used by permission of *The Claremont Daily Eagle*.

MICHAEL CLARKSON: "Searching for the Catcher in the Rye," *The Niagara Falls Review*, November 1979. Used by permission of the author.

JOHN DUGDALE: "Eighty Years of Solitude," *The Guardian*, December 30, 1998. Used by permission of *The Guardian*.

BETTY EPPES: "What I Did Last Summer," *The Paris Review*, Summer 1981. Copyright 1981 Betty Eppes. Used by permission of the author.

LACEY FOSBURGH: "J. D. Salinger Speaks About His Silence," *The New York Times*, November 3, 1974. Copyright © 1974 The New York Times Co. Reprinted by permission.

ERNEST HAVEMANN: "The Search for the Mysterious J. D. Salinger," *Life*, November 3, 1961. Copyright 1961 Life Inc. Used by permission of Life Inc.

MICHIKO KAKUTANI: "From Salinger, a Dash of Mystery," *The New York Times*, February 20, 1997. Copyright © 1997 The New York Times Co. Reprinted by permission.

ALFRED KAZIN: "J. D. Salinger: Everybody's Favorite," *The Atlantic*, August, 1961. First published in *The Atlantic* © 1961 by Alfred Kazin, reprinted with the permission of The Wylie Agency.

ARNOLD LUBASCH: "Salinger Biography is Blocked," *The New York Times*, January 3, 1974. Copyright © 1974 The New York Times Co. Reprinted by permission.

JOYCE MAYNARD: "At Home in the World: A Memoir," Picador, 1998. Reprinted from *At Home in the World*. Used by permission of the author.

MARY MCCARTHY: "J. D. Salinger's Closed Circuit," *Harper's*, October, 1962. "J. D. Salinger's Closed Circuit" from *The Writing on the Wall and Other Literary Essays*, copyright © 1962 by *Harper's Magazine* and renewed by James Raymond West, reprinted by permission of Harcourt, Inc.

LOUIS MENAND: "Holden at Fifty," *The New Yorker*, October 1, 2001. First published in *The New Yorker* © 2001 by Louis Menand, reprinted with the permission of The Wylie Agency.

J.B. MILLER: "Salinger and Me," *Salon.com*, July 6, 1999. Used by permission of the author.

ARTHUR MIZENER: "The Love Song of J. D. Salinger," *Harper's*, February, 1959. Copyright © by *Harper's Magazine*. All rights reserved. Reproduced from the February issue by special permission.

SARAH MORRILL: "A Brief Biography of J. D. Salinger," From the author's website, April, 2002. Copyright © April 2002, February 2006, by Sarah Morrill. Reprinted by permission.

CHRIS OFFUTT, CAROL OSBORNE and MIKE STRACCO: "Letters to J. D. Salinger," The University of Wisconsin Press, 2002. Reprinted from *Letters to J. D. Salinger*. Used by permission of the authors.

DIPTI R. PATTANAIK: "The Holy Refusal: A Vedantic Interpretation of J. D. Salinger's Silence," *Melus* 23.2, Summer, 1998. Used by permission of *Melus*.

JOANNA SMITH RAKOFF: Joanna Smith Rakoff: "My Salinger Year," 2002. A different version of this piece originally appeared in *Book* magazine. Used by permission of the author.

MORDECAI RICHLER: "Summer Reading; Rises at Dawn, Writes, Then Retires," *The New York Times*, June 5, 1988. Copyright © 1988 The New York Times Co. Reprinted by permission.

RON ROSENBAUM: "The Catcher in the Driveway" © 1997 by Ron Rosenbaum. This article originally appeared in *Esquire* magazine under the title, "The Man in the Glass House and then again, along with the post-script, in his collection, *The Secret Parts of Fortune*, Random House 2000. Reprinted by permission of the author.

MARGARET SALINGER: "Dream Catcher," 2000. Reprinted with the permission of Simon & Schuster Adult Publishing Group from *Dream Catcher: A Memoir* by Margaret A. Salinger. Copyright © 2000 by Margaret A. Salinger.

DAVID SKINNER: "The Sentimental Misanthrope; Why J. D. Salinger Can't Write," *The Weekly Standard*, February 22, 1999. Used by permission of *The Weekly Standard*.

SUSAN STAMBERG: "Margaret Salinger, Daughter of J. D. Salinger, Discusses Her New Book, Dream Catcher," National Public Radio's Morning Edition, September 7, 2000. Credit: © 2000, National Public Radio, Inc. Reprinted by permission of National Public Radio.

DANIEL M. STASHOWER: "On First Looking Into Chapman's Holden: Speculations on Murder," *The American Scholar*, Summer, 1983. Used by permission of the author.

JOHN UPDIKE: "Anxious Days for the Glass Family," *The New York Times Book Review*, September 17, 1961. Copyright © 1961 The New York Times Co. Reprinted by permission.

EUDORA WELTY: "Threads of Innocence," *The New York Times*, April 5, 1953. Reprinted by the permission of Russell & Volkening, Inc., as agents for the author's estate. Copyright © 1953 by Eudora Welty, renewed 1981 by Eudora Welty. The review originally appeared in *The New York Times*.

JONATHAN YARDLEY: "J. D. Salinger's Holden Caulfield, Aging Gracelessly," *The Washington Post*, October 19, 2004. Copyright © 2004 *The Washington Post*. Reprinted with Permission.